Billy
It was really nice of you to drive your car to me. I'll take the car out while you're gone.

Regards,
Bob Davis

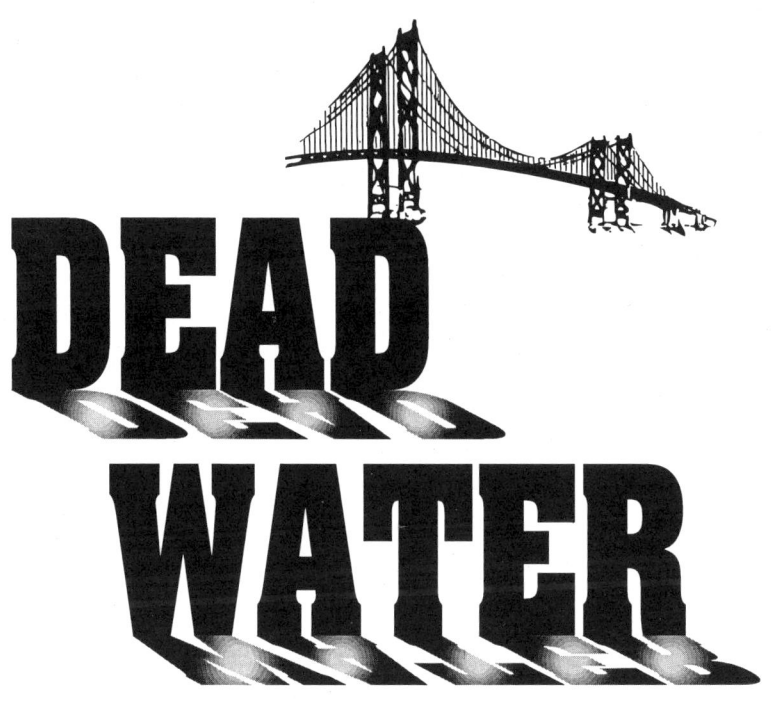

DEAD WATER

The Klindt Affair

**PAT GIPPLE
MATTHEW CLEMENS**

©1995

ACKNOWLEDGMENTS

In *Dead Water*, the writers have endeavored to re-create events that took place more than a decade ago. The book is about the brutal murder of Joyce Amelia Klindt. The only account we have of that tragic day came from her husband, James B. Klindt. Since his version contradicts trial testimony and defies logic, we have relied heavily on depositions, court transcripts, videotapes, newspaper articles, and interviews with those involved. There is also a certain amount of conjecture, a reconstruction of dialogue, and the introduction of relevant information through the voice of a fictional character. Taking all of this into account, we believe we have pieced together a reliable version of the major events as the story unfolded during the years of 1983 and 1984.

Joyce Klindt was the victim of a horrific crime. We have tried not to lose sight of that fact. In reality, there were many victims. Some do not want this painful memory exhumed. We have changed their names in an attempt to protect their privacy.

The State of Iowa versus James B. Klindt was one of the earliest proceedings to introduce genetic evidence. The case set precedent and actually made law.

Media coverage was extensive. We owe a debt of gratitude to Judy Pochel of the *Rock Island Argus*, to William Ryberg of the *Des Moines Register*, and to Bill Theobald and Alma Gaul of the *Quad-City Times* for their diligent reporting.

Special thanks go out to Marlowe Bergendoff, our editor; to Dr. Roald Tweet for his insight; to Tom Yeggy for legal counsel; to Dimensional Graphics for the art work; and to all of those who helped bring *Dead Water* to market. We would be remiss not to acknowledge the man whose cooperation made this book possible, Scott County Attorney William E. Davis. This is your story, Bill.

P.G. & M.C.

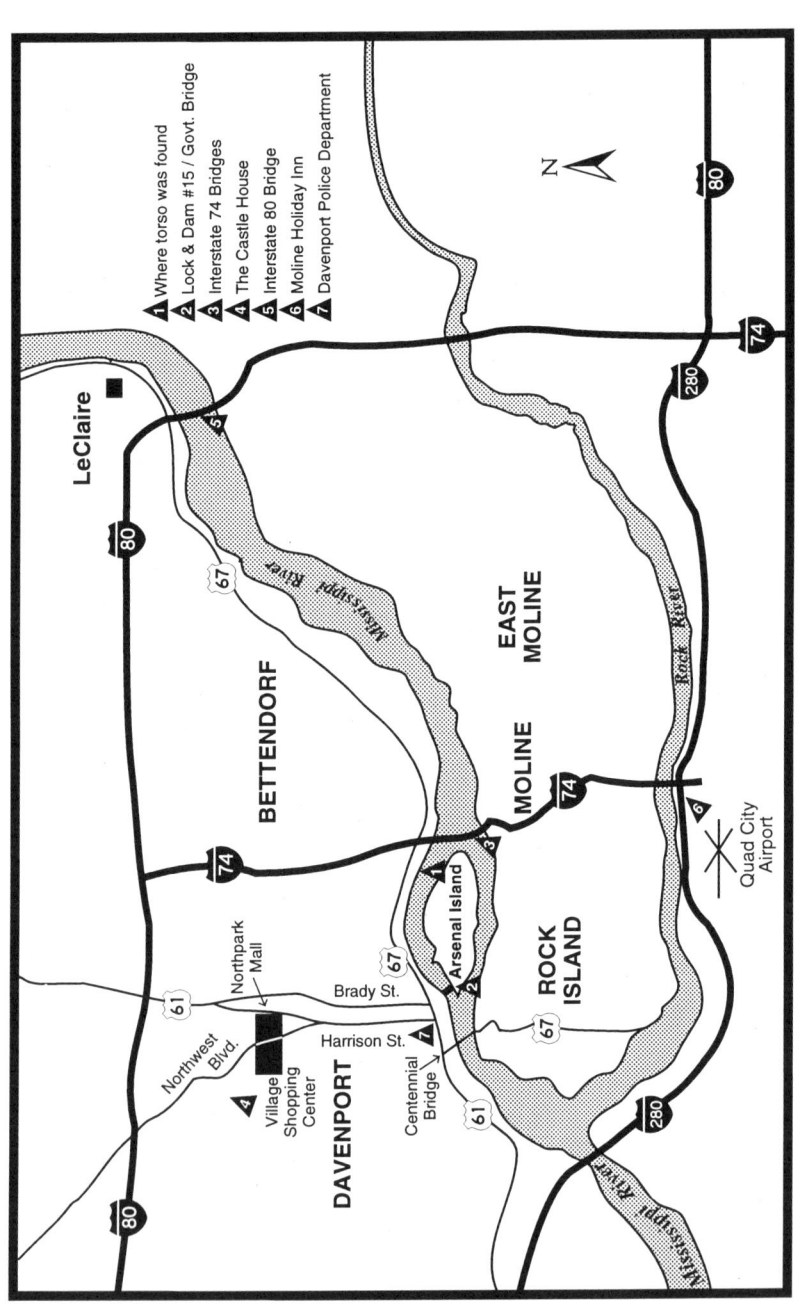

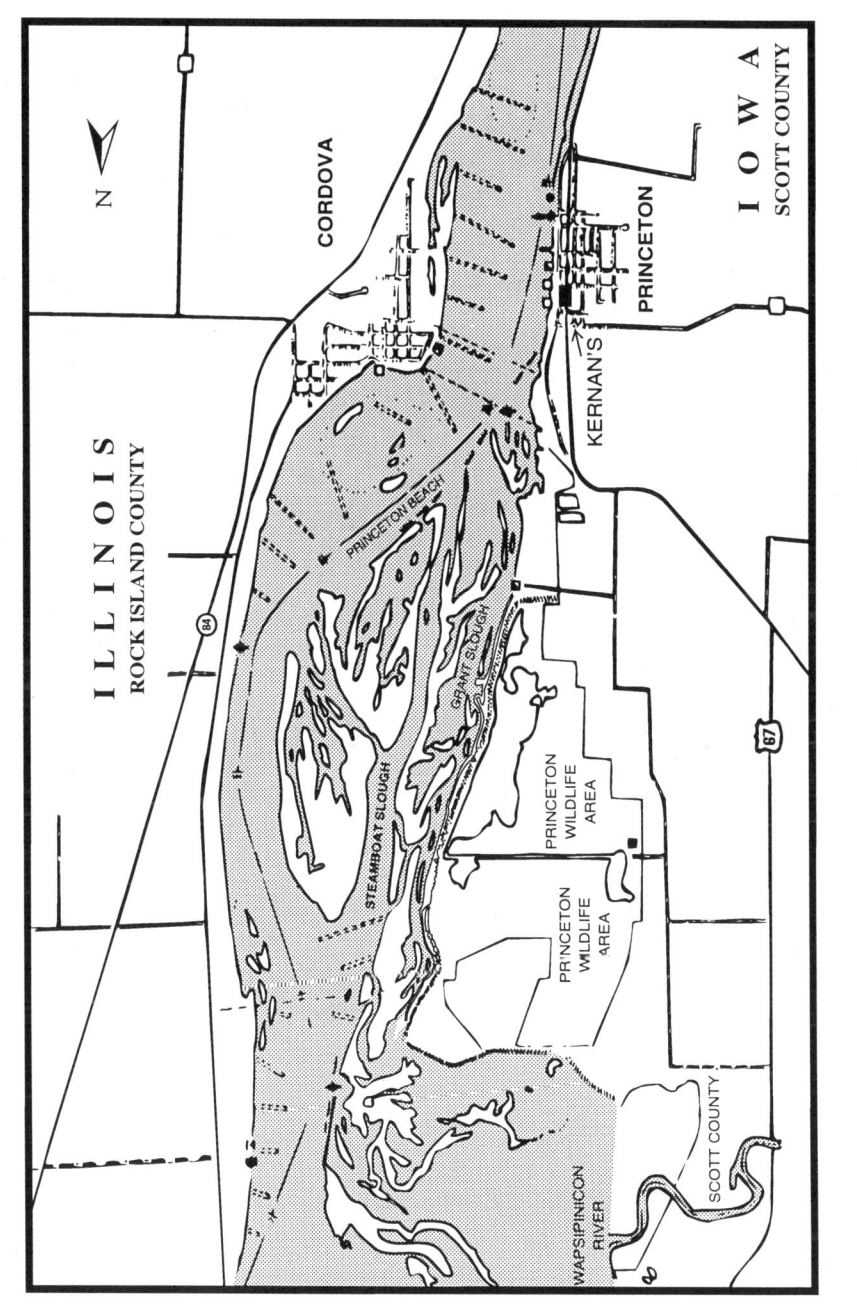

The Mississippi is not shy about surrendering the dead. Once a body finds its way into the Great River, whether by suicide, accident, or the nefarious act of another, it is a given the remains will reappear at some undesignated time downstream. Flesh and bone have a specific gravity only slightly higher than water, and as soon as a corpse is unleashed, it is swept along by the current, bouncing from shore to shore, eventually bobbing in limbo, hung up atop a rock wall or resting in the shallows on a mud flat in what fisherman so aptly call "dead water."

THE CASTLE HOUSE—Jim Klindt's International Scout is parked in drive. (1983 photo courtesy of Sgt. Rick Chase)

PART ONE

HOMICIDE

Personals

Information wanted as to the disappearance of or location of Mrs. James (Joyce) Klindt last seen on 3/18/83   Call 326-7785

The notice was first published on March 25, 1983, in the *Quad-City Times*. It was paid for by Clifford and Elizabeth Reed, a Davenport, Iowa, couple worried about a friend and former neighbor who had been missing for a week. The telephone number listed was that of the Detective Bureau of the Davenport Police Department. The advertisement ran unchanged until April 5, 1983. At that time the Reeds added monetary incentive and revised the wording, offering: "$500 for information leading to the whereabouts of Mrs. James (Joyce) Klindt." Three days later, they doubled the reward. No one responded to their plea, which remained buried in the newspaper's classified section for another six days, expiring, along with hope, on April 14.

Homicide

One hundred and seventy miles west of Chicago, Interstate 80 arcs across the Mississippi, connecting the Land of Lincoln to Where the West Begins. Traffic moves at a dizzying pace, and tourists crossing the span catch only a fleeting glimpse of the river. They come over a hill and drop into the valley, greeted by a very long bridge and a picture postcard view. The Mississippi rolls beneath them, stretching out and widening on both sides of the bridge. They are staggered by its size and captivated by its beauty — travelers riding a moment in time through a scene that is ever-changing.

Blizzards of May flies hatch in the river, mouthless insects that swirl in the headlights and spatter like sleet against the windshield, covering the roadway with waxy death. Humidity wakes in the blazing haze of summer. Storm clouds build to colossal tops. Thunderbolts split the raindrops and rumble throughout the valley. October brings crisp clear skies. Autumn's colors are reflected along the shores. Februaries are starkly beautiful, the white of snow on ice. Bald eagles add to winter's splendor, great migratory predators that soar above the frozen passage and fish the open waters below the nearby lock and dam.

It is springtime, and the valley is lush. The shadows of evening extend to the Illinois shore. A distant tugboat, pushing a string of barges three abreast, cuts a silver trail in the dark water. Small domed isles, covered with foliage, rise like painted turtles from the surface. Houses dot the riverbanks. At the edge of the flood plain, wooded bluffs climb above the valley floor before giving way to gently rolling farmland. Grain and livestock produced on those rich acres contribute greatly to the local economy, but the inhabitants are not totally dependent upon agriculture for their livelihood. There is also an abundance of industry, commerce made possible by the river.

Dead Water

On the Iowa side, Highway 67 follows the Mississippi as it snakes southwest along the state's eastern border, past the Green Gables Marina, Lock and Dam Number 14, and the mile-long ALCOA aluminum plant. On the outskirts of Bettendorf, the river bends toward the setting sun. Another mile takes the channel beneath the majestic suspension bridges of Interstate 74, twin spans linking Bettendorf to Moline, Illinois. Bettendorf merges on the west with Davenport, a city of 100,000, and the two communities sprawl for miles along the north shore of the river.

Davenport, the largest city on Iowa's eastern border, is part of the bi-state metropolitan community known as the greater Quad Cities. The other three municipalities, Rock Island, Moline, and East Moline, stretch along the opposing shore.

Downtown Davenport sits unprotected on a narrow flood plain no more than seven blocks in width. The district has borne the brunt of numerous floods, and there is an on-again off-again struggle between pragmatists wanting to build a dike and aesthetes who cherish the view — an issue that seems to surface and recede with the waters.

Summers on the levee have long been filled with music, from symphony concerts to Dixieland jazz. But it took gambling to bring people to the waterfront year-round. The area is bustling with tourists and townsfolk eager to try their luck on the President Riverboat Casino. Since the big boat's arrival, new businesses have sprung up, old ones have been revived, and construction is booming.

All of this is a far cry from the economic crisis the city faced little more than a decade ago — a time when it was more prudent to leave the district than to stay.

In 1983, Davenport was suffering through one of the worst years in memory, mired in the unrelenting depths of recession. The business district resembled a ghost town, a double-barreled

Homicide

casualty of the faltering economy and an ongoing flight to the suburbs. Many buildings in and around downtown had fallen into disrepair. Some structures, like the Vale Apartments, one-time home to President Reagan, were beyond salvage.

While most professionals chose to remain within the district, the mass exodus of clothiers, five-and-dimes, and department stores put contingent businesses at risk. Retail shops closed and remained shuttered as tenants relocated in shopping malls. Restaurants, having fewer patrons, were forced to shut their doors. Saloons a century old dried up.

Terrible weather added to the misery. March, which came and went a lion, ushered in "the cruelest month." Nearly five inches of precipitation fell in the first two weeks of April, showers of snow and sleet and rain. Day upon day of overcast skies heightened the pervasive gloom along the riverfront, ominous clouds of hard times to come.

The economy turned to rust. Some factories closed. Others, on the strength of the dollar, moved overseas. Layoffs were common. Jobs were lost. Foreclosures and bankruptcies grew. Unemployment, which had risen with interest rates, spiraled out of control. By mid-April, one of every five adults in the bi-state area was out of work.

1

TORSO

Davenport, Iowa
(Friday, April 15, 1983)

The street lamps flickered on at dusk. Not that anyone noticed. The Friday evening crowd of yuppies, enticed by two-for-one drinks and live entertainment, had already scattered. Happy hour was over in downtown Davenport.

There were a few cars in front of The Dock, a popular riverfront restaurant, just west of Lock and Dam Number 15. A solitary troubled figure stood at water's edge, leaning against the pitted black guardrail. His dark eyes scorned the twilight, making methodical sweeps of the river.

The Mississippi ran muddy and deep, just two feet below flood stage. Water gushed beneath the dam's mammoth rollers and caromed off the concrete retaining wall, throwing a fine mist above the dull and constant roar. A water-soaked log was pulled into the maelstrom, momentarily dragged into the depths before exploding to the surface, sinking, then gliding submerged and dangerous in the swift current. Clumps of debris rushed past like ducks on swirls of foam.

Detective Lt. Ted Carroll pushed himself from the railing and angled across the levee parking lot, detouring around the public boat ramp. He stepped up on the curb and followed the walkway west into LeClaire Park, stopping beside one of the antique lamp posts lining the riverbank to light a cigarette. At the far end of the park, the band shell stood a silent citadel in the darkness. Farther west, beyond John O'Donnell Stadium, traffic streamed up the ramps and across the Centennial Bridge, flickering headlights of last-minute filers traveling to

Homicide

the Rock Island Post Office for pre-midnight postmarks on their tax returns. A cloud bank grew above the span's five arches, a gray wall of worry bringing premature darkness and the promise of unwanted rain. The searchlight of a tugboat flashed across the backdrop, its blue-white beam seeking out the buoys marking the channel.

The roar from the dam was at the detective's back, distant now and shielded by the restaurant. The wind had lain down for the night, but it was a deceptive calm. The turbulence rolled past, cloaked in silence and darkness.

The smell of the river rose up around him, invading the cold dank air. He tossed the cigarette to a watery grave, turned, and trudged back to his unmarked car.

Lieutenant Carroll slid behind the steering wheel and glanced at his image in the rearview mirror. The eyes staring back at him seemed lost. He ran a hand across his stubbled chin and glanced at his watch. Eight o'clock. He slammed the door and twisted the ignition key.

He could not stop thinking about the woman. Finding her, or what was left of her, had become an obsession. Nicotine and caffeine had kept him going for twenty-eight straight days now, and God knows how many nights, digging for leads, interviewing suspects and witnesses. It was not by chance that he always returned to the river.

Joyce Amelia Klindt, 33, had disappeared from her fashionable home in northwest Davenport on Friday, March 18, 1983. She said no good-byes and there was no sign of struggle. Many presumed she had simply run off, fleeing an unhappy marriage. Others, including the authorities, believed she had been murdered.

The police had a prime suspect, the woman's husband, James B. Klindt, a prominent Davenport chiropractor. The doctor had motive and lacked a suitable alibi, but the evidence against him was all circumstantial. For neither a shot nor a scream had been heard the morning Joyce Klindt vanished.

Lieutenant Carroll was helpless, trapped within the framework of the law. He was just one lost soul in a desperate search for another. Without the woman's body, there was nothing he could do.

Davenport-Bettendorf Border
(Saturday, April 16, 1983, 9:05 a.m.)

Thomas Mosher was forty-three. At one time he had made a scant living as a commercial fisherman. Eventually the responsibility of family forced him to find more gainful employment. But he still spent most weekends fishing the Mississippi River with his son.

Dennis Mosher, twenty, had learned to fish by the time he was eight. The eldest of three children, he had inherited his father's gear, a collection of trammel nets, box traps, and jump lines. The river was in his blood.

A commercial fisherman spends every day on the river—at least those days the river allows him to work. It is a rugged life in good times and even tougher during a recession.

Early that morning the Moshers had put their skiff in at the public boat ramp in Moline, Illinois. They would not have gone out at all, except the owner of a Chicago fish house had called Dennis the previous night needing carp for his smoker. It was a raw day, sleeting and windy. Chunks of ice floated in the channel. The small boat hugged the Illinois shoreline as the two men moved cautiously downriver checking their nets. The take was poor.

"I think we're wasting our time, Dennis. You wanna head back?"

"Might as well. Can't see no reason to freeze our butts off for nothin'."

Homicide

Because of the icy wind, they crossed to the leeward side before heading home. Two hundred feet from the Iowa shore, near a big mud trap just east of Lindsey Boat Harbor, Thomas Mosher spotted something floating near the bank.

"What do you make of that?" he asked.

Dennis squinted. "Looks like a cardboard box hung up on the rock ledge."

"I don't think so," said the older Mosher. "It's a body."

"That ain't no body, Dad."

Thomas Mosher knew better. "Take my word for it, son. It's somethin' I've seen before. You better head on up to the bridges and call the police."

Dennis was not convinced. He took a closer look, nearly losing his breakfast, before steering the small craft upriver to a public boat ramp.

"Here's a quarter for the phone," Thomas said. "I'll stay here with the boat."

The call came in to Bettendorf dispatcher Pat Brick at 9:16 a.m. She sent Gary Richardson, a Bettendorf police officer, to the Twelfth Street boat dock. Richardson met the Moshers at the foot of the I-74 bridges a few minutes later.

"You the fellows who called the police?"

Dennis was excited. "We found a body."

"A human body?"

"Yeah. But just part of a body," Thomas replied.

"Where?"

"It's downriver a ways," Dennis said. "If you get in the boat, we'll take you there."

"Can't I drive down and meet you?" asked Richardson.

"No. You can't get to the body from down there," Thomas explained. "There's no road across the railroad tracks and the bank is like a cliff. You better come with us."

The officer was wary. He could feel the bite of the bitter wind through his police parka. He glanced at the ice floating in the choppy water and then at the small aluminum boat, a sixteen-foot skiff overloaded with fishing gear and reeking of fish.

"Okay," he said reluctantly. "Give me a minute to call the station and let them know what's going on."

Richardson radioed Pat Brick and told her he was leaving his squad car. He grabbed a walkie-talkie, clipped it to his belt, then tramped back down the ramp to the waiting boat. After making his way to the bow, the officer sat facing forward on the cold metal bench. He pulled on the parka's hood and cinched it tight. "Let's go," he called over his shoulder.

The boat moved slowly, staying along the shoreline, avoiding the whitecaps and ice in the main channel. Still, the ride was rough, and Richardson steadied himself by grasping the sides of the small craft.

Twelve blocks downstream, near the Davenport-Bettendorf border, the skiff neared some bushes. "Well, we're gettin' closer now. It should be right up around some of these shrubs and stuff," said Thomas.

Dennis stopped the boat about twenty feet from what looked to be part of a body. A single white gull hung like an albatross above the remains. Richardson squinted into the haze, partially blinded by wind-blown tears. His throat was incredibly dry, and he was unsure if the throbbing he felt was coming from the boat's idling motor or his pounding heart.

"Let's get in a little closer, double check," the officer said.

Thomas Mosher eased the boat nearer the shore and Richardson stepped onto the rocks. As he bent for closer inspection the officer gagged, the color draining from his wind-burned face. The body had been ripped in half, torn apart by some incredible force. The head, arms, and rib cage were gone, the bowels eviscerated, the legs severed at the thighs.

The patrolman took a deep breath and released it. "Jesus!"

Homicide

He glanced over at Thomas Mosher. A droll smile ran across the fisherman's weather-beaten face.

"Don't mean to be disrespectful," Mosher apologized, "but this is the sixth body I've found in this godforsaken river in the past twenty-eight years. A guy sort of gets used to it."

Richardson, an evidence technician on the first shift, took the walkie-talkie from his belt and called the station. "Bring a camera, Mike. We got a real doozie on our hands. Somebody's chopped up a woman and dumped her in the river."

Sgt. Michael Halfman, the police photographer, and Det. Chris Kauffman arrived a few minutes later. Halfman and Richardson snapped numerous photos. Kauffman took a statement from the Moshers and wrote down their address and telephone number. "Thanks a lot, fellows. You've been most helpful."

Detective Kauffman returned to the station and notified Dr. Roland Perkins, the Scott County coroner, of the discovery. In turn, Perkins phoned Halligan-McCabe Funeral Home and asked them to pick up the torso and deliver it to Mercy Hospital.

Kauffman then phoned the Scott County Courthouse. Assistant County Attorney Realff Ottesen had come in to clean up some paperwork.

"Mr. Ottesen."

"Yes."

"This is Detective Kauffman of the Bettendorf police. A little while ago a couple of commercial fishermen found part of a body floating in the river just above the Davenport border. It's a white female. We think it might be the remains of the missing Klindt woman. If that's the case, I think the Davenport police should handle it even though the body was found in Bettendorf."

"Did you say part of a body?"

"Yeah, the lower trunk. She's been cut in half just above navel and her legs have been severed at the thighs. Looks like she's been in the water quite a while."

"Where are they taking the body?"

"Mercy Hospital."

"I appreciate the call, Chris. I'll find Bill Davis, let him know. Would you get hold of Ted Carroll?"

"Sure."

Lieutenant Carroll was off duty that morning. Kauffman phoned him at home.

Chief of Detectives Lt. Ted Carroll, forty-seven, was a veteran cop. He had been a member of the Davenport Police Department for eighteen years, his last thirteen in the Detective Bureau. An unpretentious man, Carroll shunned publicity and believed hard work to be a way of life. He expected no recognition. Commitment held its own reward.

Carroll's wife, Jan, was an assistant in the Scott County sheriff's office. They had three children and lived in a modest home in northwest Davenport. Carroll was a family man, happily married to his love and running partner. The couple could often be seen, after work, jogging down Fourth Street and along River Drive.

"Hello," Carroll answered in his distinctive graveled voice.

"Ted, this is Chris Kauffman. Half-hour ago a couple of fishermen found part of a woman's body floating in the river just above Lindsey Park. I think it might be Joyce Klindt."

"What part of the body?"

"Lower trunk."

"Just the pelvis?"

"That's pretty much it, Ted."

"Is the torso still in the water?"

Homicide

"Yes. We're taking pictures right now."

"Has Perkins been notified?"

"A few minutes ago. He's having the body picked up and taken to Mercy Hospital."

Carroll's mind was spinning. He dialed Rick Chase, an evidence technician. "Rick, find Chapman and get over to Mercy. The Bettendorf police just found a floater. They think it's Joyce Klindt. I want you guys there for the autopsy."

Word of the fishermen's discovery spread rapidly through the bi-state community. Within an hour the riverfront was inundated with reporters and curious onlookers.

Lieutenant Carroll had driven to Bettendorf and was standing on the grassy riverbank surveying the scene when he heard someone yell. He turned to see Scott County Attorney William E. Davis bounding toward him. There was little doubt the feisty prosecutor was upset.

Bill Davis, the chief law enforcement agent in the county, had made a name for himself trying tough cases. When he first received word the Klindt woman was missing, he had contacted Acting Police Chief Charles Borgstadt. Davis was pleased to hear that Ted Carroll would head the investigation. The prosecutor had relied on the lieutenant in the past. He trusted and respected the tight-lipped detective, who like Davis had a passion for justice.

"Damn it, Ted. Why is the county attorney always the last to hear? I just found out about all this ten minutes ago. Hell, I was just down the street in the East Village. Do you think it's Joyce Klindt?"

Carroll, a former Marine with a square jaw and a craggy face, stared down at Davis. The lenses of the prosecutor's wire-rimmed glasses were covered with mist, and droplets of rain clung to his salt and pepper beard. "Can't say for sure," the detective rasped, "but my gut says it is."

Davis nodded and rolled up the collar of his trench coat. He watched in disgust while a local television station filmed the entire event. "This is a goddamn zoo. How'd the media get here so fast?"

"Don't know," the detective replied.

The two men looked on until the torso was fished from the water. Satisfied everything was under control, Davis turned and headed for his car. "Call me when you get a make on the woman."

Lieutenant Carroll did not respond. There was no reason to ruin the prosecutor's weekend. The detective was familiar with a new forensic procedure using genetics. But the science was still in its infancy. Identifying a body part without the aid of fingerprints or dental records would be next to impossible.

After Davis had gone, Carroll brushed past reporters and climbed into his car. He drove west on River Drive, eventually angling onto Fourth Street. The smooth one-way had been surfaced with blacktop, hiding warped brick and the scars of a defunct trolley system. He parked a few blocks later behind the Davenport Police Department, a rectangular stucco building located at the base of Harrison Street hill.

The detective slid from behind the wheel, stepping across sidewalks broken and upheaved by the constant freezing and thawing of an Iowa winter. He entered the police station and strode through the maze of corridors leading to his office. The Klindt file was on his desk — a three-ring binder of interviews, hand-written notes, and newspaper clippings. Carroll sat for a time staring at the notebook and recalled the night Joyce Klindt was first reported missing.

Homicide

Davenport Police Department
420 Harrison Street
Davenport, Iowa
(Friday, March 18, 1983, 8:05 p.m.)

Lieutenant Carroll and Sgt. Steve Lynn, the watch supervisor, were interrupted by desk officer Mike Edinger's knock. Sergeant Lynn, a handsome man with coal-black hair and tortoise-rimmed glasses, glanced through the open doorway at the rookie cop. Desk clerk Evelyn Martin was standing by his side. "What is it?" asked the sergeant.

"I hate to bother you, sir," Edinger replied, "but we've got a problem."

Lynn peered inquisitively at the baby-faced officer. "A problem?"

"Yes, sir. We seem to have two conflicting stories on an attempt-to-locate a missing Davenport woman, Joyce Klindt. Evelyn's got a subject on the phone, a Dr. James Klindt, who says he's trying to find his wife, and I've got three people in the outer lobby who want to file a missing person report on the same woman."

Lynn turned toward Carroll. "You've had some dealings with Jim Klindt, haven't you?"

"Let's just say I know a lot about him."

"So, what do you make of all this?"

The detective shrugged. "From what I know of Klindt, I'd guess the woman probably took a powder."

"How long has she been gone, Mike?"

"Since early this morning," Edinger replied. "That's the problem I mentioned earlier, sir. According to procedure, I'm not supposed to fill out a missing person report for seventy-two hours, but the people out front aren't interested in policy. They want action. What should I do?"

Dead Water

"Good question," Lynn replied. "What was the gist of your conversation with the doctor, Evelyn?" the sergeant asked, turning his attention to Martin.

"He told me that he and Mrs. Klindt are going through a divorce, that they had an argument this morning, that she got real upset and walked out. He said he was worried about her, that he was afraid she might hurt herself. He stated he gave her $4,000 in cash as part of the divorce settlement before she took off, that he hasn't seen her since. All in all, he doesn't sound too concerned."

Lynn turned back to the young patrolman. "But the people in the lobby, they're worried, right?"

"Worried and upset."

"Did they tell you why?"

"They feel the Klindt woman is in grave danger."

"In danger? From whom?"

"From her husband, I guess."

"Did the caller give you an address, Evelyn?"

"Yes, sir. It's on Royal Oaks Drive."

"Is there anyone available to stop by the Klindt home and ask the doctor a few questions?"

"Not till the third shift comes on."

"That's Officer Girt's area, isn't it?"

"Yes, sir."

"When she gets here, send her in."

"What about the missing person report?" Martin asked.

"Another couple of hours isn't gonna make any difference. Girt should have a better handle on it after she talks to Klindt."

"What should we tell the people out front?"

"Take their names and tell them we're sending an officer to the house to check it out."

2

A VOICE FROM THE PAST

There were others thinking about Joyce Klindt the morning the torso was discovered. Ron Iossi, married to the missing woman's first cousin, Diana, was also at the river. He had heard the news on his CB radio. Iossi later followed Halligan-McCabe's utility van to Mercy Hospital. The autopsy was about to begin when he phoned Elizabeth Reed. Elizabeth; her husband, Clifford; and Joyce Klindt's aunt (Diana Iossi's mother), Celeste Ralfs, were the trio who had driven to the Davenport Police Department the night of March 18 to report Joyce missing. Iossi confirmed Mrs. Reed's worst fear, telling her the torso of a white female had been found in the river and that it was probably Joyce. Elizabeth hung up without saying good-bye and vomited into the kitchen sink.

(Friday, March 18, 1983, 8:30 p.m.)
Having received little satisfaction from their visit to the police department, the Reeds, along with Celeste Ralfs, returned to the Reed home on Marquette Street. They were greeted at the front door by Elizabeth's mother, Emily Grant. Mrs. Grant, 80, had silver hair and normally wore a lovely smile. Tonight her face was ashen. Worried eyes peered through wire-rimmed spectacles. "Did you find Joyce?" she asked.

Elizabeth shook her head. "No, we went over to the house and talked to Jim. He called Joyce's mother while we were there. Told Ginny that Joyce was missing. He made up some story about her going to Pennsylvania. We knew he was lying, so we went to the police."

Dead Water

The old woman sighed, "Dear God."

"Celeste," Elizabeth said sadly, "I think you'd better phone Ginny, too. Tell her what we suspect."

"I'm not up to it, Liz. Do you suppose you could do it?"

Elizabeth tried to be firm. "She is your sister, Celeste."

"I know," said Mrs. Ralfs, "but we'll both be in tears if I call. I've got her number in my purse."

Elizabeth grudgingly picked up the receiver and dialed long distance. Joyce Klindt's parents, Eugene and Virginia Monahan, lived in Granite City, Illinois, across the Mississippi from St. Louis, Missouri.

Elizabeth knew Joyce's devotion to her family, a caring daughter who never forgot a birthday or special occasion. Joyce was especially close to her parents and spoke to them often by phone. She also took responsibility for arranging get-togethers during holidays. And so the call the Monahans awaited had not been the one placed by Jim Klindt earlier that evening informing them their only daughter was missing. They had been expecting Joyce to phone, inviting them to Davenport for Easter, just two weeks away.

Elizabeth did not want to be the bearer of bad tidings. Understanding the close relationship Joyce held with her family added to the difficulty of the call. Mrs. Reed had a sinking, almost nauseous feeling when Joyce's mother answered. Mrs. Monahan's rueful voice sounded a million miles away.

"Ginny, this is Elizabeth Reed. We were over at Jim's house when he called you earlier."

"That was strange, wasn't it?" Virginia said. "Jim hasn't called us in years, not even when Joyce comes to visit. Do you have any idea what's going on?"

Elizabeth did not respond to the question. "Celeste and I think you and Gene should drive up to Davenport right away."

Homicide

Virginia Monahan's voice was barely audible. "You think something terrible has happened, don't you?"

Elizabeth blinked back tears and searched for the right words. None were forthcoming. Her voice cracked with emotion. "Ginny, we think Joyce is dead."

The passing silence was followed by a brusque good-bye. The messenger was slain.

"Are they coming?" asked Celeste.

"I don't know," Elizabeth replied.

"Well, what did Ginny say?"

"She didn't say anything."

Elizabeth did not have time to worry about Mrs. Monahan. She immediately phoned Katie Ryan. Katie's husband, Jeffrey, a close friend of Jim Klindt, had been best man at the private ceremony in which Jim Klindt and Joyce Monahan exchanged marriage vows in Granite City. Katie had been very curt when Elizabeth phoned her earlier in the evening.

"I'm sorry I was so rude," Katie explained. "Jim stopped over here around six-thirty. He was a real mess. Jeff gave him a tranquilizer and Jim laid down on the couch for a while. He wasn't ten feet from me when you called."

"Did you talk with Joyce today?"

"Not since early this morning. I called to remind her I needed a ride to the bank. She was supposed to pick me up around nine-thirty. I can't drive. My foot's in a cast.

"Jim called a little after nine, said Joyce wouldn't be able to take me. He told me he and Joyce had separated, that she had gone to Lancaster, Pennsylvania, to visit her brother."

The Reeds had a second phone line. While Elizabeth was talking to Katie Ryan, Clifford spoke to their attorney, Thomas Schebler. "I don't know, Tom. Something's just not right. We've got to do something."

"If it's really bothering you," Schebler said, "you might give Realff Ottesen a call. He's the assistant county attorney."

Clifford called Ottesen and explained the situation. "What do you suggest?" Reed asked.

"If it were me," said Ottesen, "I'd go back down to the police station and ask to see a detective."

"That settles it," Clifford announced. "Grab your coat, Liz. We're going back downtown."

Celeste Ralfs then phoned her daughter, Diana Iossi, at Kernan's, upriver in Princeton, where she was having dinner with her husband. Celeste told Diana that Joyce had been missing since morning.

"What'd Diana have to say?" asked Elizabeth.

"She and Ron will head back to Davenport as soon as they've finished eating. Ron's going to call a couple of his cop friends to see if they can meet him here at the house. I'll stay here with Emily and wait."

Davenport Police Department
(Friday, March 18, 1983, 9:50 p.m.)

The Reeds returned to the Davenport Police Department. They were ushered into Lieutenant Carroll's office. Clifford Reed introduced himself and his wife to the detective.

"Ted Carroll," the detective replied, shaking Reed's hand. "Ma'am," he said, acknowledging Elizabeth with a nod. "Please sit down."

Elizabeth Reed, forty-seven, a well-dressed woman with frosted hair, seemed to anticipate Carroll's invitation, plopping on a straight-backed chair. She looked exhausted, but fatigue could not hide the concern in her pale blue eyes. Clifford Reed, fifty-five, thin, high-strung and mustached, was far too nervous to sit.

"I take it you're the people who stopped in earlier this evening."

"Yes," Clifford replied. "We're worried about a friend of ours, Joyce Klindt."

Homicide

"You suspect foul play?"

"I'm afraid so," Clifford sighed. "We think something terrible has happened. She's been missing since early this morning."

"You wanna tell me about it?"

Elizabeth Reed responded. "They were going through a messy divorce. A week ago, Joyce retained Sy Raben as her attorney. He's the best in town, you know. She told me her husband had threatened to kill her if she hired a lawyer."

"You're talking about the chiropractor?" Carroll asked, scratching notes on a legal pad.

Elizabeth gave the lieutenant a dubious glance. "You know Jim?"

"Let's just say I know who he is," the detective replied, declining to elaborate. "Could you start from the beginning?"

"We were next-door neighbors," Elizabeth said, "until the Klindts moved into their new house a few years back. Joyce called me a couple of weeks ago. She was worried. I hadn't seen her since January, but I knew back then she and Jim were having problems. Said she needed to talk, that Jim had gone off the deep end. She didn't explain. She didn't have to. I suggested we have dinner at the Ground Round."

Carroll stopped writing and ran his left hand through his slicked-back hair, revealing "TED," a self-inflicted tattoo on his ponderous forearm. "When exactly did she call, ma'am?"

"It was on Monday ... March seventh. I ... I'm not sure of the time."

The detective glanced at his desk calendar. "And did you meet for dinner?"

"Yes, on Wednesday."

"The ninth?"

"That's correct. Joyce told me she didn't want Jim to know where she was, so she hid her car in our garage. On the way to the Ground Round, she said Jim hadn't given her any money

Dead Water

in weeks. Honest to God, the woman didn't even have any change in her purse. We'd always gone dutch in the past and she was humiliated that I had to pay for her dinner. I really felt sorry for her.

"While we ate, Joyce explained that Jim had filed for divorce and that it was about to be finalized. It was uncontested, but Jim had promised her half. Joyce told me she knew he was lying, but she didn't have money to retain a lawyer. I wrote her a personal check for $200."

"How did she know he was lying, I mean about giving her half?"

"Joyce and a friend of hers, Katie Ryan, went down to Jim's office the following Sunday. Geri Klindt, Jim's mother, let her in. Joyce found the divorce decree and had it copied."

"Okay," said Carroll. "When exactly did Dr. Klindt find out Joyce had hired a lawyer?"

"I'm not sure. Couldn't have been more than a week ago."

"Did Joyce tell you how the doctor reacted when he found out she had retained Sy Raben?"

"Well, I wasn't there," Elizabeth replied, "but I know he was furious."

"How did you learn that?"

"From Jim's mother, Geri."

"Is there anything else you can tell me?"

The Reeds exchanged glances. Instinct told the detective the couple was withholding something important. He didn't press. "You did the right thing, coming down here and all," Carroll continued. "If Joyce doesn't show up by Monday, I'd like you to get in touch with me. If anything comes up before then," he added, handing Elizabeth a card, "you be sure and call."

"There is one more thing," Clifford said reaching into his suit coat pocket. He produced an audio cassette and handed it to the lieutenant. "Jim has always bragged about being friendly with lots of cops and you just admitted knowing him. But I

Homicide

guess we've got to trust somebody. I've been carrying this around with me all night. It's gotten pretty damn heavy."

"What's on it?"

"It's an argument between Joyce and Jim."

The detective's dark eyes flashed. "How'd you get hold of it?"

"Joyce brought it over last night," Elizabeth replied. "Cliff and I were over at Spector's for the annual St. Patrick's Day dinner. You know, corned beef and cabbage. Mother was home alone at the time."

"Your mother lives with you?"

"Yes."

The detective made a note. "Go on."

"Mom said Joyce was really excited when she arrived."

"About what time was that?"

"Must have been around eight. Anyway, Joyce asked if I was home. Mom told her no, we were out to dinner, but we shouldn't be too late. I guess Joyce seemed real disappointed. Mom asked if she could help.

"Joyce told her, 'I'm just gonna bust if I don't share this with somebody.' Then she pulled a small tape recorder out of her purse. Diana Iossi, that's Joyce's first cousin, had helped her set it up in the Klindt kitchen yesterday afternoon.

"Joyce asked Mom if she wanted to hear it. Well, to be honest, she didn't, but she couldn't say no. Joyce had always treated her so nice. My mother's diabetic and her eyesight's poor. Joyce looked in on Mom and helped prepare her insulin injections when we were out of town.

"Cliff and I walked through the front door a few minutes later. I don't think I've ever seen Mother so glad to see me.

"Joyce didn't bother to rewind the tape. She just let it run, explaining it was an argument she and Jim just had and she was going to use it for leverage in the divorce, that she got him to admit to all sorts of things. 'You're not gonna believe it,' she said.

"'Oh, I don't know,' I replied. 'After what you told me last Wednesday night, I think I'd believe just about anything.' But I was shocked. I remember sitting sort of dazed on the couch. And poor Cliff, he got so upset he had to leave the room.

"Joyce was so engrossed with the tape, she didn't even notice that Cliff was gone. She'd interrupt it from time to time saying, 'Do you believe he actually said that?'

"When the tape ended, Joyce scooped up the recorder. 'I gotta go,' she said. 'Bart will be home soon.'

"I think Bart was over at his tutor's. He's had some problems in school. Joyce loved that boy. Took him every place and really fretted when he was home alone, even if it was just for a few minutes. Jim keeps a lot of guns in the house. Once when Bart and a friend were playing with a pistol, it went off. The bullet went right through Bart's mattress and the bedroom floor. Jim eventually found the slug in the basement.

"Anyway, I said good-bye, gave Joyce a hug and told her, 'Everything will be all right, you'll see.' She was already out the door when Cliff called after her."

Clifford cut in. "I'd heard enough to be concerned. I caught up with Joyce in the drive. 'You'd better leave that,' I told her. 'There's no telling what Jim might do if he finds that tape.'

"Joyce said, 'You're probably right, Cliff,' and handed me the recorder. 'One more thing,' I told her. 'You stay in touch. If I don't hear from you or I can't find you, I'm going straight to the police with this.'

"'I'll phone first thing tomorrow,' Joyce promised. Then she backed out of the drive, smiled, and waved good-bye."

Elizabeth's eyes glistened and her voice choked with emotion. "That's the last time we saw her."

Homicide

"That check you gave Mrs. Klindt, did she ever cash it?"

"I don't know. Joyce kept lots of stuff at our place," Elizabeth replied. "I'd given her a key and the use of a spare bedroom. The check could be in a dresser drawer."

"What else did she keep at your house?"

"Some clothes, her good jewelry, and some documents."

"Is there anyone at your house now?"

"My mother and Joyce's aunt, Celeste Ralfs. Celeste was with us the first time we came down to the station. When I saw how upset Mom was, I was afraid to leave her alone. Celeste volunteered to stay with her until we got back."

"Then your mother knows what's going on?"

"Oh, she knows, all right. She worked as a legal secretary most of her life. She doesn't miss much. She and Joyce were real close."

Lieutenant Carroll stopped writing. The last line struck him as strange. It was the second time during their conversation that Mrs. Reed had spoken of Joyce Klindt in the past tense. "I'll wait until you get back home before I send an officer to pick up Joyce's things," Carroll said. "Let's have a listen to that tape."

The forty-five minute cassette aired an ugly domestic argument between the Klindts. It contained some harsh accusations by Joyce and shocking admissions by the chiropractor. There was rough talk of drug use, tax evasion, even adultery. But it was the end of the tape that piqued the lieutenant's interest. "You hurt me last night," Joyce said in a wounded voice. "You held my head down in the covers and told me you were gonna cut me up in little pieces, that I was gonna die."

After the tape had run its course, the conversation between the detective and the Reeds flagged. The lieutenant knew there was nothing he could say that would allay the couple's fears. He tried to console them with words like "Joyce will probably turn up" and "threats are often made during domestic arguments," but his voice sounded hollow. It got to the point where Carroll wondered who he was trying to reassure, the Reeds or himself?

"Why don't you two go home," Carroll said, standing up. "Try to get some sleep."

He would find out later that the Reeds ignored his advice.

3

IN THE BEGINNING

James Barry Klindt was born in St. Louis, Missouri, on July 1, 1948, to Dick, a chiropractic student, and Geraldine, a doting mother. A year later, Dick graduated from Logan Chiropractic College and moved the family to Davenport, Iowa, where he became a successful chiropractor.

Jim Klindt was a pampered boy, handsome and tall, standing well over six feet by the time he was fifteen. His parents bought him a used car before he could legally drive and a new Corvette while he was still in high school.

Despite his having the best of everything, friends and acquaintances remember Jim Klindt as a good kid, unspoiled by the gifts and attention lavished on him by his parents. Athletic and popular, he was named "Prep of the Week" by the *Times-Democrat* (now the *Quad-City Times*) for winning the state's 120 high-hurdles championship in 1966 and was voted king of the "turn-around" dance that same year.

After graduation, Klindt attended Iowa State University in Ames for a year before transferring to his father's alma mater, Logan Chiropractic College, in St. Louis. Dick Klindt was thrilled to learn that Jim had decided to follow in his footsteps.

Founded in 1935, Logan was small school, graduating only about fifteen students annually. Klindt lived in the men's dormitory, Keystone Hall, during his first two years.

One afternoon, he stopped on a St. Louis freeway to help a young woman change a tire. That shy eighteen-year-old was Joyce Amelia Monahan, the daughter of a Granite City, Illinois, schoolteacher. She and Klindt met again that evening at a local drive-in and began dating.

Dead Water

Joyce Monahan's parents were less affluent than her suitor's, but she came from a loving family. Her mother, Virginia, a homemaker, was very supportive of her only daughter, and Joyce had two brothers who looked out for her well-being. Joyce worked in the payroll department of the Mississippi Glass Company in St. Louis. But the job afforded her little financial freedom, so she continued to live with her parents.

James Klindt was Joyce Monahan's only "real" boyfriend. The couple fell in love and were married in a private ceremony in Granite City in August 1969. Only the immediate families and a few close friends attended. The newlyweds moved into a small townhouse in St. Louis, where they lived during the week, spending their weekends with Joyce's parents in Granite City. On July 24, 1970, Bartley James Klindt was born.

Jim Klindt returned to Davenport in 1971 with his wife and newborn son. Joyce was elated with the move. Her mother's sister, Celeste Ralfs, lived in Davenport, and Mrs. Ralfs's daughter, Diana, was Joyce Klindt's favorite cousin. The young women had been best friends since they were four years old. During adolescence, Joyce had spent two weeks each summer visiting the Quad Cities. Joyce and Diana had strengthened their relationship while they were pregnant, and in truth, acted more like sisters than cousins.

After passing the Iowa boards, Jim joined his father's practice. Six years later, a heart attack forced Dick Klindt into retirement. By that time the young chiropractor had more than two thousand patients, so it was rare, indeed, to meet someone in the quiet river community who did not know, or at least know of, Jim Klindt. The charismatic chiropractor then recruited a boyhood friend, Dr. Dennis Hagemann, to be his associate.

The young family lived with Klindt's parents for about a month before finding their first home. Dick and Geri Klindt lent them $24,000 to buy the house, located two doors north

Homicide

of the Reed home on Marquette Street. Even though the Reeds were older, the couples soon became friends.

Jim Klindt and Clifford Reed had similar interests and often went hunting and fishing together. On occasion, the Reeds would spend an afternoon on board one of the doctor's boats.

Joyce and Elizabeth frequented area health clubs and held memberships in Nautilus and Elaine Powers. Even though Joyce suffered from asthma, she struggled to stay in shape, working out frequently to keep herself physically attractive.

The Reeds' daughter, Heather, baby-sat Bart, and she too formed a friendship with Joyce. Both Heather and Joyce enjoyed shopping, spending hours together at North Park Mall.

For the seven years the Klindts and Reeds were neighbors, the two couples got along well. The Klindts seemed happy.

Eventually, Joyce introduced the Reeds to her aunt, Celeste, and her cousin, Diana. By that time, Diana had married a local businessman, Ron Iossi, and lived on an acreage near Walcott, a farming community west of Davenport.

In 1976, Jim Klindt borrowed another $14,000 from his parents and custom-built what would come to be known as "the castle house," a strange combination of modern and medieval architecture, at 1220 Royal Oaks Drive, six blocks north of their first home on Marquette Street. Shortly after they moved into the unusual dwelling, the *Quad-City Times* ran a feature on it, complete with photographs, for the newspaper's Home section. The house was sparsely furnished, so Elizabeth Reed lent the Klindts several pieces she had brought back from Europe.

Joyce Klindt was at the height of her glory, vibrant and attractive. She was a good cook and enjoyed playing the hostess, wearing frilly dresses and expensive jewelry. She may have seemed more like a princess than a housewife to some, for the brick turret which rose above the roof line on the

Dead Water

southwest corner of her new Tudor-style home created the illusion of a medieval castle.

Following the move, the Klindts spent less time with the Reeds. The couples still went out for Chinese food from time to time and shared an occasional Sunday brunch, but they were never as intimate as when they were neighbors.

A short time after he moved into the his home, the doctor's personality began to change. Those who knew the chiropractor blamed his erratic behavior on drugs. Local psychics ascribed to another theory, saying it was the house that was evil. Either way, Joyce found herself living a lie, her dreams tarnished by the grim reality that her husband was using cocaine.

By late 1982 Joyce Klindt's world was collapsing, her thirteen-year marriage in shambles. The rift between the couple widened. Jim Klindt became distant and aloof. He had a "bad habit" and a "new friend." The doctor's drug use and his clandestine extra-marital affair eventually destroyed the couple's social life. In December, Joyce suffered the final humiliation. The chiropractor filed for divorce.

Elizabeth Reed had heard rumors that the marriage was in trouble. In mid-January of 1983 she invited the Klindts to dinner. They arrived in separate cars. The evening was strained. Jim came late and left immediately after the meal.

Iowa has a statutory ninety-day waiting period, and the "uncontested" divorce would not become final until mid-March 1983. Joyce had been led to believe the proceeding was on hold, not finding out until March 13, the day she first read the divorce decree, that Jim Klindt had lied, that he was about to seize the couple's home and take custody of their only child. Joyce avoided default by retaining her own lawyer a week before the ninety-day waiting period ran its course. The legal postponement, however, had placed her life in jeopardy, for the doctor had made it very clear to Joyce that if she contested the divorce, he would kill her.

4

A FRIEND REMEMBERS

While the Mississippi is one of the world's great waterways, extending 2,436 twisted miles from Lake Itasca, Minnesota, to the Gulf of Mexico, it is also a monumental divide, carving the boundaries of ten states and splitting America in half. Those who live in locales bisected by the Great River understand its divisiveness. Bridges do little to close the gap.

The term Quad Cities would presume one big community, but in reality, unity is restricted by the river. Common ground is found on Arsenal Island which lies between the cities, approximate to the Illinois shore. The island is home to the Rock Island Arsenal, a huge military complex which manufactures arms and munitions for the U.S. Army. A major Quad City employer, the arsenal provides hundreds of jobs and pours millions of dollars into bi-state city coffers, the importance of that money amplified by the recession.

The island is linked to downtown Davenport by the Government Bridge, a massive one-hundred-year-old structure with rails atop and roadway below. On the island side of the bridge, a perfectly-balanced swing span rotates in giant circles, allowing tall boats to enter the lock. The section, which is longer than a football field and weighs over 2,000 tons, is lifted by compressed air and is turned by an old trolley motor, revolving on a giant circle of bearings.

Both Clifford and Elizabeth Reed held jobs on Arsenal Island. They commuted together, crossing the Government Bridge each workday. The Reeds were employed by the U.S. Army—Clifford as an industrial engineer in facilities

Dead Water

management working for the Material Command, his wife as a program analyst for the subordinate Armament, Munitions, and Chemical Command division. Elizabeth did not hold a college degree, but she was an intelligent woman and had climbed the General Schedule pay scale at an exceptional rate of speed, eventually earning the same pay of her husband.

At the request of Lt. Ted Carroll, the Reeds returned to the Davenport Police Department for a third time on Monday afternoon, March 21. Joyce Klindt had been missing for three days. It was through these extensive interviews that the detective was able to piece together that fateful day of March 18, 1983.

No one had better recall than Elizabeth Reed. She began with the story of her last conversation with Joyce Klindt. She told Carroll that Joyce fulfilled the promise she had made the night of March 17, phoning her at work the following morning. Elizabeth said she was relieved to hear her friend's soft voice.

The Rock Island Arsenal
(Friday, March 18, 1983, 8:20 a.m.)

"Hi Liz. It's me."

"Joyce, I'm glad you called. I was just thinking about you. Has Jim left yet?"

"He left all right. He took the Jetta."

"Why would he take your car?"

"I don't know. He said he was taking Bart to breakfast at Harlan's and then dropping him off at school. I asked him to take the Scout and he mumbled something about it being low on gas. I said, 'Well then, drive the Cadillac.' He said it was in the garage and he didn't have time to move the Winnebago. I told him, 'So, take the Winnebago.' He said 'I'm tired of driving that piece of crap.' When I reminded him that he didn't

Homicide

mind driving it at night he got real defensive. 'WHAT'S THAT SUPPOSED TO MEAN?' I had a notion to tell him it meant I was sick and tired of removing used condoms from it every morning, but he was already upset and I felt I'd pushed him enough. He said he wouldn't be gone long.

"Maybe it wasn't such a good idea, I mean, me giving you my other set of car keys," Joyce fretted. "Not that it matters. I'm scared to drive any of his cars, anyway."

"Do you want me to come over and pick you up?" Elizabeth asked. "You can drive the Chevy."

Joyce declined. "No, that's okay. Jim said he'd be right back."

"Are you coming over this evening? I picked up an Arsenal application for you."

"I'll be over, but probably not until after eight. I've got a busy day. I'm taking Katie [Katie Ryan] to the bank at ten, then I'm going to the mall before I meet with Reverend Gamb. You don't think he's upset because I canceled the last appointment, do you?"

(Joyce Klindt did not have any religious affiliation. Reverend Gamb was the Reed's minister at Zion Lutheran Church. Joyce had canceled an appointment with him earlier in the week.)

"Don't worry about it. I explained the situation. He understands what you're going through."

"Anyway, after I meet with Reverend Gamb, I'm going to stop by Scott Community College, and maybe AIC [a local business college] and look into enrolling in some courses. I usually pick Bart up after school."

"You sure you don't need a car?"

"No, Jim will be back soon."

Elizabeth could hear dishes rattling in the sink and knew Joyce was on the kitchen phone. It had a long extension cord which allowed her to move freely while she talked.

Dead Water

The conversation came to an abrupt end. "I gotta go now. Jim's home."
"Call me at noon, okay?" Elizabeth pleaded.
"I will," Joyce assured her.

When Joyce failed to "report in" at noon, Elizabeth sensed something was wrong. She tried to phone Joyce around 12:30. No one answered. She tried again at 3:00. Still, no answer. The call she placed to Zion Lutheran Church heightened her fears. Joyce had not shown for her one o'clock appointment. Co-pastor Al Negsted told her that Reverend Gamb had waited for Mrs. Klindt until around 2:15 before leaving the rectory for another appointment.

Elizabeth panicked. Near tears, she phoned her husband. "Cliff, I can't find Joyce," she said breathlessly. "I've called her house twice and she missed her appointment with Reverend Gamb. Has she called you?"

"No," Clifford replied. "I'll let you know if I hear from her." It was obvious from the tone of his voice that he too was concerned.

Elizabeth then phoned Klindt's chiropractic associate, Dr. Dennis Hagemann.

"I can't talk now, Liz. I'm busy with a patient."
Elizabeth persisted. "Have you seen Joyce?"
"No, not today," Hagemann replied.

Elizabeth told Lieutenant Carroll that she and Clifford had left the arsenal earlier than usual Friday afternoon. "Of course, we were delayed. They were working on the bridge, and one lane was closed."

"Seems like it's either construction, or that damn swing span is open," Carroll replied. "Must be one of Murphy's laws. Happens every time you're in a hurry."

Homicide

Elizabeth said that after she and Clifford arrived home, a little after three, she made arrangements to baby-sit her granddaughter, and then resumed her hunt for Joyce. She phoned Katie Ryan at Thoms-Proestler to ask if Joyce had driven Katie to the bank that morning. Ryan had just left work. She tried Katie's home. No answer. She phoned Joyce's aunt, Celeste Ralfs. Mrs. Ralfs had not heard from Joyce. She called Reverend Gamb at his home. Joyce had not phoned him to cancel her one o'clock appointment.

Bishop's Cafeteria
Second and Brady
Davenport, Iowa
(Friday, March 18, 1983, 5:45 p.m.)

That evening, the Reeds, their granddaughter Marcy, and Elizabeth's mother, Emily Grant, drove downtown for dinner. Bishop's Cafeteria was half full.

Elizabeth was sick with worry. All efforts to locate her friend had come up empty. More than nine hours had passed since she had spoken to Joyce. Elizabeth found her appetite had also vanished. She toyed with her food, unable to get the ominous words spoken eight days ago out of her mind. At the time, Joyce was sitting wide-eyed and naive, across from Elizabeth in a booth at the Ground Round. "Jim told me if I hired a lawyer, he'd kill me."

Clifford Reed finished his dessert and stacked the empty saucer on his dinner plate. Elizabeth, in a world of her own, was absentmindedly helping her two-year-old granddaughter with her meal when she heard the clatter of plates. She remembered Joyce had been washing dishes the last time the two women had talked on the phone. "Cliff," she said, "I'm terribly worried about Joyce. Would you try to call Katie again?"

"Sure," he replied. "There's a pay phone in the lobby."

Dead Water

Clifford returned to the table shaking his head. "I talked to Katie. She acted real strange when I asked her if she knew where Joyce was. Said, 'I wish I did. Hope it's nothing bad. I can't talk right now,' and hung up."

Elizabeth glanced up. "'Hope it's nothin' bad?' Why on earth would she say something like that?"

"You know her better than I do," Clifford replied.

A short time later, the family left Bishop's and headed up Brady Street hill. The clock in Palmer Chiropractic College's clock tower read six o'clock. Elizabeth turned to Clifford. "I want to run by Joyce's," she said.

Clifford parked the car in the Klindt driveway. As soon as Elizabeth opened the car door she could hear the stereo blaring. The rock and roll playing inside was so loud that no one heard her knock. She pounded a second time. Bart, twelve, finally opened the door.

Elizabeth was forced to yell. "Where's your mother?"

Bart had trouble hearing her. Elizabeth could see a neighbor boy jumping on the furniture. "Turn down the stereo," she snapped, "and tell your friend in there to settle down."

Bart obeyed and returned to the door.

"Where's your mother?" Elizabeth repeated.

"She's out of town."

"Who told you that?"

"My dad."

"Did she leave while you were here?"

"No," he replied. "She was gone when I got home from school."

Elizabeth went back to the car. "Bart doesn't know any more than we do," she said. "Joyce was gone when he came home from school. He told me his dad said she'd left town."

"You want to wait around?" asked Clifford.

"No, there's nothing we can do here. Let's go home."

Homicide

Elizabeth could not shake the feeling. Something was wrong, dreadfully wrong. As soon as they arrived home, she was back on the phone, talking this time to Jim Klindt's mother, Geraldine.

"Geri, have you seen Joyce today?"

"No," she replied. "Jim called me this morning, said he thought she went to Pennsylvania to see her brother."

"Did she phone you before she left?"

"No."

"Geri, I'm really concerned. Joyce was supposed to call me at noon. Katie doesn't know where she is, and she hasn't called you. Don't you think that's a little strange, I mean Joyce leaving town without telling anybody?"

"It sure is."

"Well, I think we'd better find Jim and get some answers. By the way, I just left their house. Bart's there with one of his little friends and the stereo's blaring."

"Kids!" Geraldine sighed. "I suppose Dick and I had better get up there."

"Cliff and I will meet you."

After hanging up, Elizabeth called Katie Ryan. "Katie, we're still looking for Joyce and no one seems to know where Jim is. Do you know what's going on?"

Katie was abrupt. "Sorry, I can't talk now," she said, hanging up the phone.

Elizabeth phoned Celeste Ralfs again, explaining that Bart was home alone and that Geri had told her Jim said Joyce had gone to Pennsylvania. "We're meeting Dick and Geri at Joyce's."

"I want to go with you," Celeste insisted. "We've got to find out what's going on."

Dead Water

The Castle House
1220 Royal Oaks Drive
Davenport, Iowa
(Friday, March 18, 1983, 7:10 p.m.)

The Reeds picked up Celeste, and the trio arrived at the castle house the same time as Jim Klindt's parents. The gray evening was giving way to darkness.

Jim Klindt was standing by the curb, next to the mailbox. The chiropractor was an imposing figure — bald, mustached, and six-foot-six-inches tall. He was casually dressed, wearing scuffed boots, faded blue jeans, plaid shirt, and a brown leather jacket.

Elizabeth jumped from the car, almost before it stopped, and lunged at him. "Where's Joyce?" she yelled.

"I don't know," he said. "When I came home this morning, I found her sitting on the bed holding a gun to her head."

The response angered Elizabeth. "Oh, come on, Jim. She was doing dishes. I was talking to Joyce on the kitchen extension when you walked in this morning."

Klindt glared at her, turned, and stomped into the house. Dick Klindt caught up with him and placed a consoling hand on his son's shoulder. The others followed through the open door.

Inside, the atmosphere was so intense no one bothered to sit. Geraldine Klindt seemed as concerned as Elizabeth. "What did you do with Joyce?" she demanded.

Elizabeth was more aggressive. She fueled the confrontation, repeatedly calling Jim a liar. Klindt moved toward Mrs. Reed, his red face not six inches from hers, telling the same story over and over.

"When I got home, Joyce was sitting on the bed with a gun. I took it away from her. She took some clothes and left. I don't know where she went."

Homicide

"Don't give me that," Elizabeth said. "I told you Joyce was in the kitchen when you came through the door this morning. I know. I was talking to her on the phone. She would have told me then if she was leaving town."

The chiropractor tweaked at his bushy mustache. "What did you say to make her so despondent?" he asked.

Elizabeth would not allow Klindt to switch the blame. "I didn't say anything, Jim. And you know as well as I do that she wasn't despondent. Now where is she?"

Klindt responded through clenched teeth. "I told you. I don't know! Maybe she went to Pennsylvania to see her brother."

But Elizabeth would not back off. "You're lying, Jim. She's not the type to just skip out. Besides, you and I both know she never has anything ironed. It would have taken her all day just to get ready."

Elizabeth's assault continued until Dick Klindt mercifully interrupted. "Jim, you've got to call her parents," he said.

It took some persuading, but Dick finally convinced his son to call Granite City. Jim stalled for a moment, glanced at his mother, then Elizabeth, and decided he would rather face the Monahans. He reluctantly picked up the phone. "Ginny, this is Jim," he said speaking to Joyce's mother. "I thought I'd better give you a call. Joyce is missing ... Oh, I'm sure she's okay. She left here around ten this morning. We're going through a trial separation. I think maybe she went to Lancaster ..."

He paused.

"I don't think so," Klindt replied. "She's been real despondent lately, you know, losing custody of Bart and everything ... Okay. I'll let you know as soon as she turns up."

Clifford Reed had heard and seen enough. "We're getting out of here," he said.

Elizabeth was unwilling to leave. "Not yet," she replied.

Clifford was emphatic. "Yes, we are!"

Elizabeth could not summon the energy to argue. Celeste Ralfs followed them through the door. As they trudged down the drive, Clifford turned to Elizabeth. "He's killed her," he said, his voice trembling. "We've got to go to the police."

(Friday, March 18, 1983, 11:00 p.m.)

After Clifford and Elizabeth Reed had surrendered the tape to Lieutenant Carroll, they drove back to the castle house. Dick Klindt's Chevette was still parked behind the Winnebago in the driveway. It seemed obvious that the police officer, promised some three hours earlier, had not yet arrived.

Dick and Geraldine Klindt were talking to Jim in the open doorway when the Reeds pulled to the curb. When the chiropractor saw their Buick, he said good-bye to his parents and hurried back inside.

Elizabeth met Geraldine on the front steps, put her arm around the big woman's shoulders, and walked her down the drive. Geraldine Klindt was cold with fright, shaking so badly she needed help getting into the compact car. The cruiser arrived as the Klindts backed onto Royal Oaks Drive.

(Friday, March 18, 1983, 11:25 p.m.)

Thinking the Reeds had gone directly home from the police station, Ted Carroll dispatched Patrolman Greg Glandon to their residence to pick up Joyce Klindt's belongings. Glandon arrived about the same time as Diana and Ron Iossi, who were just returning from dinner in Princeton. The couple's two police friends were already there.

After being asked bluntly to leave the castle house by Officer Gayle Girt, the Reeds left the policewoman alone with Jim Klindt and headed south on Marquette Street. They could see flashing red lights six blocks away and arrived home puzzled by the scene. Their street looked like a parking lot for squad cars.

Homicide

Officer Glandon impounded everything Joyce had stored with the Reeds except her clothing and returned to the station. Ted Carroll looked through the missing woman's possessions. "Did the Reeds ever show up?" the detective asked.
"They arrived a few minutes after I got there," Glandon replied. "The place was a madhouse."
"A madhouse?"
"There must have been a dozen people, including a couple of police officers."
"City cops?"
"No. One was with the Scott County Sheriff's Department. The other fellow was from the Metropolitan Enforcement Group. Friends of the family, I guess. Anyway, they were planning to go out and look for the missing woman's car."

(Saturday, March 19, 12:30 a.m.)
Officer Gayle Girt did not return to the Davenport Police Department until well after midnight. She had phoned Lieutenant Carroll around 11:50 p.m., requesting permission to fill out a missing person report. The detective was pacing the lobby when Girt walked through the door. "So, how's the good doctor?" he asked.
"Oh, he tried to be gracious, but I felt like an intruder."
"Sounds like Klindt," Carroll quipped. "Why don't you give me a verbal. You can type the report later."
"Sure," Girt replied glancing at her notes. "When I arrived at Klindt's residence a small car was leaving. A man and a woman were standing in the drive. They said they were waiting for me. Evidently they knew Sergeant Lynn was sending an officer to the house."
"It wasn't the Reeds by chance?"
"I believe that was their name."
"That's the couple who came down to the station to report Mrs. Klindt was missing. They were pretty concerned. Must

have driven straight back to Klindt's house after they left my office. Go on."

"They followed me up to the house. Kind of a spooky place, isn't it? Dr. Klindt opened the door. Sort of scowled when he saw the Reeds behind me.

"I introduced myself and told him I was there to check on the location of his wife. The doctor told me he hadn't seen her since morning. I asked if he minded if I came in and looked for myself. He said he didn't object, but I could tell he didn't like it when the Reeds followed me inside. I scanned the living room. The house was a mess. Newspapers and magazines scattered everywhere. I went into the kitchen. Dirty dishes were stacked on the counter and in the sink. While I was looking around, the woman ... what was her name?"

"Elizabeth."

"Yeah, Elizabeth. Anyway, she and Dr. Klindt were really going at it, so I asked her to leave. She just stood there and glared at Klindt. Wasn't very happy with me, either."

Carroll smiled. "No, I don't suppose she was."

"After they'd gone, I asked Dr. Klindt if I could take a look upstairs," Girt continued. "He said, 'Sure. Follow me.'

"The steps leading to the loft and the basement are inside the turret. The spiral staircase wraps around the outside wall of the fireplace. I followed Klindt up to the master bedroom. A blue handgun, a Ruger revolver, was lying on the king-size bed — a six-shot double-action .357 magnum. I opened the cylinder and found that it held five rounds of live ammunition. I noted the empty chamber was in line with the barrel and the firing pin. I dumped the bullets into my hand and put them in my breast pocket.

"Klindt pointed at an occasional chair. 'Joyce was sitting right there,' he said. Then he told me the hammer was cocked and she was holding the gun in both hands between her legs and pointing it at the floor. He stated he remained calm and

Homicide

said, 'Joyce, don't move,' before taking the gun away from her.

"After that, he told me they sat on the bed and talked and cried while they discussed the divorce. Then Joyce packed a couple of suitcases and left.

"I looked at that bed. If anyone had been sitting there earlier, the bed spread would have been wrinkled. But it wasn't. In fact, the bed was the only thing in the entire house that was neat. The closets were a disaster, and the large sunken black tub in the upstairs bathroom was coated with a grimy film. In the adjoining rec room, clothes were stacked in baskets beneath the pool table. And when we walked back down the staircase, I noticed cobwebs under the steps.

"The whole time, Klindt continued to ramble about the things his wife had taken with her and the $4,000 in cash he had given her just before she left.

"There was a pistol range in the basement and a storage area with large plastic garbage bags stacked against the outer wall. There were two cars parked in the garage, an International Scout and a Cadillac. The plastic windows of the Scout were old and clouded. I opened the passenger door and looked inside and peeked through the windows of the Cadillac.

"A Winnebago motor home was parked in the drive and there was a big boat out back. I shined a flashlight through the windows. Didn't see anything irregular. That's when I returned to the house and called you for permission to fill out the missing person report."

"Did you check the trunk of the Cadillac?"

Girt seemed embarrassed. "No sir, I didn't."

"Don't worry about it. If he killed her, he had all day to dispose of the body."

"When I sat down with Dr. Klindt to fill out the report, he was overly helpful. He continued to volunteer information about his wife being an asthmatic, that she took all her

Dead Water

medications with her, and about divorce being messy. Then he said the oddest thing."

Carroll leaned forward. "And what was that?"

"He said, 'Thank God I don't have a girlfriend. That'd really be a problem.'

"Well, I glanced up from my paperwork. I didn't quite believe my ears. 'What did you say?' I asked. And he repeated it."

"Anything else?"

"Only that he seemed calm, confident, and well-rehearsed."

(Saturday, March 19, 1983, 12:55 a.m.)

It was nearly one o'clock before the front porch light was turned off at the Reed home. Celeste Ralfs had been the last to leave. After the Reeds climbed into bed, the house fell deathly quiet. The grandfather clock in the living room broke the silence, chiming once. A short time later, Clifford started to sob.

Elizabeth was so concerned about her husband's mental state that she phoned Kenneth Gamb. The minister came right over. Reverend Gamb tried to help Clifford come to grips with his feelings, but Clifford was so distressed that he continued to cry for more than an hour. He would say later that he felt betrayed by the chiropractor.

Reverend Gamb left around 2:30. The Reeds crawled into bed, physically and emotionally exhausted. Sleep did not come quickly, nor did it last. At 5:30 Saturday morning, the telephone rang. It was Ron Iossi. "We've found Joyce's car."

5

LOST WEEKEND

Holiday Inn of Moline
6902 27th Street
Moline, Illinois
(Saturday, March 19, 1983, 6:35 a.m.)

The sun had risen by the time Clifford Reed swung the Buick Electra around the back of the Moline Holiday Inn.

"There's Ron's truck," Elizabeth said.

Ron Iossi climbed down from his truck cab and yawned. "Cliff, Liz ... You remember Warren Welke, don't you?"

"Sure. You were at the house last night," Clifford replied thrusting out his hand. "Things were kind of a blur."

"Know what you mean," Welke replied.

"Warren here is a MEG officer," Iossi said.

"Metropolitan Enforcement Group," Welke explained. "The Jetta's parked over there behind the dumpster," he said. "I felt the hood right after we found it. The engine was cool. Even checked out the guest registers of the other motels in the area. If Joyce is around, she's using another name."

"Maybe she registered under Joyce Monahan," Elizabeth suggested.

"We thought of that," said Iossi.

"Oh!" Elizabeth replied, unable to hide her disappointment.

"Anyway," Iossi said, "if you don't mind standing watch for awhile, we'd like to go inside, get a donut and a cup of coffee and check out the rooms."

"Sure," Clifford said. "Take your time."

Iossi and Welke returned to the Jetta an hour later.

Dead Water

"No luck," said Iossi. "We knocked on every door. If they didn't answer, we went back to the lobby and called their room on the house phone." He grinned. "We did manage to upset a lot of guests."

"It could have been worse," said Welke. "Ron wanted to set off the fire alarm."

"You didn't by chance notify the Davenport police, did you?" asked Elizabeth.

"I called them a couple of hours ago," Welke said. "Told the desk officer that we'd found Joyce Klindt's Volkswagen Jetta. We're out of Davenport's jurisdiction. He said he'd relay the information to the Moline police."

The conversation lulled for a moment. Iossi took a deep breath and stared at the Reeds. "How well do you two really know Jim?" he asked.

"Pretty well," Clifford replied. "We were neighbors for seven years."

"Well, I can't stomach the S.O.B.," Iossi said bluntly. "Held a gun to my head one night. Said he'd blow my brains out if I ever told Joyce he ran around on her. That's not all of it. He's into drugs, too ... big-time."

Clifford shook his head sadly.

"I'm not the only person he's threatened," Iossi continued. "Katie Ryan told Diana that one time she and Jeff were having dinner at the Klindt house and Jim got so mad that he picked up a carving knife and threatened to cut Joyce's head off."

The group resumed the vigil and discussed their options.

"Too bad we can't get into the trunk," said Iossi.

Elizabeth reached into her handbag. "I've got the keys."

The key was not needed. The trunk was unlocked.

"It looks just like it did last Wednesday," she said. "Joyce was trying to get ammunition for the divorce and I helped her load a small safe from her garage into the trunk. We took it to a Bettendorf locksmith." She laughed. "I think the poor guy thought we were criminally insane. He didn't want anything to do with opening that safe. Anyway, Joyce's bowling bag was sitting in the middle, and her trench coat was folded to one side. Nothing's been moved. Do you think we could take a look inside the car?"

"Guess it wouldn't hurt," Welke said, unlocking the door. "But don't touch anything."

The bucket seat on the driver's side was shoved all the way forward. "Is Joyce real little?" Welke asked.

"She's small," Elizabeth said, "but she'd have trouble fitting behind the wheel. What bothers me is the car was a mess on Wednesday. I know, because my purse fell over and everything dumped on the floor. When I bent over to pick it up, there was junk everywhere. It's been vacuumed and washed. Joyce isn't the type to have cleaned out her car."

"There's not much more we can do here," said Welke. "Besides, I've gotta run."

"Thanks for the help," Clifford said. "Do you suppose you could call the Davenport police again before you leave?"

After the two men had gone, Elizabeth turned to her husband. "If they don't get here pretty soon, Cliff, I may drive the Jetta back to Davenport myself."

Clifford talked her out of it.

It was noon when the Reeds left the Holiday Inn. The Moline police still had not shown.

(Sunday, March 20, 1983, 1:05 p.m.)

Four inches of snow fell on Sunday, as if the relatively mild winter had saved its fury for the final day of the season. By noon, the wet white shroud had covered lawns, bent boughs, and turned the city streets to slush.

Elizabeth Reed braved a storm of fears, delivering two containers of beef stew to the Klindt house, a peace offering of sorts. Mrs. Reed was apprehensive. If the doctor had murdered

Dead Water

Joyce, as she suspected, he was truly a dangerous man. Elizabeth knew one of the chiropractor's maxims was: "Nobody ever crosses Jim Klindt." She had second thoughts after ringing the bell and was relieved when Bart answered the door. "Dad's not home," he said. Elizabeth placed the Tupperware bowls on the kitchen counter and explained to Bart how to microwave them before she left.

Jim Klindt phoned Elizabeth Sunday night and thanked her for the stew. She considered telling him that Ron Iossi had found the Jetta but decided against it. While on the phone, Mrs. Reed renewed her inquiry. "Jim, what clothes did Joyce take with her?"

"Oh, I don't know, just some stuff in the house."

"What suitcase did she take?"

"She didn't take a suitcase."

"Well, how did she get her clothes into the car?"

Klindt began to stall and become evasive. "I ... I carried them out for her."

"Where did you put them?"

"In the trunk."

"Lay off," Clifford whispered. "Lay off."

Elizabeth ignored him. "Were they on hangers?"

"Yeah," the doctor replied.

Elizabeth knew Klindt was lying. The only clothes Joyce hung up were those that no longer fit. Everyday clothes were piled in laundry baskets beneath the pool table, unironed until needed.

It became obvious that the chiropractor wanted to terminate the interrogation when he went on the offensive. "Elizabeth, *was* Joyce seeing another man?"

"Jim, she never had eyes for anyone but you."

Klindt was silent for a long time, then quietly said good-bye.

After she hung up, Clifford shook a finger at her. "You're provoking a cobra."

6

SUSPECT

Before they left the police station on Monday afternoon, March 21, the Reeds asked Lieutenant Carroll if there was anything else they could do to help. The detective suggested they place an advertisement in the classified section of the *Quad-City Times* listing the Detective Bureau's telephone number.

That evening, Dr. James Klindt finally showed up at the police station, seventy-one hours after reporting his wife missing. The chiropractor would not have come at all had Lieutenant Carroll not phoned him under the pretense of asking the doctor to aid in the investigation. Carroll had requested that Klindt bring a recent photograph of his wife.

Davenport Police Department
(Monday, March 21, 1983, 7:05 p.m.)

Lieutenant Carroll knew Jim Klindt only by reputation. The two men had never met. The chiropractor had been under scrutiny ever since an informant had told a police officer that Klindt trafficked in cocaine. That was a secondary concern now. With the finding of the Volkswagen, more important questions needed to be answered.

The detective was taken aback by Klindt's size, so tall he seemed to duck his head entering Carroll's small office. The strength of the doctor was not reflected in his handshake, but his hands were large and powerful. Suddenly the detective was remembering something Elizabeth Reed had said, that Klindt used to brag he could kill by merely applying pressure to any of seventeen different points of the human body. "Have a chair, Doctor."

"Thanks."

"The reason I asked you down," said the detective, "is to inform you that we've located your wife's car. The Jetta was found abandoned Saturday morning behind the Holiday Inn."

Revealing the car had been found was two-fold in purpose. First, Carroll meant to catch Klindt off guard. Finding the car was not the reason the detective had given when he had asked Klindt to come to the station. Second, Carroll was careful not to divulge which Holiday Inn. There are three in the Quad Cities, and Jim Klindt was "familiar" with all of them.

The chiropractor seemed surprised. The detective suspected Klindt's reaction was not so much that the car was found as that it had been found so quickly. When the chiropractor did not ask which Holiday Inn, Carroll surmised it was because Klindt already knew.

"I've been worried all weekend," Klindt said. "She was carrying a lot of money. I gave her $4,000, all in hundreds, before she left the house last Friday. Now that you've found the Jetta, I'm even more concerned. Were her clothes in the car?"

"No," Carroll replied.

Klindt continued. "She didn't take a suitcase. I loaded the stuff loose in the back seat. Most of her clothes were on hangers. She also took her hair dryer, curlers, and makeup. You know, stuff like that in a paper bag. She left the house around ten."

"Any ideas on where she might have gone?" Carroll asked.

"No."

"The front seat of the Jetta was moved all the way forward," said the detective. "So she must have been driving. Since the car is registered in your name, and I've got no reason to hold

Homicide

it. I'll have a couple of officers drive you over so you can claim it."

Klindt nodded. "I want you to know that I appreciate all you're doing."

The conversation was interrupted when Carroll's phone rang.

"Excuse me for a moment," the detective said. "Lieutenant Carroll speaking."

"Lieutenant, this is Clifford Reed. I've just heard that Jim Klindt was seen out on the river near Princeton last Friday morning driving his airboat."

Carroll remained expressionless. "That's very interesting. I'll check it out. Thanks."

"If that's all," Klindt said standing, "I'll be going."

The detective stopped him. "If you don't mind, Doctor, there is one more thing."

Klindt did not like the tone of the detective's voice. He sat down gingerly, not leaning back.

Carroll stared at the chiropractor for a moment, his deep-set eyes concealing his thoughts. He scratched a thick graying sideburn with the forefinger of his left hand.

"Would you tell me what you were doing in Princeton the morning your wife disappeared?"

Klindt squirmed in the chair and stumbled a response to the unexpected question.

"Not at all," the chiropractor replied. "I ... I received a call from a friend of mine. Wednesday night," he said shifting his eyes away from the detective's glare ... "I think ... he told me the high water was banging my airboat into the cement. I ... I went up to move it before it ... it got damaged."

Lieutenant Carroll realized he had caught Klindt off guard. For the first time, he felt the doctor's cool facade crack. Keep the pressure on him, Carroll thought. Don't let him breathe. He hasn't rehearsed this part.

"Did you take your airboat out on the river, Doctor?"

"A ... just b ... briefly," Klindt sputtered.

"Why would you do that? I mean, with the river flooded, being so dangerous and all?"

The questions were getting tougher. Klindt took out a handkerchief and mopped his brow. "Well, it'd been sitting there for a long time. I ... I just wanted to make sure it'd still run."

"How long were you out on the water?"

"I ... I'm not sure. Forty-five minutes ... maybe an hour."

"Gee, I guess you got it running pretty good, huh?" The detective stared at the chiropractor, waiting for a reaction.

Klindt did not respond. He sat quietly, fidgeting from time to time like a schoolboy caught in a lie. "Can I go now?" he finally asked.

"Yeah, I'm through, Doctor," the detective rasped. "For now."

The chiropractor gave a worried glance over his shoulder as he headed for the door. Two uniformed officers were waiting just outside Carroll's office to drive Klindt to Moline Holiday Inn so he could reclaim the Volkswagen Jetta.

Lieutenant Carroll would learn later that Jim Klindt was so glad to get out of Carroll's office that he talked continually on the way to Moline. Officers Schulz and Glandon made mental notes while the doctor rambled.

"You think you know somebody," Klindt had said, "then she pulls a stunt like this. Even took the $4,000 I had hidden. Told me I was never gonna get it back. I'll bet she's in California or Florida by now ... She always liked the ocean and warm weather."

When they arrived at the Moline Holiday Inn, Officer Schulz pointed out that whoever parked the Jetta obviously did not

Homicide

want it found. He also asked Dr. Klindt if it was okay for the officers to take a look at the car before he drove it back to Davenport.

"No problem," Klindt had replied.

Glandon found nothing of relevance and turned the car over to Klindt. "It's all yours."

Klindt seemed to be waiting for the two officers to leave. Officer Glandon sat patiently in the cruiser, watching the doctor while Schulz filled out a report. After a few minutes, Glandon climbed out and walked over to the Jetta. "Something wrong, Doctor?"

"Ah ... No."

"You wanna see if it'll run?" asked Glandon.

The chiropractor had slid the bucket seat back as far as it would go, but he still looked cramped inside the small car. Glandon tried not to smile. Klindt twisted the key in the ignition. The engine turned over, but the car did not start. Klindt acted surprised.

"Pull the hood release and I'll take a look," Glandon said.

The chiropractor obliged.

"I got some bad news, Doc. Seems whoever left this here didn't want it moved. The distributor wire's missing."

"Probably vandals," Klindt said glumly.

"We'd like to stay around and help," the officer said, "but we've got to check out the motel and the airport while we're over here. You'd better call a tow truck."

Carroll laughed when he heard the story. But he was also curious. Why would anyone disable the car?

7

FOOTSTEPS

Lieutenant Carroll spent the following week trying to retrace the movements of the chiropractor on the day Joyce Klindt disappeared. He drove to Princeton, looking for anyone who might have seen Klindt out on the flooded river the morning of March 18.

Princeton, Iowa
(Tuesday, March 22, 1983)

The village of Princeton lies on Iowa's eastern border, eighteen miles upriver from where the torso was found. While much of the area's support comes from farming, Princeton is a bedroom community of about a thousand residents, many of whom commute to work in nearby cities.

Princeton is not a wealthy town, but for most of its inhabitants, money is far down the list of life's priorities. Those who live there do so because they love the water. For them, "river rat" is more a term of affection than an insult.

Like so many hamlets built along the Mississippi, Princeton is "a mile long and two blocks wide." U.S. Highway 67, also known as "The Great River Road," follows the length of the village and is paralleled by the Soo Line's tracks until the two intersect at the north edge of town.

Princeton's business district extends along both sides of River Drive on the north edge of town, a block east of Highway 67. None of the buildings exceeds three stories in height, and the panorama of the river from the western hillside is virtually unobstructed. Kernan's, a riverfront restaurant with a stunning view, is the most notable business in Princeton. Its

Homicide

spacious dining room has large plate glass windows with views up and down the river and across to the Illinois shore.

Just north of Kernan's, across a sloping parking lot and asphalt drive, is Al Grosz's home, and adjacent to the house, his business, Al's Garage. The area behind the two structures has been fenced off to keep pedestrians from cutting through his property, and there is a small docking facility at the river's edge which Grosz leases to boaters.

North of Al's Garage lies the Princeton Beach Marina, where a paved boat ramp leads down to wooden docks that rise and fall with the level of the water. Above the ramp, the marina's cement block building holds supplies and spare parts for boat repair. The structure is set on higher ground, safe except when the river floods.

Lieutenant Carroll's first stop was the Princeton Beach Marina, where he interviewed the marina owner, Chuck Seitz. Seitz, and his girlfriend, Marie Smith, had spent the morning of March 18 fighting a losing battle against the rising river.

"I guess it was around nine-thirty ... nine-forty-five, when we first noticed Dr. Klindt," Seitz told Carroll. "Marie and I were busy rearranging sandbags against the marina's outer wall. The river was cresting and we got hit pretty hard. Must have been a foot of water inside the building.

"It was really cold last Friday, thirty-eight, maybe forty degrees. It was raining and the wind was blowing. Marie and I decided to take a break, walk down to Kernan's, get a cup of coffee, and warm up. That's when I saw Jim."

Seitz pointed at the dock behind Al's Garage. "Dr. Klindt leases space from Al. The airboat was winched right over there, maybe sixty feet from here."

"When did Dr. Klindt move the boat?"

"I heard he and his boy came and got it over the weekend."

"Do you know where he stores it?"

"Not for sure," Seitz replied. "He used to store it on a farm over by Dixon, but I don't think he keeps it there anymore."

"Isn't it sort of unusual to have an airboat in these parts?"

"Yeah. I've seen others, but there's only one like Klindt's."

"What makes it different?"

"It's a black Hurricane Aircat. You know, like they use in the everglades. Got this big Cadillac V-8 engine and a huge propeller housed in a wire cage."

"Do you know why he moved it?"

"Yeah. The flood waters had lifted the boat off those rubber rollers over there, and the waves were banging its hull into the sea wall. The stern was nearly under water."

Carroll's eyes narrowed. "You're sure it was Dr. Klindt you saw?"

"It was Klindt, all right. I didn't see him arrive, but he's easy enough to recognize. He was stooped over, bailing water out of the airboat. Besides, I spoke to him later."

"Did he take the boat out of the water on Friday?"

Seitz scratched his head. "He might have put it on a trailer, but I don't think so. I'm almost sure I saw it in the water Saturday morning."

"If it was your boat, would you have gotten it out on Friday?"

"Long before that, but then I wouldn't have gone out on the river Friday, either."

"So Dr. Klindt was still on the airboat when you returned from your coffee break?"

"Yep. He'd finished bailing and was cranking the engine. It wouldn't start. He's a real good customer, and I thought about offering him a hand. I saw him glance up, so he knew I was here, but he didn't ask for help.

"When he finally got it running, he made a couple of passes past the marina. The wake knocked over a bunch of sandbags. I was really upset. Marie and I had worked half the morning

Homicide

setting them in place. A few minutes later he idled up to the marina's dock and asked if I could pump him some gas.

"I was still hot. I remember telling him to take it easy with that goddamn boat, that he'd just destroyed one hell of a lot a work. Then I explained the pumps weren't set up for high water."

"Jim hollered back, 'Sorry,' and headed north. I don't have any idea how far upstream he went or where he found fuel. Marie and I left a few minutes later. I'll tell you one thing, you'd have to be nuts to go out on that river last Friday."

"I really appreciate the information," Carroll said. "Do you know of anybody else who might have seen Klindt last Friday?"

"Check over at Kernan's. I know Shirley Burmeister was working that morning. She served us coffee."

"What about the owner of the garage next door?"

"No," Seitz said shaking his head. "I'm sure Al was out of town."

Lieutenant Carroll walked south around Al's Garage and house and entered Kernan's. Shirley Burmeister, a waitress and barmaid, remembered seeing Jim Klindt the morning of March 18. Tall and thin, Burmeister was a stereotypical waitress, forty-something with black horn-rimmed glasses and bleached hair.

The restaurant had not yet opened for business when Carroll sat down with her. She puffed nervously on a chain of cigarettes and chatted incessantly about the morning of March 18. Burmeister told Carroll she had just finished setting up the salad bar and was taking a coffee break.

"I was sitting in the dining room on the upper level, when I saw this very tall man with a mustache walking down the drive between the restaurant and Al Grosz's house. He was wearing a navy windbreaker with the hood pulled over his head and tied around his face. He was carrying a dark plastic garbage bag in each hand. He put them on his airboat and took off like a bat out of hell."

"Did you see the man's car?"

"No. It must have been parked up the slope."

"Did you see him return?"

"Uh-huh. He made several trips out onto the river. Loaded the airboat with garbage bags and returned empty."

"You could see the boat was empty?"

"It was empty, all right. I remember, because I was curious at first. I mean, why would anybody go out on the river on such a miserable day. It was cold and rainy and the water was real choppy. When he came back and carried two more bags down to the boat, I got mad. I thought some outsider was dumping his garbage into the river."

"Then you didn't know at the time it was Jim Klindt?"

"No. Not until later."

"Which way'd he head when he left the dock?"

"I'm not sure. I think he went straight out and then turned south toward LeClaire. But I didn't watch where he went after that. That boat goes awfully fast, and the river's pretty wide here. He could've turned back upriver."

"Okay. So he came back and loaded the airboat a couple more times, correct?"

"I'd guess he made four or five trips in all, but I was working, so I'm not positive. I could always hear him return, though. The boat's so noisy it rattled the windows when he got close to shore. And like I told you, I was kind of leery about this fellow dumping garbage into the river."

"How long was he out on the river?"

"All total, I'd guess an hour. After we opened, sometime around eleven, I took another break. I was sitting with Roger Becker, he's one of our regulars, when this Klindt fellow made his last trip. I remember asking, 'Hey Roger, who's that crazy ass out on the river?' He said, 'Oh, that's Dr. Klindt.'"

Homicide

Lieutenant Carroll knew that Jim Klindt would never have taken the main highways to get to Princeton, not if he had Joyce's body in the back of the Scout. Klindt was an avid hunter, and he knew the back roads north of town. The detective remembered Joyce had told Elizabeth Reed, during their final phone conversation, that the chiropractor took her Jetta because his Scout was out of gas. Carroll stopped at every service station on the north edge of Davenport. Don Giammetta, the owner of Fred's 66 on Northwest Boulevard, remembered seeing Klindt the morning of March 18. So did his cashier, Lea Edwards. Giammetta was a high school classmate of Jim Klindt; Edwards, an acquaintance of the chiropractor.

Fred's 66 Service
7627 Northwest Boulevard
Davenport, Iowa
(Thursday, March 24, 1983, 9:30 a.m.)

"About what time of the morning did Klindt stop here?" Carroll asked Giammetta.

The station's owner shrugged and looked to his cashier for help. "I'm not sure," said Edwards. "It seems like it was fairly early, right after I came in. I can check the cash register receipts if you like. That should give us a pretty good idea of the time. I changed the tape last Friday morning. It was a small purchase. Around two dollars."

Carroll was puzzled. "Jim Klindt put two dollars worth of gas in his car?"

"Not in his Scout, in a gas can."

"A gas can?"

"That's right. A two-gallon gas can."

"So how will the register tape help?"

"All cash purchases go on the tape. Two dollars ought to be easy to spot. If it was early and we weren't very busy, it should be right at the start of the tape."
"What time did you come in?"
"Around eight o'clock."
"And he was driving the Scout?"
Giammetta nodded.
"Where did he park?"
Edwards pointed. "Over there, at the far pump."
"Did you see him get the gas can out of the Scout?"
"Yeah. He opened up the tailgate."
"Could you see inside?"
"Not from this angle."
"Dr. Klindt came inside to pay?"
"That's right."
"What was his mood?"
"Same old Jim," said Giammetta.

Carroll wondered why Klindt would make such a small purchase. Maybe to prime the airboat's engine or to pour into its empty tank. But two gallons of gas would not take a boat powered by a V-8 Cadillac engine very far, certainly not out on the river for nearly an hour.

There was also something else bothering the detective. Klindt had not put gasoline in the Scout. Had he lied to Joyce about the Scout being out of gas? Was his only purpose in taking the Volkswagen Jetta to keep Joyce from leaving the house that morning?

The detective spent much of the afternoon checking filling stations along the river above and below Princeton. No one remembered seeing Jim Klindt. The question of where the chiropractor found gasoline for the airboat went unanswered.

Homicide

Despite Elizabeth Reed's urgent phone call the night of March 18, Virginia and Eugene Monahan did not arrive in Davenport until March 28. The parents of the missing woman were interviewed by Carroll and Det. James Van Fossen of the Criminal Investigation Division.

Davenport Police Department
(Monday, March 28, 1983, 3:05 p.m.)

"What do you think happened to your daughter?" asked Van Fossen.

Eugene Monahan's reply was matter-of-fact. "We have no doubt that she's dead and that Jim murdered her."

The candid reply caught Van Fossen off guard. "What makes you think that?"

"Because Joyce told me over the phone that Jim said he would kill her if she hired a divorce lawyer," Virginia replied.

Later that evening, the Reeds received a threatening phone call. Clifford Reed immediately informed Ted Carroll. It seems Jim Klindt had noticed the small advertisement the Reeds had taken out in the *Quad-City Times*. Geraldine Klindt had phoned Elizabeth to ask if she and Cliff had paid for the ad. When Elizabeth replied they had, Mrs. Klindt responded, "Well, Jim's furious with your meddling. I'd be very careful if I were you."

Lieutenant Carroll stopped by the Reed house and filed a report on the incident. While there, he also assessed the Reed's security. "Tell you what, Cliff," the detective said. "I know some people at Per Mar. I think it'd be smart to have them install a security system. I'll put a rush on it if you want."

"Appreciate it, Ted."

"One more thing," Carroll said. "I'll send a squad car by your house on the hour. At night, leave a light on in that spare bedroom Joyce used. If there's trouble, turn it off."

8

THE AFFAIR

Davenport Police Department
(Tuesday, March 29, 1983, 7:10 p.m.)

Ted Carroll rubbed his eyes, lit a Camel, and choked down a swallow of tepid coffee. It had been a long day. Across the desk, Jim Klindt sat rigid on a straight-back chair, his gaze fixed on the detective. Eight days had passed since the chiropractor had last visited the police station. Klindt appeared gaunt, his eyes sunken. Lieutenant Carroll wondered if he too looked that bad. Despite fatigue, Carroll was eager to question Klindt again. After their last go-round, he suspected the chiropractor was not in a similar frame of mind.

Klindt recounted his story once again, describing for the first time what Joyce was wearing the morning she disappeared. "The last time I saw her, she had on a blue corduroy jumpsuit and a black ski jacket. I gave her $2,000 and she left."

"Two thousand? Did you say TWO thousand, Doctor?"

"Yeah. I remember going to the Brenton Bank drive-up that morning, withdrawing $2,000 and giving it to Joyce."

Carroll recalled that during the first interview the chiropractor had specifically told him $4,000. The detective did not have time to dwell on the discrepancy.

"That's not all she took. She stole $34,000, my expensive gold ring, and two insurance checks I'd hidden in a furnace duct."

"Let me get this straight, Doctor. You're now telling me your wife took another $34,000?"

"Yeah. I wanted my money back. That's why I went looking for her car that afternoon."

Homicide

"About what time was that?"

"Maybe two ... two-thirty."

"Let's back up a minute. Joyce left at ten, you went to Princeton, moved your boat. I figure half-hour up, half-hour back, and an hour out on the river. It's noon, Doctor. What did you do then?"

"I remember calling Terry from Kernan's around noon. I told her me and Joyce had agreed on a trial separation, that Joyce had left town."

Carroll leaned forward. "Terry? Who in hell is Terry?"

"Well, you're probably gonna find out anyway. I've been dating another woman. Her name is Terry Keuhn. She's a beautician here in town."

The words exploded in Carroll's ears. The suspect was having an affair.

"We met for lunch," Klindt continued. "After that, I went back home and discovered the money was missing. So I drove to the Holiday Inn looking for her car."

"The Holiday Inn? You mean in Moline?"

"No, not that one. The one up on Brady Street. But I didn't find it there. I found it at Randall's Super Valu in North Park."

The detective was puzzled. "Go on."

"I watched the car until I had to pick my son up at school."

"What time was that?"

"Around three-thirty."

"You drove back home?"

"Not right away. First we went to Payless Cashway. Bart had a friend with him, and they needed some supplies for a science fair project. After that, I went home and helped the boys get started."

"Okay, then what happened?"

"I went back to Randall's. The Jetta was still parked in front of the grocery store, but Joyce had taken her clothes out of the back seat."

Carroll wondered, if Klindt knew the clothes had been removed, why, in their first interview, had he asked if the clothes were in the car? "The clothes were gone?"

"Yeah. That's when I called Terry again. I told her to pick me up at the Quad City Airport after she got off work. I drove the Volkswagen to Moline and parked it behind the Holiday Inn, moved the seat up, pulled the distributor wire, and walked to the airport to search for Joyce."

"You pulled the distributor wire?"

"Yeah. Just in case Joyce found it. I didn't want her to get it started."

"And why would she be looking for her car in Moline, when you said she left it at North Park Mall?"

"I thought she went to the airport."

Carroll was astonished. "You thought your wife was at the airport?"

"That's right. She had plenty of cash. I thought maybe she took a cab to the airport and took a flight out of town."

"Why wouldn't she drive her car? Wouldn't that be more practical than taking a cab?"

"Not if she was trying to throw the cops off her trail."

"But why in the world would you move the car and hide it behind the Holiday Inn?"

"I thought you guys would look harder if you couldn't find the car."

"That doesn't make any sense, Doctor. At that point we weren't even looking for your wife. In fact, you didn't report her missing until five hours later."

"Well, that's why I moved it."

Carroll pressed for a better explanation but did not receive one. Klindt stubbornly stuck to his story, seemingly offended

Homicide

that the detective would question his honesty. When the lieutenant could not get a satisfactory response, he asked his final question. "Why'd you shove the seat forward?"

"I wanted to make it look like a short person, a woman, had been driving the car."

The detective stared at Klindt, shaking his head in disbelief.

Following the interview, Lieutenant Carroll began adding up the pieces. There were accusations made against the doctor by friends and relatives of the missing woman, as well as major holes in the chiropractor's story. When added to the fact the couple was going through a messy divorce and that the police held a tape cassette in which he threatened her life, the circumstantial evidence seemed insurmountable.

Carroll had the reputation of being a "hat-band detective," a cop who kept a tight rein on his reports. He revealed little information to his superiors and even less to the prosecuting attorney, unless he was absolutely sure where it was all leading. But it was the extra-marital affair that caused this cautious cop to awaken Scott County Attorney William Davis from a sound sleep. The prosecutor thought enough of Lieutenant Carroll and his conclusions to meet the detective and Sgt. Mike Hammes at Terry Keuhn's apartment.

Chateau Knoll Apartments
29th Street and Middle Road
Bettendorf, Iowa
(Tuesday, March 29, 1983, 10:30 p.m.)

Terry Keuhn's mother, Ruth, who shared the apartment with her daughter, seemed stunned when she answered the door. Her bleached-blonde hair was in rollers, and she wore a bathrobe. She looked suspiciously at Davis, a man for whom she had worked for the past six years.

"This is not a social call, Ruth. We've got a woman missing, and we just found out tonight that her husband is having an affair with one of your daughters. We need to ask you both some questions."

Terry had heard the knock. She came out of the bedroom, wearing skin-tight blue jeans and a T-shirt. She acted as if she was expecting someone else and seemed shocked to see the county prosecutor and two detectives standing in the living room.

Bill Davis interviewed Ruth.

"There's not much I can tell you, Bill. I know about Terry's dating Jim Klindt. It's not for me to judge. I don't condone their actions, and I don't condemn them."

"Evidently the chiropractor's kept the relationship pretty low-key. This is the first we've heard about it."

"Of course he kept it low-key. Jim's a married man. He's got to be careful. It's gotten to the point where if someone knocks on our apartment door and Jim's here, he hides in the closet."

Carroll and Hammes eavesdropped for a time before turning their attention toward Terry Keuhn.

Theresa Ann "Terry" Keuhn, 26, was a cosmetologist. Attractive and single, the petite brunette with big brown eyes and dimpled chin had been a patient of Dr. Klindt's ever since her mother Ruth had taken Terry, then seventeen, in for an adjustment. Her liaison with Klindt had begun in September of 1982.

The two had run into each other by accident one Wednesday night at John D's Emporium, a cocktail lounge located in the Bettendorf Holiday Inn. Wednesday night was "girls' night out" and Terry Keuhn was with friends that evening, as she was the next time she saw Klindt a week later. The third time they met, the date had been prearranged. Terry came alone.

Homicide

The couple had a few drinks at John D's before driving across the river to a Rock Island bar. Later, they had sex.

It did not seem to bother Terry that the chiropractor was married. She continued to see Klindt and have sex with him almost daily. Twice a month, the couple would travel south to Burlington, Iowa, and spend the weekend at the Pizazz, a motel with a variety of restaurants and nightclubs under one roof. In January of 1983 and February of 1984, she had flown with him to Las Vegas. Once, while Joyce and Bart were visiting Joyce's parents in Granite City, Illinois, she had shared the Klindts' king-size bed.

At 10:00 o'clock on the evening of March 19, 1983, Terry Keuhn left her Bettendorf apartment, excited about meeting Jim Klindt. She drove to northwest Davenport and parked less than a block from his house at 1220 Royal Oaks Drive. Creeping up the driveway, she opened the motor home's unlocked door. A moment later, the doctor slipped beneath the garage door and joined her in the Winnebago. Around 11:00 Klindt got dressed and went back into the house. Keuhn departed a moment later, leaving the neighborhood as softly as she came.

Terry Keuhn understood the day was not far off when she would be the mistress of the big house with the turret. Until then, her relationship with Jim Klindt must remain a secret. She was glowing and carefree driving home. She truly believed that Joyce Klindt, the major obstacle in her plans and biggest threat to her security and happiness, had simply vanished.

During the interview with Terry Keuhn, Lieutenant Carroll gained new perspective on what transpired the afternoon March 18, 1983.

"Jim called around one from Kernan's," Keuhn told Carroll. "Said he was on his way back from Princeton. He asked if I was busy. I told him I was just finishing up with an appointment."

"What do you do for a living, Terry?"
"I'm a cosmetologist."
"Where do you work?"
Terry lit a cigarette and drew heavily. "Family Affair Fashions."
"In Davenport?"
"Uh-huh. On West Locust?"
"Why did Jim call you on the eighteenth?"
"He wanted me to pick up some hamburgers and a couple of Cokes at Wendy's and meet him for lunch."
"Where did he ask you to meet him?"
"In front of his house."
"Had you ever been to his house before?"
"Just once."
"When?"
"One night, a long time ago. I'm not sure of the date. Joyce had taken Bart to Granite City."
"You slept over?"
Terry giggled. "Why not?"
"Okay. Let's get back to the afternoon of March eighteenth. Didn't that seem a little unusual, I mean meeting him right in front of his own house?"
"I guess. I never really thought about it."
"Weren't you nervous, I mean, meeting Jim in broad daylight in front of his house."
"Not really. He said Joyce had left town."
"Who arrived first?"
"I did. Jim pulled into the driveway a few minutes later."
"What was he driving?"
Terry puffed on the cigarette. "The Scout."
"Then what happened?"
"He parked in the driveway, got into the Winnebago, and motioned me to follow. We drove to the shopping center."
"Which one?"

Homicide

"North Park."

"That's a big place, Terry. Where in North Park?"

"In front of Alexander's."

Carroll was perplexed. "Alexander's ... The bar?"

Terry nodded.

"Alexander's isn't in North Park, Terry. It's across Northwest Boulevard in the Village Shopping Center."

Keuhn rolled her eyes. "Oh! That's right."

"What happened?"

"I got out of my car, and we both got in the back of the Winnebago."

"What kind of mood was Jim in?"

"He seemed a little down."

"What did he say?"

"He said he had news. I asked if it was bad. He said, 'No, actually it's good,' that Joyce and he had split up, and then he told me that she had left town that morning for a trial separation."

"What was your reaction?"

"I was thrilled. I remember saying, 'Really?' and throwing my arms around his neck and kissing him. I asked him to tell me all about it."

"What was Jim's response?"

"He said there wasn't much to tell, that he threw her stuff in the back of the Jetta and gave her $2,000 in cash and she left. I couldn't believe my ears. 'Two thousand dollars?' I asked. 'Is that all?'"

"Then what happened?"

"Like I said, Jim was a little down. He didn't want to talk about it, so we ate. I left a few minutes later. I had another appointment."

"But you heard from him again later that afternoon, didn't you?"

"Yeah. He called around four-thirty."

"What did he want this time?"

"He said he was at the airport and he needed a ride home."

"The Quad City Airport in Moline?"

"Uh-huh."

"Tell me about that phone conversation."

"He asked what time I got off. I told him I was busy with a customer, but that I'd be done in about an hour. He asked if I could pick him up at the airport. I said, 'Sure, as soon as I'm finished.' He told me to hurry, but if I didn't see him there, not to worry, because he'd found Joyce."

"He told you he was at the airport looking for Joyce?"

Terry grew very serious. "I know what you're thinking. I thought the same thing. He'd said earlier that she'd already left town."

"Did you ask him to explain why he was looking for her?"

"Yes. He said, 'It's a long story. I'll explain when you get here.'"

"Did he?"

"No."

"Did he ever explain to you what he was doing at the airport."

"No."

"So, you finished your hair appointment and then you picked him up?"

Terry nodded. "Yeah."

"Can you recall what he was wearing?"

"Uh-huh. Blue jeans, a brown leather jacket, and a hat. I remember, because I didn't see him right away."

"Who drove back across the river?"

"I did. He was upset."

"Did he tell you why?"

"He asked, 'Am I hard to see, or what?' I told him I didn't know what he meant. 'I'm six-six and standing up on the curb

Homicide

waving a goddamn red flag and you drive right by me,' like I was supposed to know he'd be wearing a hat."
"He didn't usually wear a hat?"
"Not very often."
"Okay. Go on."
"Jim apologized. He patted my leg. 'This hasn't been the best of days. Thanks for picking me up, honey.' I could tell something was still bothering him. So I asked what was wrong. He didn't answer for a long time. He seemed down, worse than he was at lunchtime. 'She took a lot more than I thought,' he said. 'Jeez, you're kidding?' I said."
"Did he say how much more of what she took?"
"No. He didn't want to discuss it anymore. We drove to North Park Mall."
"Why North Park?"
"That's where Jim left the Winnebago. 'I have to call Bart,' he said. I pulled up to a curbside phone near Randall's Super Valu and Jim called home."
"When he talked to Bart, did he ever mention Joyce?"
"Not that I remember."
"Jim didn't ask if she had returned home, or anything like that, did he?"
"No."
"Then what'd you do?"
"After we got into the Winnebago, he slumped to the floor. He talked about how confused he was, about Joyce leaving and all. I said I didn't understand. I told him I thought he wanted her out of his life."
"What was he confused about?"
"I think he was trying to decide whether to go to the police, or not."
"Anything else happen before you left?"
Keuhn's face flushed pink. She hesitated for a moment then said, "No."

70

"Did you see Jim later that night?"
"No."
"Did he call you later that night?"
"I called him, but there were people at his house and he said he couldn't talk."
"How about the night before, the evening of March seventeenth?"
"No, I didn't see him."
"Did you speak to him on the phone?"
"No."
"Do you know where he was?"
"No."
"You're sure?"
"Uh-huh."

Following the interviews, Davis climbed into his station wagon and headed home. Carroll, who had ridden with Sergeant Hammes, was quiet during the ride back to the police station. Hammes finally broke the silence. "What'd you think of Terry?" he prodded.
"I think she's got stars in her eyes."
"Then you think Klindt acted alone?"
"I didn't say that," Carroll replied. "We know from the tape he stormed out of his house after arguing with Joyce the evening of March seventeenth. Terry just told us she didn't see Klindt that night. Where do you suppose he was?"
Hammes thought for a moment. "Scoring cocaine?"
"That doesn't take all night. I've got this feeling someone else is involved in his wife's disappearance."
"You think he had an accomplice?"
Carroll nodded. "That's exactly what I think. Probably someone strung out on drugs. Could even be a woman. From what I've heard, Klindt has had a number of affairs."
"But he's head over heels about Terry."

Homicide

Carroll snorted. "Klindt only loves himself. He has no loyalties. Using people, that's his strength."

"So who are you talking about?"

As usual, Carroll was evasive. "If I find out, Mike, you'll be the first to know."

Davenport Police Department
(Wednesday, March 30, 1983, 12:06 a.m.)

It was after midnight when Carroll called the Klindt residence. The chiropractor answered in a groggy voice.

"Doctor, this is Lieutenant Carroll. We want you to come back down to the station."

"You mean tonight?"

"Right now, Doctor."

"Jesus, don't you guys ever sleep?"

Carroll hung up grinning. "When Klindt gets here," the lieutenant said, "read him his rights, have him sign a waiver, and let him stew for awhile."

An hour later, Klindt was quizzed by detectives Carroll and Hammes. The chiropractor's pupils were dilated, his eyes glazed. Klindt repeated a similar story, admitting he had been having an affair with Terry Keuhn since September 1982. The detectives then played the cassette. The chiropractor, unaware that Joyce had taped the argument, seemed baffled. "That's not my voice," he said flatly.

"Look, Doctor. I suggest you listen for a moment before you deny something that's easy to confirm."

Five minutes passed.

"I guess it's me," Klindt admitted. "But that doesn't prove anything. It was just an argument between me and my wife."

Carroll was derisive. "No, Doctor. It doesn't prove a thing. It's circumstantial, isn't it?"

By the time the tape ended, the chiropractor was squirming in his chair.

"Not pleasant stuff, Doctor. Spitting in a woman's face and threatening to kill her and cut her up into little pieces."

"That was just dramatics."

"What about these pictures of drug paraphernalia allegedly photographed in your home?"

"I don't deny it. That's my stuff, but it's just for show. I picked it up at the Curiosity Shop [a local head shop]. That's how I got out at night. I told Joyce I had to deal drugs to support my cocaine habit. It was just an excuse."

"What about that $9,800 you admitted to owing suppliers?"

"Same reason. I made it up to get out of the house. The drugs in the picture are phony. I admit I smoke pot. Everything else is just turkey [fake]."

"If it's all right with you, Doctor, we'd like to search the Winnebago you've got parked out front."

Klindt hesitated. "Okay. I already told you, I smoke some pot. There's some in the motor home."

Inside, they found hashish and two small bags of white powder. When told the search had yielded something besides marijuana, Klindt replied, "Oh, yeah, that's right. There probably was a little MDA [a psychedelic] in the vehicle." The police impounded the drugs.

"Tell me about this $34,000. Where did it come from?"

"I was hiding it from the IRS. It's money I'd skimmed."

Why, Carroll wondered, was the chiropractor so anxious to confess to tax evasion? Was he trying to cloak a much bigger crime?

"We want you to sign a consent to search form allowing the police to search your house. You got any problems with that?"

"No."

"I also want you to take a lie detector test."

"I ... I'd better check with my attorney on that."

Homicide

It was nearly dawn when the police got to Klindt's house. The place was a mess, stacks of dirty dishes and piles of soiled clothing. Guns everywhere. Nothing of relevance was found.

At 3:00 that afternoon, Lieutenant Carroll received a call from Klindt's attorney. "Ted, this is Ned Wehr. I want you to know that Jim Klindt will not be taking that polygraph you requested. And if you have further questions about his wife's disappearance, make sure you direct them through me."

An hour later, Carroll received another call. It came from Tammy Dickinson, a sales clerk at Peterson's Department Store at North Park Mall. She told the detective she remembered selling Jim Klindt a woman's gold herring-bone chain just before Christmas. The chiropractor had returned to Peterson's on March 26, 1983, during a 60 percent off sale on gold jewelry. He had picked out several bracelets and necklaces of matching herringbone and tried to charge them to Joyce's credit card. When Dickinson checked with the main office, she discovered the card had been canceled in January. Klindt wanted the credit card reinstated, saying he was the one who had asked for the cancellation. Dickinson told him that according to Peterson's records, Joyce had canceled the credit card. The reason listed: an impending divorce. Embarrassed, Klindt paid for the jewelry with a $100 bill and wrote a $700 "BankAmerica check" for the balance.

The search for Joyce Klindt continued for another fortnight. It seemed ironic the name of the missing woman, which for days had dominated the front page of local newspapers, could no longer be found, even in the personals. The initial noise of the presses had died. They were about to come alive again, this time with a vengeance.

9

PROBABLE CAUSE

Mercy Hospital
1401 West Central Park
Davenport, Iowa
(Saturday, April 16, 1983, 12:05 p.m.)

Halligan-McCabe delivered the lower trunk of a white female to Mercy Hospital shortly after noon. The odor of formaldehyde filled the morgue. The torso was placed in the middle of a stainless steel table, appearing a lurid green beneath the bright fluorescent lights.

The autopsy began promptly at 12:30. Dr. Perkins and Dr. Peter Stephens assisted Dr. Kimball Thompson. Davenport police evidence technicians Cary Chapman and Rick Chase were in attendance, along with a Bettendorf police detective, Phil Redington. Chase took photographs and videotaped the entire procedure.

Thompson worked at a methodical pace, speaking without emotion into a microphone dangling from a cord above the table. He removed residue clinging to the exposed exterior wounds of the torso and placed it in a clear plastic bag before beginning dissection and measurement.

"'Jane Doe' has been cut in half some three inches above her navel. Her legs had been severed above the knees, the stub of the left leg is three and a half inches longer than the right.

"A deep gash, five-sixteenth of an inch in width, runs the width of her back just above the crease of the buttocks. It penetrated four and one-half inches into the pelvic bone, and the woman's intestines have been drawn up through the lateral

Homicide

portion of the wound. The laceration seems to have been made by the rotating blade of a power saw, possibly a chain saw."

At 2:17 that afternoon, Officer David Schafer of the Bettendorf Police Department found what he believed to be human gastro-intestinal parts near the Twelfth Street boat ramp in Bettendorf. Detective Kauffman ordered these additional remains be bagged and delivered to the Mercy Hospital autopsy room. The autopsy was interrupted at 2:50 for an examination of the viscera. They were determined to be the entrails of an animal.

Dr. Thompson continued the autopsy. "There are numerous bruises on the torso, as well as an array of small moles and birthmarks on the lower back ... There are stretch marks and the woman has an episiotomy scar, indicating that she has given birth ... She has not been sterilized ... No IUD is present ... There is no appendectomy scar, nor any other visible scars anywhere else on the torso ... The hips measure approximately thirty-nine inches in circumference."

Thompson determined she had not been sexually assaulted. The organs remaining intact were deemed normal. He took a urine specimen from the bladder to check for drugs and plucked a sample of pubic hair.

Early Sunday morning, Rick Chase delivered Dr. Thompson's preliminary autopsy report to Ted Carroll. The detective stopped reading halfway through, not moving for more than a moment. He now knew why the chiropractor had filled the two-gallon gas can on the morning his wife disappeared. His square jaw was rigid, and his steely eyes bore into the wall. He calmly picked up the phone and called Magistrate Linda Molyneaux. "This is Lieutenant Carroll. I need a search warrant. I've got probable cause for a murder."

Dead Water

The Castle House
(Sunday, April 17, 1983, 8:35 a.m.)

Rick Chase tried not to damage the French doors, forcing them with his shoulder. The dead bolt held. The youthful patrolman ignored his colleagues taunts, calmly smoothed his mustache with the thumb and forefinger of his right hand, then flung his two hundred pounds against the entry. Wood splintered.

"It's a damn good thing you don't earn your living as a cat burglar," Lieutenant Carroll said wryly. "I hope to God the neighbors aren't trying to sleep."

Chase grinned. "Serves 'em right. They should be in church."

Initially, the four officers — Carroll, Blank, Lambdin, and Chase — had tried to gain entry without destroying property. They had knocked on all doors and windows in an attempt to rouse anyone inside the house. No one had answered.

"You and Lambdin take the upstairs, Sergeant," Carroll told Blank. "I'll check the basement. I want to take a look at the shooting gallery that Girt mentioned in her report. Rick, search the garage, will you? See if the doctor owns a chain saw."

A few moments later, Chase called for the detective. "Lieutenant, you better come see this."

Carroll climbed the steps and ambled into the garage. "What've you got, Rick?"

"Klindt has two identical Stihl chain saws. One of them's brand new, hasn't even been out of its packing crate. You think maybe he's planning on ditching the old one?"

"Or maybe he had two chain saws to begin with, and he's just replacing the one he threw overboard," Carroll surmised. "Grab the used saw and bring that open can of oil. You didn't happen to see a two-gallon gas can, did you?"

"No," Chase replied.

The detective yelled upstairs. "You guys find anything?"

Homicide

"Just a hairbrush. We removed the hair and placed it in a plastic bag."

"If you're done," said Carroll, "let's get the hell out of here. We still have to go to Klindt's storage shed. It'd be nice to have Sunday dinner with the family for a change."

The officers then proceeded to Northwest Storage on Hickory Grove Road, where they removed human hairs from inside two acrylic blonde wigs. All items seized were taken to back to the station to be processed by the evidence technician.

Carroll returned to the Davenport Police Department around noon. Three telephone messages lay on his desk. His wife, Jan, received priority. She had a roast on. He told her he would be home in an hour. Carroll then phoned Bill Davis and chatted briefly about the search of Klindt's home and storage shed. The lieutenant stared at the last message. The woman had called four hours ago. Her name was unfamiliar. She lived in Cordova, Illinois. He dialed long distance.

"Marilyn Lampo, please."

"Speaking."

"Marilyn, this is Lieutenant Carroll of the Davenport Police Department."

"Thanks for returning my call, Lieutenant. The reason I phoned is because of the story in the *Times* this morning about finding that torso in the river. It's been nearly a month ago, but I finally put two and two together. My daughter and I saw Dr. Klindt out on the river the morning of March eighteenth."

"You're sure?"

"Well, as you probably know, Cordova is across the river from Princeton. The river is very wide here, but we saw a man running the main channel along the Illinois shore. He was driving a black airboat. He sped past the large sandbar, maybe two hundred yards from our house, then disappeared into Steamboat Slough. The sound of his engine faded for a time.

Dead Water

Then we saw him again, skirting the islands and heading upriver.

"I remember because that was the only boat either of us saw on the river that morning. It was a terrible day, cold and windy. The water was very high. From what I read in the paper, it had to be Dr. Klindt."

Lieutenant Carroll called his wife again, told her to put Sunday dinner on hold. He drove to Cordova and interviewed Mrs. Lampo.

Early the following morning, Monday, April 18, Carroll went to Princeton. He had made arrangements for boats and skin divers to search the sloughs upriver from Princeton, especially Steamboat Slough, for additional body parts. The trip was a waste of time. Dragging the river was aborted due to high winds.

That same morning, Jim Klindt was more than willing to talk to reporters. He had returned home Sunday night to find his house ransacked. The chiropractor decried the police action. "I wasn't even home," he said. "When I came in, it looked like a tornado had hit. They damaged everything, between six and eight hundred dollars, just for the three doors they kicked in. I phoned my lawyer and insurance company."

The doctor was livid, criticizing the police and the press. "Marital problems probably caused my wife to run off. People are pointing a finger at me and they shouldn't. My private life is private. I've been implicated unfairly in this investigation. I feel like I'm in limbo, caught here in a nightmare. It's not very pleasant, and you wonder what the recourse is."

That Monday afternoon, Dr. R. M. Perkins issued a statement to the press on the autopsy. "A chain saw was used to butcher the body of an unidentified white woman," the

Homicide

coroner said. "The torso could have been in the water from one week to three months. Without additional body parts, identification will be impossible."

In an affidavit made public that same day, the Davenport police claimed to have an audio cassette in their possession which implicated James Klindt in the murder of his wife. The cutting chain on the saw seized at Klindt's home was five-sixteenth of an inch across, the same width as the saw used to cut up the torso.

10

THE FOURTH ESTATE

An important element in any criminal action is publicity. In fact, there is a direct correlation between the atrocity of a crime and the attention it receives in the media. While television and radio tend to report events with some objectivity, newspapers are less constrained. Each paper has its own strategy and leans toward columnists whose style fits the publication's particular agenda.

Three newspapers dominated coverage of the Klindt case: the *Des Moines Register*, the *Quad-City Times,* and the *Rock Island Argus*. Bill Ryberg, the eastern Iowa correspondent for the *Register* wrote conservative, almost poetic, columns based on observation and fact. Bill Theobald of the *Times* stirred public passion with sensational reports, enhanced by larger-than-life photos and block headlines. But it was Judy Pochel, a fledgling reporter for the *Argus*, who developed a keen insight into Klindt's character.

Pochel, a plumpish woman in her mid-twenties with a dimpled smile and saucers for eyes, was the picture of innocence; youthful features disguised her dogged tenacity and guile. Although she had been with the *Argus* less than two years, Pochel was assigned lead reporter on the Klindt story.

She quickly gained Jim Klindt's ear, contacting him by phone on March 19, 1983, the day after his wife disappeared. Her article reflected the chiropractor's calloused reaction to his wife's disappearance. "She's gone," Klindt had told her. "She took everything I had. I'm glad she's gone. All she ever did was spend a lot of money and run up my charge cards."

Homicide

The following week Pochel pressured the chiropractor for an interview. Klindt finally agreed, asking the reporter to come to his office. During the interview, the doctor simply reiterated what he had initially told the press. Pochel wanted more. She continued to hound the doctor by phone, pushing so hard the chiropractor once hung up on her. But in the end, the brash young reporter gained Jim Klindt's trust.

Pochel had been among the throng on the riverbank the morning the torso was found. During the ensuing month, her insolence had completely alienated Bill Davis. That morning, she had waited for the prosecutor to leave the scene before approaching Ted Carroll and asking the detective if he believed the body was Joyce Klindt. Carroll had turned and walked to his car, brushing the reporter off with a gruff "No comment."

After the crowd had dispersed, Pochel returned to her Rock Island office, certain the body was that of the missing Davenport woman. If the torso was Joyce Klindt, the reporter felt she had the inside track to one of the most electrifying stories in the newspaper's history.

The afternoon of April 16, 1983, Pochel flipped through her Rolodex for Klindt's office number, eager to inform the chiropractor of the fisherman's find. She was looking for his reaction to use as a direct quote for her story. Klindt's business associate, Dennis Hagemann, answered the phone. Pochel was told Dr. Klindt was in Chicago attending a chiropractic convention. When Hagemann said he did not know which hotel Klindt was staying in, Judy dialed a friend in Chicago and asked him to locate the chiropractor.

By 7:00 Saturday evening, Pochel had not heard back. The deadline for the Sunday morning paper neared, her article finished except for the Klindt quote. Pochel typed in her byline and waited. The phone rang at 7:15. She was told that Jim Klindt was not registered in any hotel or motel in Chicago unless it was under an assumed name. If fact, there was no chiropractic convention being held that weekend in the Windy City. Pochel leaned back in her chair and wondered if Hagemann was trying to protect Klindt. That seemed unlikely. She was sure Klindt had lied to his associate about the convention. But for what reason?

During the four-week interval between Joyce Klindt's disappearance and the time the torso was found, reporters received few details from the authorities, although they had pestered both Ted Carroll and Bill Davis for pertinent information: Were the police close to breaking the case? Did they think Joyce Klindt was dead? Was Dr. Klindt the only suspect? Was his arrest imminent?

On April 18, when Pochel learned of the affidavit, she phoned Bill Davis and asked him about the audio cassette. Davis told Pochel to check it out for herself, that affidavits are public information. Frustrated by another put-off, Pochel grew irate. She accused the prosecutor of withholding important details about the case from the press. Davis told Pochel she was entitled to her opinion, but he did not have time to cater to her whims, he had a job to do. Pochel's scathing retort, which included a reference to "the public's right to know" brought a violent response. Davis slammed down the receiver.

Undaunted, Pochel phoned Ted Carroll. "It's my understanding that you're the one who filed the Klindt affidavit, Lieutenant. Do you expect to arrest him soon?"

"I've got nothing to add," Carroll said. "At this point ... we can't establish the man has done anything."

The media followed the Davenport police to Princeton on Wednesday, April 20, where calmer waters allowed frogmen to search the sloughs for additional body parts. None were found. That afternoon, an East Moline woman, Laura Meyers, claimed she had spotted a leg floating in the Mississippi

Homicide

downriver from Davenport near Buffalo, Iowa. "It was horrible," Meyers told the press.

Verl Holtz, the lockmaster at Lock and Dam Number 16 in Muscatine, Iowa, told reporters he was on the lookout for body parts, but that he didn't expect to find any. "I'm not sure if a leg would float," Holtz said. "Even if it did, the dam's wide open."

Public interest in the Klindt case continued to grow. The community was divided into two camps: those who thought that Joyce Klindt had merely run off and those who thought she was the victim of foul play. The hometown *Quad-City Times* sensationalized the event. The *Times* report of an interview with Davenport psychiatrist Truce Ordona was a typical example. "There's no doubt that there's intense interest in the case," Ordona said. "Sadly, most of the comments have come in the form of macabre jokes."

(Two of the jokes were Jim Klindt served 'lady fingers' for lunch and paid an 'arm and a leg' for his Cadillac.)

"Why?"

"Simply to relieve the pressure," Ordona replied.

"What kind of person is capable of butchering another with a chain saw?"

"Usually, they are controlled individuals who keep their emotions bottled up and are preoccupied with this violent act inside them, and then they just let it erupt. A lot of these people usually have stored up anger towards people in their past ... they usually do this to someone they perceive as invulnerable or as a threat to themselves, and the act of cutting somebody up in this fashion does two things. Number one, it eliminates the problem. And number two, it gives them the power to remove the identity of the person by reducing them into chopped-up pieces, so that the whole of the personality disappears. It is a very primitive, almost infantile, response to anger."

Judy Pochel, feeling the chiropractor vulnerable, phoned him Thursday morning, April 21, 1983, conceding to Klindt she felt he had been treated unfairly in the press. She added she would print his side of the story if he would give her a second interview. He told the reporter he would think about it. Thursday night Judy received a phone call from Dr. Klindt, granting her the interview. Judy would say later that the chiropractor seemed nervous when she arrived at his office Friday morning.

Klindt Chiropractic Clinic
1941 West Third Street
Davenport, Iowa
(Friday, April 22, 1983, 9:00 a.m.)

"What I'm about to tell you is confidential, strictly off-the-record," Klindt told Pochel. "Is that okay?"

Judy nodded.

"I took Bart to school that morning. When I came back Joyce was sitting upstairs on the bed with a loaded pistol pointed at her head. I thought she was going to kill herself and I said 'Joyce, don't do it.' I slowly walked over to the bed and took the gun away.

"Joyce was really upset. Bart had told her earlier that he had decided to live with me. She was scheduled to move out of the house that day." The chiropractor's eyes were moist and his voice wavered. "You know, I loved my wife. After thirteen years, you gotta feel something. It was just a good marriage gone bad.

"Anyway, I gave her $2,000 and helped her load her clothes into the car. That's when I discovered the part for the airboat on the floorboard. I had purchased it a week earlier. I put the

Homicide

part in the garage, and the dog got out. I was gone for about fifteen minutes trying to get my dog back. When I returned, I found all of Joyce's things on the front porch. I loaded them back into the car again and watched her leave.

"After she got into the car, she told me, 'Move that boat because it's half mine.' She left with a smile on her face.

"The river was high so I went to Princeton to check on my boat. I put the part on, got it started and took it out on the river. I decided to do a little fishing, and I threw the gill net overboard. That's when I lost my keys. I drifted into some trees and had to cut the branches away with an axe to free the propeller. I no sooner got the boat started ..."

Judy interrupted. "You said you lost your keys in the water. How'd you get it started?"

Klindt plowed on, avoiding the question. "That's when I found a hoop net with a turtle in it. I took the turtle, put a five dollar bill in the net, and went back to shore."

The reporter studied Klindt's face. Even she knew turtles hibernated until early June. "You took a turtle out of a hoop net and put five dollars back in the net and put the net back in the water?"

Klindt didn't blink. "That's right. When I returned home, I discovered Joyce had taken $30,000 out of our safe. I went looking for her to get my money back. I found her car parked over at North Park and I waited for her. It was getting late, so I picked up Bart at school, took him shopping for some material for a science fair project, and took him home.

"I told Bart I needed to run some more errands and left. I returned to North Park and found the car in the same spot. Her clothes were gone. That's when I became suspicious.

"I called my girlfriend and told her to meet me at the Quad City Airport. I drove to Moline, checked out the airport, drove to the Holiday Inn, and parked the car. I moved the seat forward so the cops would look harder for my wife."

Dead Water

Judy Pochel left Klindt's office shaking her head. The off-the-record interview went unpublished for nearly a year.

On a wind-swept Tuesday, April 26, 1983, the media and a pack of interested spectators filled the Scott County Associate Court. Attorney Harry DeLange, an associate of Ned Wehr, accompanied Jim Klindt. The chiropractor was brought before Judge Jack Broderick on drug charges. The arrest stemmed from Lieutenant Carroll's search of the chiropractor's Winnebago motor home in the wee hours of the morning of March 30. Klindt was indicted for possession of both hashish and MDA.

Early in May 1983, Ted Carroll learned that Terry Keuhn had moved out of her mother's Bettendorf apartment. He wondered why. Lieutenant Carroll, knowing that Ruth Keuhn worked in the county attorney's office, asked Bill Davis for help. Davis learned from Ruth that the relationship between the two women had become strained. They argued constantly about Jim Klindt, and Terry had rented a one-bedroom flat at the Racquet Club Apartments in Davenport, less than a mile from the castle house. Ruth said she thought the chiropractor was behind the move.

On May 11, 1983, after going to court, Klindt finally got his chain saw back, sans cutting bar and chain blade. It was a small and short-lived victory for the chiropractor. The Davenport police played tit for tat, adding a third drug, cocaine, to the previous charges.

Two weeks later, Klindt's attorney, Ned Wehr, entered a not guilty plea to all drug charges. The trial was set for August 9.

Homicide

"I was tricked," Klindt told reporters, "into giving the police statements which resulted in drug charges being filed against me. My attorney's gonna file a motion saying the search and seizure at my house and motor home was illegal, so it won't be admissible as evidence in my upcoming trial."

On June 18, Klindt filed a burglary report stating that items and coins valued at more than $400 had been stolen from his home. Reported missing were hundreds of fifty-cent pieces, tools, a tape recorder, and a bayonet. Initially, he had reported a color TV had also been stolen, but he later said he had found the set in a wooded area near his home.

It is probable the missing tape recorder and the coins were being held in the Davenport Police Department's evidence locker. It might be presumed that Joyce used part of the coin collection to retain Sy Raben.

During the greater part of the murder investigation and despite the efforts by the officers involved, there were days, sometimes weeks, when very little happened. And though lulls occur in any investigation, the Klindt case became a matter of endurance. Regardless of the portrayals of intrigue and glamour, Lieutenant Carroll held a painstaking and thankless job. He worked long pressure-packed hours, using extreme care in gathering evidence, being equally careful not to impinge on individual rights.

A week passed, and another, with no new developments in the case. As the cold wet spring gave way to the heat of summer, Jim Klindt dropped from the public eye. His desire to work waned and his chiropractic practice dwindled. He seemed content to spend his free time at the Racquet Club Apartments playing tennis and championing virility. He also vacationed in the Bahamas that summer with Terry and Bart. He returned looking tan and fit.

Dead Water

It was during the summer of 1983 that one of the authors of this book first came in contact with Jim Klindt. The chiropractor was playing tennis with Terry Keuhn at the Racquet Club Apartments on the court next to Pat Gipple and his daughter, Erin. It was a hot sticky afternoon in July.

Klindt seemed jovial as he volleyed with the beautician, hitting soft shots across the net. When one of Keuhn's short lobs bounded high in center court, Klindt's judgment seemed to leave him. He put all of his leverage into a ferocious overhand from close to the net. The ball rocketed off the strings. Keuhn had no chance to defend herself. The ball struck her in the stomach and rebounded to the net. Tears welled up in the young woman's eyes. "What made you do that?" she yelped.

Klindt was unapologetic. "It just happened."

Keuhn glared at him. "You realize you have a reputation for treating women unkindly."

"I know," Klindt grinned. "I'm a real lady-killer, ain't I?"

They both laughed and laughed.

On August 9, Jim Klindt was found guilty of a minor possession offense, fined $300 and court costs, and given two years probation.

In October, lead evidence technician Cpl. Dennis Kern became involved with the search for Joyce Amelia Klindt. Kern, an eight-year veteran of the Davenport police force had just returned the FBI Academy in Quantico, Virginia. He was briefed on the case by Ted Carroll and Rick Chase.

On October 19, Corporal Kern spoke with Dr. Peter Stephens about determining the blood type in decomposing body tissue. Stephens referred Kern to the Southwest Institute of Forensic Science in Dallas, Texas. This was the third time

Homicide

Southwest had been recommended to Kern. The Division of Criminal Investigation in Des Moines and the Illinois Department of Law Enforcement had both endorsed the Dallas institute.

The laboratory, which was affiliated with the coroner's office in Dallas, had an excellent professional reputation in blood/tissue analysis. Kern phoned the institute and was transferred to Benita Harwood in the serology section. He explained to Ms. Harwood that the Davenport police were seeking positive identification on the lower trunk of a white female which had spent considerable time submerged in frigid water. She requested a two-inch square section of muscle tissue and a one-inch section of either rib or vertebrae. Harwood explained to Kern that the tissue and bone samples must be kept frozen during transport.

Halloween arrived. Davenport resident Willie Wisely took full advantage of the Klindt story, masquerading in a hideous bald mask and "blood-stained" smock and carrying a mannequin's torso and a chain saw into local bars. He won the first place prize at Alexander's, fifty dollars, for best costume.

On November 7, Dr. Kimball Thompson removed the two sections requested by Harwood, packed them in dry ice, and forwarded the samples via air freight to Dallas.

Harwood phoned Kern on December 13 and told him the torso was blood type A (the same type as shown on Joyce Klindt's medical records). Harwood had also searched for and found six other enzymes. She asked that blood samples be taken from the missing woman's parents to determine if they could have parented the torso.

Dead Water

On December 27, 1983, at Mercy Hospital in Davenport, blood samples were drawn from the Monahans and Federal Expressed to Harwood. The results of the tests were phoned to Kern on January 12, 1984. The written report received four days later stated that the torso could be the offspring of Eugene and Virginia Monahan: the blood groupings present in the torso existed in less than one-half of one percent of the Caucasian population.

Harwood said that blood samples from the missing woman's husband and son would help narrow the identification process even further. Kern met with Carroll and prosecutor Bill Davis in order to have a search warrant issued for blood samples of James and Bartley Klindt. The warrant was issued by Judge J. Hobart Darbyshire the following day.

Lieutenant Carroll and Corporal Kern tried to serve the warrant at both Klindt's office and his home. Neither Klindt's parents nor his son knew his whereabouts. The officers decided not to serve the portion of the warrant concerning Bart until the boy's father was present. Klindt phoned Kern three days later, at 7:30 a.m. on Friday, January 20, 1984.

"This is Jim Klindt. I'm calling to see if a search warrant naming me exists. My parents said they read something about it in the *Times*."

"That's correct, Doctor. It calls for blood samples from you and your son."

"Is there any way to get out of it?"

"I'm not a lawyer, Doctor, so if you have questions about the warrant, I'd suggest you call one."

"It costs money to talk to my lawyer. It costs money when he contests something, and my lawyer contests everything."

"Tell you what, Doctor. If you want, I'll come over there and pick you up and take you to the magistrate who issued the warrant. You can explain your situation to him."

Homicide

"That ... that's not necessary," Klindt stammered. "I was just wondering if it could wait until after the weekend."

"I don't have a problem with that. How about seven-thirty Monday morning at Mercy? Bring Bart."

When Acting Chief Borgstadt found out about the delay, he became adamant. "Ted, call Klindt. I want his ass over at Mercy this afternoon for those blood tests. The goddamn media's been hounding me all morning. I don't want anybody hanging around when he and his son show up at the hospital."

The blood was drawn without incident at 4:00 that afternoon and shipped to Southwest Institute.

Ten months had passed since the Moshers discovered the torso floating in the Mississippi. While Carroll had searched Scott County, Kern had scoured the nation for evidence that Joyce Klindt was still alive, or for proof that she was dead. He had sought missing persons reports from nearby states, acquired a list of unidentified white females held in morgues around the country, and had run a nationwide driver's license check. He found only one other Joyce A. Klindt, a physician in upstate New York.

When the results of the forensic serology tests were combined with the diligence of Ted Carroll and Dennis Kern, it seemed a statistical certitude that the torso and the missing woman, Joyce Amelia Klindt, were one and the same. Yet, despite reasonable conclusions, a death certificate was not issued. Even more staggering, in view of the wealth of circumstantial evidence, no arrest had been made.

11

DENIAL

Satisfied that the torso was Joyce Klindt, Lieutenant Carroll shifted his focus to homicide. The investigator reviewed the evidence and widened the scope of his inquiry, thus beginning a relentless quest for her killer. Insignificant leads took on greater stature. Unimportant names gained prominence. Witnesses deemed hostile were reconsidered and questioned, often revealing more information than those friendly to the State.

Davenport Police Department
(Monday, January 23, 1984, 1:00 p.m.)

Terry Keuhn appeared at the Davenport Police Department to answer a subpoena. After Carroll read her the Miranda warnings, Keuhn refused to initial the rights waiver form, requesting that an attorney be present before she answered any questions. The detective brought in Assistant County Attorney Realff Ottesen who explained the consequences of noncompliance. Ottesen swore Keuhn in, and she talked of her relationship with Jim Klindt and of his actions the day Joyce disappeared.

Keuhn's statement, although more detailed, was basically the same account she had given Ted Carroll the night he learned she was the mistress of Jim Klindt.

Terry gave her address as 1941 West Third Street. She had moved from the Racquet Club Apartments on October 1, 1983, into a room in the home of Dick and Geraldine Klindt. (Carroll knew that Keuhn spent many of her nights in the house with the turret.) Keuhn also stated she had left her job

Homicide

at Family Affair Fashions in October, borrowing $3,000 from Jim Klindt, to set up her own shop across the hall from Klindt's chiropractic office in his parent's large home. She paid no rent. Klindt had made room for Ms. Keuhn by "asking" his associate partner, Dennis Hagemann, to find new quarters. Hagemann departed gracefully. By then, the relationship between the two chiropractors had become strained.

As the interview came to a close, Lieutenant Carroll asked Keuhn a final question, one that had been bothering him for some time. "I'm hearing rumors that Jim has witnesses that have spotted Joyce recently. You know who they are?"

"No. But Jim told me he has two witnesses who've seen Joyce alive and have not been contacted by the police."

"It's not my job, Terry, to determine guilt or innocence," said Carroll. "The purpose of any investigation is to find the truth. Things look bad for Jim right now and if he's withholding relevant information, he's only hurting his own cause. Here's my card. If Jim actually has witnesses, I want to talk to them."

Terry was about to leave the station when she received a phone call.

"You can take it in my office," said Carroll. "I'll wait outside."

Keuhn spoke for a few moments. "Lieutenant Carroll," she yelled. "It's Jim. He wants to talk to you."

Carroll realized for the first time the close tabs that Jim Klindt was keeping on Terry Keuhn. The chiropractor was angry. "You son-of-a-bitch, Carroll. What are you doing calling Terry down there? She don't know nothin'."

"In case you haven't heard, Doctor, I'm conducting a murder investigation. Which brings up another question. Terry told me you've got witnesses. I want their names."

Dead Water

"You can go to HELL," Klindt screamed and slammed down the receiver.

Davenport Police Department
(Tuesday, January 24, 1984, 1:30 p.m.)

The following day, in a videotaped one-on-one interview, Ted Carroll questioned the suspect's mother, Geraldine Klindt. Mrs. Klindt, a large woman with white hair, was well-rehearsed, often anticipating and constantly interrupting the detective in mid-sentence, not so much to answer a question as to change the subject. She spoke rapidly, injected opinions, and made disparaging remarks about her daughter-in-law. She speculated wildly on Joyce's whereabouts, said the missing woman was out to frame her son, and made ludicrous accusations of complicity by Elizabeth Reed and the Monahans.

From the onset, Carroll was convinced that the headstrong woman was not only paranoid, but living in a state of denial. There was little doubt that Geraldine Klindt believed the system was out to get her son, and she was willing to do anything to throw the police off track or place the blame elsewhere.

Early in the interview, Lieutenant Carroll treaded lightly, allowing her to prattle. He was empathetic toward the family, admitting the local newspapers had sensationalized the event. He wondered aloud how Jim could endure such stress and said he felt sorry for Bart.

Geraldine stated that the last time she had seen her daughter-in-law was on March 15, 1983. She remembered because Joyce had called and told her Bart wanted to come over to see his grandma.

She said that when they arrived Joyce handed her a dish she had borrowed and apologized for keeping it so long. When

Homicide

Bart left the room the conversation turned to the divorce. Joyce was upset and started talking against Jim.

Mrs. Klindt told Carroll that was the first time her daughter-in-law informed her she had retained a lawyer, "I told her, 'Well, finally ... Good!' We were sympathetic to her, too. I loved that girl, better than a daughter, until I found out she'd taken Jim. So, I wasn't too upset on March eighteenth, until Elizabeth Reed called."

When she paused to take a breath, the detective slipped in a question. "Then that was the first time you'd heard she'd left, March eighteenth?"

"Seven o'clock p.m., I'm pretty sure ... Elizabeth Reed."

"Okay. She was the first person that called you?"

"Yes, and she said, 'Have you seen Joyce today?' I said, 'No,' and I didn't think anything of it, because I hadn't seen her since Tuesday. But Elizabeth wouldn't let it drop. She said, 'Something's happened to Joyce, I know it has.' She got me upset enough that I went up to see Jim. I've never seen such overacting in all my life."

"Everybody was all excited?"

"Oh ... she was. Nobody else was."

"Just Elizabeth?" Carroll asked.

"She was the only one that was excited. We met the Reeds at Jim's house and Elizabeth shocked Jim when she flew at him like a tornado. She practically accused him of mur ... what everybody's thinking here and over at the county attorney's office.

"Say," Geri continued, changing the subject. "I asked Jim, 'What suitcase did she take?' 'She didn't take a suitcase,' he said."

"Yeah," Carroll replied, "that's what Jim told me."

"That's why Jim knew Joyce went to North Park, to buy luggage," Geraldine explained.

"That makes no sense," Carroll replied. "Joyce had been gone seven hours, and it doesn't take seven hours to buy a suitcase. Besides, Jim said he found the Jetta in front of Randall's Super Valu, and you don't buy luggage in a grocery store."

"Do you think she took a cab?" Geri asked.

"I checked all the cab companies," Carroll replied. "She didn't take a cab. So the only other option for her leaving there would be somebody picking her up."

"Oh, for heaven's sake. Then she must have had help. I always thought she had help, but what good does it do?" Geraldine complained.

"But I've got a problem with that too. We've got a lady going through a divorce ..."

Mrs. Klindt would not hear anything that might incriminate her son. She was off again, launching into another tirade against her daughter-in-law, saying Joyce constantly carped about the settlement. "Everything I heard was money, money, money, or Jim was no good, he was a druggie, he was a dealer, he was this and that ... and oh, did you know, Joyce got a $200 weekly allowance?"

Ted Carroll had been inside Jim Klindt's residence twice — the day they found the chain saw and the night the police searched the house for drugs. Unlike most men, the lieutenant noticed a home's interior. Part of his ability to observe stemmed from the inquisitive nature of his job, but the detective was also a woodworker. If Joyce received an exorbitant allowance, it certainly was not reflected in her home's second-hand furnishings.

According to Elizabeth Reed, nearly everything in the house except the bedroom suite, the kitchen appliances, and a large oriental rug Joyce had bought in anticipation of the *Quad-City Times'* story, came from Dick and Geraldine Klindt. The two

Homicide

wingback chairs, the sofa, and the end tables were all hand-me-downs. There was one handsome piece Carroll admired, an ornate antique desk, a bequest from Jim's grandmother. The elderly woman had lived with the young chiropractor and Joyce until into her nineties. Dick and Geraldine made sure Jim was compensated for taking care of grandma, allowing him to cash her social security checks. Of course, it was Joyce who cared for the old woman.

Geri rambled on, bitter that Joyce rarely visited, or seldom invited Dick and her to "Jim's" house, that it was not until the divorce was filed that she became friendly.

Carroll tried briefly to regain control of the interview. After two attempts, he gave up, sitting back in his chair until the woman unwound. When she paused, the lieutenant picked up where he had left off. "But, as I said, the problem I got ..."

Mrs. Klindt interrupted him in mid-sentence with a loud frustrated sigh.

"... is here's a lady that's gonna get a divorce she doesn't want. She hires an attorney to represent her side ... Her attorney tells her not to leave that house."

Carroll tried to explain the best he could, between frequent interruptions, that in a divorce action the wife nearly always got the home as well as custody of any children and that the $34,000 in cash Jim alleged she had taken was just as much Joyce's as it was his, and that if she had taken the money, she had done nothing illegal, that Jim had no recourse, because he had not listed it in the divorce assets.

Lieutenant Carroll then mentioned he had another problem. "Problem" seemed to be the magic word that tripped Geraldine's trigger. She interrupted again, with a gossipy inference that the Monahans, who never had any money had just bought two new cars.

"That's interesting," Carroll said, irritated. "But I'm still having a problem with this lady that's been told by her lawyer to stay in her home. She's got no reason to run. She's out for everything she can get. Right?"

"Right."

"Why did she leave her car? Why does a gal who wants everything ..."

"To build a frame."

Carroll was growing tired of the intrusions. He raised his voice, "I thought about that, Geri."

"THAT'S HONEST TO GOD WHAT I THINK," Geri shouted.

"NO," Carroll shot back. "I THOUGHT ABOUT THAT."

Mrs. Klindt was not about to let it die. "I smell a frame."

"I really did think about a frame," Carroll said lowering his voice.

"If I were going to frame someone, I'd do exactly what she did," Geri continued.

"The only problem I've got with a frame, and there's no nice way to put it. If it was a frame, then who's the volunteer I got to jump in the river?"

Geraldine sighed loudly again. "May I surmise, here?"

"Sure."

"It could be anybody."

"Except my tests are coming back that it can't be anybody," the detective said, explaining the case was in the hands of forensic experts. "Do you know how long we've been at it?"

Mrs. Klindt laughed nervously. "No, I don't."

"We're coming up on ten months."

The woman paled. "Oh, God."

"Ten months," Carroll repeated, "and everything is shaping up that in all likelihood this is Joyce."

"Oh, God ..."

Homicide

Geraldine then embarked upon a lengthy diatribe, condemning the media for "convicting and crucifying" her son. She talked of the pressure Jim was under and of his profession of innocence.

Carroll forged ahead. "Also, Geri, something came up when I talked to Terry and I heard it before, and I can't understand why that information isn't coming forward. Jim's been saying that he has two people that have seen Joyce since March eighteenth."

"He has, huh?"

"Well, why doesn't he tell me and clear the air so I can talk to him? Maybe we can clear this whole thing up by night."

Mrs. Klindt then asked if something had happened to upset her son, something which had made him so angry that he would withhold information.

A tight smile creased Carroll's lips. A police helicopter followed the chiropractor home from work nearly every afternoon, and Carroll often spent evenings in front of Klindt's house, revving the engine of his Harley-Davidson motorcycle, just to let the doctor know he was still on the case. "He's probably mad because we interviewed Terry and Jeff."

The answer did not satisfy Mrs. Klindt. She wondered if Bill Davis was responsible.

The lieutenant said he didn't know, but that Jim was only hurting his own cause by withholding witnesses. Geraldine promised to have a stern talk with her son. She then said Joyce had told her twice that she wanted to run away, that she had probably gone to Toronto or Mexico.

Carroll took a deep breath and started over. "My biggest problem is he tinkered with that damn car."

"That was stupid, wasn't it?" she said.

"Well, and I tell you what really looks bad for him, Geri, is the fact he was out on his airboat that day, and I got this lady coming out of the river."

Dead Water

Mrs. Klindt nodded. "Sure, the circumstances are terrible."

"And that Terry."

She interrupted again. "Do you know Terry?"

"Yeah, I met Terry, talked to Terry. I think Terry's got dollar signs in her eyes."

"I think most ..." Geri laughed. "That could be."

"You know what I mean?"

Geri laughed louder. "Yeah, money is wonderful."

"I know some of the guys that Terry went with before she met Jim."

"You know more than I do then."

"In fact, that's another thing I got a problem with, Geri. This I know for a fact, Jim began seeing Terry last September."

"I know. I'm about to tell ..." Mrs. Klindt suddenly stopped talking, like a child who had nearly given away a secret.

Carroll had been interrupted so many times he did not even notice, "Very clandestine."

"Have to be," she said.

"Very low-profile, low-key, everything. But March eighteenth, he has Terry meet him in his own driveway. What does that tell you?"

Geraldine thought for a moment. "Well, it could tell me they're in love and can't stay apart at all."

"Why on that particular day? Every other time it's been low-profile, hiding out ... That particular day, he has her meet him right in the driveway. That tells me you've got a guy and a girl who know the wife isn't coming home."

"It tells me it's pretty foolish," she said.

"They feel pretty comfortable that the wife isn't going to be there." Carroll continued.

"I really don't understand."

"Broad daylight, right in your own driveway, now hear me out, if you're sneaking on Thursday."

Homicide

But she did not hear him out. "Well, if that's all. The divorce is final, see. So they figure everything's just great."

Carroll challenged her. "The divorce was not final."

"Okay, I mean filed."

"Filed! Hell, it was filed back in December and they were sneaking around. Why? Why March eighteenth, all of a sudden, no more sneaking? Here we are."

Mrs. Klindt shook her head. "Well, I see it all. Joyce has left. I see your problem. You really got a case and a half."

"I've got lots of problems."

Geraldine did not want to hear Carroll's problems. She changed the subject, asking Carroll if he was looking "elsewhere." She said she had friends tell her of girls being "dropped from barges ... they have these 'fins' underneath that chop up everything."

"The lady I found was not chopped up by a boat prop."

"And do you remember the papers, the torso didn't have a baby ..."

Carroll became indignant. "They lied."

"Why would they lie?"

"Because they don't have information."

"Somebody's orders," she asked, again inferring the county attorney was involved.

"They print what they think they know."

"Humph. They're sure causing a lot of problems."

"I'll tell you right now, the torso has had a baby, stretch marks, no appendectomy scar, an episiotomy scar, all just like Joyce."

"Oh, my God."

"Just like Joyce ... Blood types, enzymes, hair color ..."

"Oh heavens, I knew nothing about it."

"I'll add it up for you, Geri ... Age group, what I have is with the age range of Joyce ..."

"Oh dear!"

"Blood type ... same blood type. There are enzymes in the blood, a mix between Gene and Virginia Monahan's, that less than one-half of one percent of all the people in that blood group ever have..."

"Rare, very rare," she said.

"Guess what? My torso's got it."

Mrs. Klindt was not convinced. She wondered if she could have the torso examined.

"Sure, sure," Carroll said. He then proceeded to reiterate his findings. "I haven't been able to uncover any evidence that would exclude the torso from being Joyce. It's coming down to where we're gonna have to say, that's Joyce."

Geraldine continued to proclaim her son's innocence.

"You know, Geri, I know things I shouldn't know. For instance, I know about the polygraphs Jim took in Des Moines and down at Per Mar. And for whatever reason, Jim has lied to me thirty times," Carroll said, insinuating the chiropractor had flunked both tests.

"Thirty times," she said shaking her head.

"Lies I can prove are lies. Over thirty times."

Geri fidgeted in her chair. The man had just called her son a liar. It was a painful reality she could neither face nor defend. So she digressed, wondering if Joyce could have had a boyfriend who had helped her, before beginning a scathing attack against Elizabeth Reed, accusing her of being the central character in a shadowy conspiracy against her son.

"Let me ask you something again," she said. "If you think it was Jim, why would he do it? He had no reason. He had the divorce going ..."

"But, okay, let me point out something. How much do you know about the divorce, Geri?"

"Just that they were going to get one."

The detective drew a line down the middle of his legal pad, the left side representing Jim, the right side, Joyce. As he

Homicide

spoke, he made hash-marks representing the division of assets.

"Jim was keeping the house, the Cadillac, the Winnebago, both boats, and the Scout. Joyce was getting the Jetta."

Mrs. Klindt stared at the page, seemingly shocked by the single slash on Joyce's side of the ledger.

Carroll continued. "There wasn't gonna be a cash settlement. He was gonna pay her no more than $500 a month. Oh, he was keeping Bart too."

"Was this in writing?"

"Yep," Carroll nodded. "It was in writing."

"Oh, my God."

"And the interesting thing, from what Jim told me, is that she stole $34,000. He made a financial statement for the divorce. It showed he never had $34,000."

"That's hiding the facts," she said, for the first time, siding with Joyce.

"Whatever," Carroll said. "He was pulling a fast one. He was gonna slip one through on her ... and you ask why? What's his motive?"

Mrs. Klindt searched for a comeback. "Women are like that too."

Lieutenant Carroll ignored her. "That Thursday, it was all set to go through court. It didn't because Joyce had a lawyer. Jim was upset about that."

"I'll bet."

"Now his little world was just collapsed. He was gonna have the house, Bart, the boats, the cars, everything ... and Terry, too. Joyce threw a monkey wrench into all that."

"I didn't know that," Geraldine said almost apologetically. "Joyce just screwed all that up for him."

"She should have gotten out," Mrs. Klindt said.

Carroll was not quite sure how to interpret the statement. Did Mrs. Klindt mean that she knew Joyce had not gotten out? "Talk about motive."

"Yeah. Well, oh my gosh, yes. You can't help ... but think what you're thinking, and I know what you're thinking."

"Sure. He had it all set. He was gonna come out smelling like a rose, and the most it was gonna cost him was $500 a month."

Geraldine shook her head. "Didn't know that either."

"She was gonna get the Jetta and a few sticks of second-hand furniture."

Mrs. Klindt became upset, almost angry, insinuating Joyce had lied to her. That her daughter-in-law had inferred she would receive between $800 and $1,000 a month after the divorce. "She didn't tell me that ... and she made me think ... Oh my ... Well, she sure fooled us again."

It was a pathetic display of ill-placed blame, and once again Carroll was not quite sure what to make of it. The detective returned to the money missing from the heating duct, stating that the only person who said the $34,000 existed was Jim.

"But I know he had money stashed in the house," Geri said.

"On the tape, in his own words, he's saying 'I don't have any money. I'm broke. But, at least I'll be rid of you.' That's his own words."

Geraldine remained combative. "He didn't want anyone to get his money. Can you understand that?"

It was Carroll who was no longer listening. "Motive, yeah, she's threatening him with income tax evasion ... drugs ..."

"I don't know what he made. I never knew, but he's certainly in debt. He owes on his house, he owes on his cars. He owes and owes and owes, and he owes us."

"Well, then I got a question. A guy owes all this, is it normal for him to have $34,000 in cash?"

"I don't know that he ever had it," she said. "It doesn't make sense."

Geraldine asked Carroll if he really believed all that talk about Jim being involved with drugs. That was, of course,

Homicide

despite the fact that she knew her son had been arrested and fined for "possession" the previous year.

"If he wasn't involved in drugs," Carroll replied, "why does he have the phone numbers of known suppliers written down?"

Carroll reviewed the long list of the circumstantial evidence for Mrs. Klindt in a logical progressive fashion. He quickly discovered he had not dented her mindset.

"Yeah, hearsay and no proof of anything. That's pretty shallow," she said.

Carroll did not flinch. "You know, I've got half a lady we pulled out of the river. Every test I can run on that lady tells me that's Joyce Klindt. The last person we can find who ever saw her alive is Jim."

"Well, I just pray that test comes back with something wrong. If it doesn't, I'm gonna have to face the facts."

"But right now, everything keeps coming back Joyce, Joyce, Joyce." The lieutenant's rough voice softened each time he repeated her name.

"Ted, from what you're telling me, I may just have to admit ..."

Carroll stared at her, fascinated by the prospect that Mrs. Klindt might possibly concede to anything. She never did.

12

LEG WORK

When Geraldine Klindt told her son about the interview, it must have been very disconcerting to the chiropractor. With the noose tightening, Jim Klindt's next act bordered on desperation.

Connie Caven, an employee in a local convenience store, phoned the Davenport Police Department and informed Lieutenant Carroll that she had been pressured by the chiropractor to give a statement to the Davenport police that she had seen Joyce Klindt alive. Caven seemed shaken by the incident. Carroll told the young woman he would be right over.

7-Eleven Food Store
1714 East Kimberly Road
Davenport, Iowa
(Tuesday, January 24, 1984, 7:20 p.m.)

"Jim phoned me here at work," Caven told Carroll, "around five o'clock this evening."

"Did he identify himself?"

"Oh, yeah. He said, 'You probably don't know me, my name is Jim Klindt.'"

"How did you respond?"

"I said I knew who he was, that he had adjusted me before. He said, 'Oh, I remember you now.' Then he explained that one of my co-workers, Sharon Campbell, had informed him that I had seen someone who looked like Joyce outside the 7-Eleven. I tried to tell him that I couldn't be positive it was Joyce, and besides, it happened months ago."

Homicide

"What'd Klindt say?"

"He pressured me. 'Oh, I'm sure it was her, but I can't say that. I need you to give the police a deposition on my behalf. They're out to get me. You can save my ass.' I told him, 'I'm sorry. I wish I could help, but I can't say for sure it was Joyce.' He hung up, and I thought that was the end of it, but he showed up a few minutes later."

"Did you see what he was driving?"

"Yeah. It was black and yellow, kind of rusted, looked like an old Jeep of some kind."

"Then what happened."

"He came in, said, 'Look, Connie. You're not the only person to see Joyce alive. I've got another witness who saw her in the same kind of car, a silver Camaro.' Then he offered to pay me for my time to go down to the police station and fill out a report.

"I kept trying to tell him I didn't know for sure what kind of car the woman was driving or if she was Joyce. He wouldn't take no for an answer. I got really scared, but I stuck to my guns. 'I'm sorry, Doctor,' I said. 'I did a double-take when I saw her looking through the window, but I can't swear it was your wife.' He stomped out, got into his Jeep, and left."

The incident gave Carroll another witness and further advanced the State's cause. The investigators continued to dig.

The next day, January 25, 1984, Corporal Kern sent copies of the autopsy report and X-rays of the torso to Dr. Clyde Snow of the Oklahoma State Medical Examiner's Office. Dr. Snow, a world-famous forensic anthropologist, had been involved with the J.F.K. assassination investigation, the identification of the victims of mass-murderer John Wayne Gacy, and the confirmation of identity for the 273 victims in the 1979 American Air Lines DC-10 crash in Chicago. Kern wanted to know if Snow could do an anthropological study and approximate the age and stature of the torso with the limited bones available. Snow said it was possible and requested that the remains be shipped to him in Oklahoma City. Kern told Snow that he and Lieutenant Carroll would deliver the torso.

Dennis Kern spent the first week of February 1984 compiling statistics. He checked with Mary Gilman of Blue Cross in Des Moines requesting data on frequency of Caesarean sections. She was unable to supply the information, referring Kern to an article published January 19, 1984, in the *Wall Street Journal*. Kern obtained a copy of the paper and noted the figures quoted came from the National Center for Health Statistics. He then phoned the NCHS headquarters in Hyattsville, Maryland.

The corporal spoke to Selma Taffel in the natality section concerning data, broken down by age, of the percentages of adult white women who have not delivered a child. He also requested the names and sections of additional sources of information available from the center.

The following day, Kern phoned Ed Graves of the NCHS concerning the frequencies of episiotomies for the United States. Graves said he would supply the information, but the data was not broken down by age or race.

On February 5, Kern walked to the Davenport Public Library and obtained a copy of the general population characteristics summary gathered during the 1980 census.

Two days later, he removed the torso from the evidence locker freezer and transported it to the morgue at Mercy Hospital. Dr. Kimball Thompson removed additional tissue samples before packing the corpse in dry ice.

Lieutenant Carroll and Corporal Kern gathered every piece of identification they owned for their trip to Oklahoma. But Kern still worried. "Isn't there some sort of penalty for transporting a body across state lines?" he asked Carroll.

Homicide

The detective grinned. "I'm sure there is."
"You're not going to check on authorization?"
"Hell, no."
"Ignorance is no excuse for the law," Kern replied.
"Dennis, we are the goddamned law. Now, get in the car."

The two lawmen drove all night, arriving in Oklahoma City at daybreak. After eating a leisurely breakfast, they drove to the medical examiner's office. It did not open for another half-hour.

At 8:10 a.m. the torso and a container of fixed bones removed during the autopsy were delivered to Mike Stroud in exchange for a signed morgue register acknowledging the transfer of possession.

The following morning the two officers met with Dr. Snow and outlined the attempts the Davenport Police Department had made in trying to identify the torso. The disheveled Dr. Snow was not what either of the officers expected.

"Anthropology is an alternative means of identification," said the doctor. "The first thing I need to do is strip the flesh off the bone."

Kern made a face.

"In my business, Dennis, you learn to laugh at disaster. Otherwise, you go bananas. Over time, a forensic scientist either becomes desensitized to the misfortune of others, or he ends up like the doctor who mourns the loss of his patients."

"Are you gonna get started today?" asked Carroll.

"Yeah. But it will take some time. I've seen the torso and there's not much bone to work with. I'll let you know my findings as soon as I put her back together."

On February 16, Dennis Kern drove to Dubuque, Iowa, and met with John C. Fridell, Ph.D., a statistician teaching at Loras College, concerning the data the corporal had obtained to date. Father Fridell said he would review the information and call Kern after considering the mathematical problems pertaining to its application.

Judy Pochel phoned Ted Carroll the following morning and the detective confirmed that Jim Klindt was the prime suspect in the murder investigation.
"When are you going to arrest him?"
"I don't foresee an immediate arrest."
The reporter phoned Bill Davis.
"I've got no comment concerning Klindt's status as a suspect," the prosecutor replied.
"Well, on Channel Four last night, you told a Kathleen Seith that you were convinced the torso was Joyce Klindt and you were confident you could prove it in a court of law. You also said that you expected an arrest in the immediate future. Are you telling me that you have other suspects?"
"No comment."

If Jim Klindt had an accomplice, Lieutenant Carroll knew Jeffrey Ryan was a logical choice. One witness had said Ryan would do "anything" for the chiropractor. Another told Carroll that Ryan used drugs and that Jim Klindt was his supplier. He also said Jeff owed the chiropractor money. In Carroll's mind, Klindt owned the man.

Both Carroll and Kern had talked with the chiropractor's "best friend" by telephone, but neither officer had spoken to Ryan in person. When Ryan refused Carroll's request for an interview, he was subpoenaed.

Homicide

Davenport Police Department
(Thursday, February 23, 1984, 3:16 p.m.)

Ryan, a stocky little man with a wispy mustache, looked extremely uncomfortable. He seemed tense and squeezed his eyes shut every few seconds in exaggerated tic. Before being sworn in by Assistant County Attorney Jim Hoffman, Ryan expressed his loyalty to Klindt. "You know, Jim's a good friend of mine," he told Carroll, "and I'd never say anything to intentionally hurt him."

Jeffrey Ryan was exactly what Carroll had expected, a bantam rooster ready for a fight.

"How long have you known Jim?" Carroll asked.

"Since the third grade."

"Did you know Joyce?"

"For the past thirteen years. I was Jim's best man at their wedding in Granite City. We've been close ever since."

"Did Dr. Klindt say anything to you about Joyce's disappearance?"

Ryan blinked nervously. "All that Jim told me was that Joyce got mad and left. That she took all his money and left. He did tell me about finding the car. Said he was gonna take it home but for some reason he got scared and took it over to the airport and hid it."

He paused for a moment and studied the detective. Carroll waited. "Jim did tell me he hadn't hurt her," Ryan added, as if it were an afterthought.

"Do you know if the doctor owns a chain saw?" asked the lieutenant.

"Yep. Kept it on the airboat."

Carroll then showed him a picture of the chain saw confiscated from Klindt's home.

Ryan shrugged. "Looks like it, I guess."

"Did you know that Dr. Klindt used drugs?"

"Sure," he said. "That's no secret. Jim's used drugs off and on for about the last five years, mostly pot. I smoked it with him once in a while. He does a little cocaine, even offered it to me a couple of times, but I turned him down."

The frank confession baffled Carroll. "Do you know anything about Jim's guns?"

"Yeah, he's got a bunch of 'em; shotguns, rifles, and a couple of pistols ... the Ruger Willie had ... maybe a dozen more."

"I've also heard that he owns an automatic weapon."

"He owns a .45-caliber Ingram, but it's semi-automatic. I even tried to make a silencer for it once."

"It hasn't been converted to a full automatic?"

Ryan squirmed. "That'd be illegal. I don't know anything about it being converted. I'm a law-abiding citizen."

Carroll smiled. The "law-abiding citizen" sitting across from him had just admitted to smoking dope and building a silencer for a machine gun.

"Where's the Ingram now?"

"I don't know. Jim told me something about it falling off the airboat."

"Who's this Willie you mentioned earlier?" Carroll asked.

Ryan's dark eyes darted about the room. "Willie Hendricks? Oh, just a guy Jim used to hunt and trap with. Lives up by Dixon."

"Tell me about the Ruger that Willie Hendricks has."

"It's just an ol' beat up pistol — a .22 single-action revolver. But Willie don't have it no more."

"What'd he do with it?"

"See, it was kind of like Bart's gun. Me and Jim and Bart went up to Dixon to get the gun back."

"When was that?"

"I don't recall. Maybe a year ago. I don't know where the gun is today."

Homicide

"Okay, Mr. Ryan, that's all I have. I appreciate you coming in."

Jeffrey Ryan rose and Carroll walked with him to the front door of the station. On the way, Ryan reiterated his loyalty to Klindt, volunteering, "If Jim did kill Joyce, I don't want to know about it and I sincerely hope you never catch him."

Davenport Police Department
(Tuesday, March 6, 1984, 1:30 p.m.)

It seemed to Carroll that no one came to the police station voluntarily anymore. Willie Hendricks was the next to be subpoenaed. Hendricks, a wiry man of six feet, was dressed in dirty overalls and needed a shave.

"Do you know James B. Klindt?" Carroll asked.

"Yeah," Hendricks replied.

"For how long?"

Hendricks scratched his head. "Five years or so."

"How did you meet him?"

"Through my brother-in-law, Jack Crofton. Jim used to store his boat at Jack's place."

"Would you call Jim Klindt a friend?"

"I guess so. We used to hunt and trap together. My wife and I had dinner at the Klindt house a few times, and they've come to our place too."

"Have you ever been out on his airboat?"

"Five or six times. Jeff Ryan usually went along."

"Do you have any direct knowledge as to the course of events which took place on March 18, 1983, the day that Joyce Klindt disappeared?"

"I don't have no direct knowledge. Only what Jim has told me and the rumors spreading around Dixon. Jim never offered any explanation of Joyce's disappearance other than she just took off."

"Did Jim Klindt have a chain saw on his airboat?"

Willie ran a hand over his stubble. "Yeah, he had one, but I never seen it."

"Well, I'd heard rumors that you moved the chain saw. Is that true?"

"No, the chain saw I moved belonged to my brother-in-law Jack. He was going through a divorce and I took the saw over to my dad's place until the divorce was over. He didn't want his wife to get it."

"Do you remember what it looked like? Color, brand name, etcetera?"

"Yeah, it was orange and white, I believe it was a Stihl."

Carroll's head jerked up. The saw Hendricks described was identical to Klindt's. Had he been looking for the wrong saw? "When did you move it?"

"Last September."

The detective filed the information and changed the subject. "Do you know a man by the name of Albert Rohse?"

Willie nodded. "Yeah, I used to work for him on his mink farm out by Donahue. I helped him grind up the meat that he fed to his mink."

"What kind of meat?"

"Mostly small animals that I caught in my traps."

"Was Jim Klindt ever out there?"

"Lots of times," Hendricks said, nodding. "He'd stop out and wait for me to get off work. We never stayed around long, always went someplace else. Rohse didn't like Jim. In fact, I don't think he liked chiropractors in general. He'd had a bad experience with one a while back. Called them quacks."

"Did you ever borrow a gun from Jim?"

"Yeah, an old pistol."

"What'd it look like?"

"It was a six-shot revolver, real beat up. I used it to kill the animals I'd caught in my traps."

"Do you still have it?"

Homicide

"No. I remember Jim and Jeff and Bart comin' out to get it."

"When?" Carroll asked.

"About the time Joyce disappeared."

"Does Jim own an Ingram submachine gun that has been altered to fire fully automatic?"

"Yeah. I've seen it."

"Ever shoot it?"

"Nope, but my wife Tina did. Fired a full clip through it one afternoon out at Jack's place."

"Jack Crofton's place?"

"Yeah. On a farm near Dixon."

"Do you know where the Ingram is now?"

"No."

"Did you know Dr. Klindt uses drugs?"

"Yes, but I wasn't involved. I don't do drugs. Besides, we did mostly outdoor stuff, trappin' and huntin'. I don't have the money to run with him at night, drinkin', chasin' women, and all those other things."

"Is there anything else that I've missed? Anything that you can add?"

"Nothin' except to tell you I don't have any knowledge about what happened to Joyce other than rumor. I don't want to know any more than I know, and I don't want to get involved."

That same day, Dennis Kern returned to Loras College in Dubuque and met with Fr. John Fridell to see if he could learn from him what percentage of the population had the physical characteristics of both the torso and Joyce Klindt. Father Fridell said he order to insure the soundness of his methodology in determining that number, he would need to confer with the statistics department at the University of Iowa.

Dead Water

Donahue, Iowa
(Wednesday, March 7, 1984, 9:30 a.m.)

Carroll and Kern traveled to Albert Rohse's mink farm the next morning. Rohse was an ornery old cuss, sort of like the critters he raised. But he was a straight-shooter, the kind of man Lieutenant Carroll respected. They had learned from Willie Hendricks that Rohse did not like Jim Klindt. Carroll quickly discovered that Rohse was not too fond of the police either.

"You Albert Rohse?"

"Yep."

"I'm Ted Carroll. This is Dennis Kern. We're with the Davenport police. If you don't mind, we'd like to ask you a few questions."

"Would it make any difference if I said no?"

"We could get a subpoena, have you come to Davenport."

"I don't want that."

"You know a Willie Hendricks?"

"Yeah. He works for me from time to time."

"You also know a chiropractor named Jim Klindt?"

"Unfortunately."

"You don't like him very much?"

The old man grinned. "That'd be an understatement."

"Willie said Dr. Klindt used to come out here once in a while. That true?"

"I guess, but he never hung around very long when I was here."

"Willie also said you have a power grinder."

"Yeah. I use it to grind up meat for my mink, like the varmints Willie traps. It's right over here by the fence."

Carroll and Kern examined the machine. "How big is that engine?"

"Seven and a half horse."

"Got a lot of power, uh?"

Homicide

Rohse smirked. "It don't clog up, if that's what you mean."

On March 8, 1984, Kern met with Father Fridell and Russell Lenth, Ph.D., at the University of Iowa. Dr. Lenth was the director of the Statistical Consulting Service at the university. Lenth reviewed Fridell's work and said the data and calculations made by the Loras professor were sound, but he felt there were additional technical factors to consider. He asked for additional time to study the data.

Clock Tower Building
Arsenal Island
(Friday, March 9, 1984, 9:15 a.m.)

The following morning, Carroll and Kern drove to the Arsenal Island, regional headquarters for the Corps of Engineers. They met with George Johnson, chief of the hydraulics branch, and S.K. Nanda, a hydraulic engineer.

The Upper Mississippi, that portion of the river above Cairo, Illinois, is divided into twenty-six "slack-water" pools, separated by an equivalent number of locks and dams. The system, built by the Corps of Engineers in the 1930's was designed to keep the channel at a depth not less than nine feet. Nicknamed the "aquatic staircase," this remarkable feat of engineering keeps the river navigable most of the year.

Carroll needed to determine the likelihood of a body moving downriver from Princeton to the Davenport-Bettendorf boundary. He soon learned the river was a very complicated place.

"What is the longest distance a corpse has been known to travel when dumped into the river?"

"I'd have to check," Johnson replied. "If memory serves me, somewhere around forty miles. The distance a body will

Dead Water

travel depends upon a lot of variables — where the body was dumped, the time of year, and the stage of the river."

Johnson unfolded a navigation chart. "Let's start with where the body was dumped."

Carroll pointed to a spot on the map. "We think here, in the sloughs just above Princeton."

"Do you know the exact date?"

"March eighteenth, last year," Carroll replied.

Nanda pulled out a journal. "The river was at flood stage last spring," he told the officers. "The gates of Lock and Dam Number Fourteen, that's the one just down from the I-80 bridges, were wide open for nearly two weeks. March eighteenth falls right in the middle of that timetable."

"How long would it take a body to make the trip?"

"I'd be guessing ... probably three days to a week."

"That fast?"

"Oh, it could take longer," Johnson replied. "If you're right and the torso was dumped into the old channel, what we now call Steamboat Slough, it could have silted in for weeks. Even if it broke loose, it wouldn't come straight downriver. There's a series of submerged wing dams that swing the current from shore to shore."

"But if the water was deep, wouldn't the body go right over the top of those wing dams?"

"Probably not. The human body is a little heavier than water."

"It's hard to believe the body was floating," Nanda said. "Not with the water temperature at thirty-eight degrees."

"You mean a body is more likely to sink in cold water?"

The engineer smiled. "I'm not sure how to answer to that," he replied. "What I was implying is cold water retards bacterial growth, sort of acts like a preservative in that it keeps the body from decomposing. It's the air bubbles created by decay that make tissue buoyant."

Homicide

"What about the speed of the current?"

"Varies," Johnson replied. "Water moves at different speeds throughout the river. On the bottom and along the shore, the river's slowed by drag. Even something as light as air causes surface friction. The flow is also impeded by bridge abutments, things like that. On the other hand, you get sort of a surge coming through dams. At flood stage, just beneath the surface in mid-channel, we're talking somewhere around six to eight feet a second.

"Let's say the torso broke loose right after it was dumped. It's too heavy to float, so it would have traveled the entire distance underwater, skipping along the bottom. That could cause numerous skin abrasions. The current swings it back to the Iowa shore, where it gets caught on the rock ledge near Lindsey Park. The torso could have hung up there for a couple of weeks. During that time, two things were happening. The river began to recede, and the water was warming up. Bacteria caused air bubbles to form in the tissue. Bingo! The torso bobs to the surface."

"Thank you for your time, gentlemen. You've answered my question. It is feasible for a body, in this case a torso, to travel from Princeton to Davenport."

"At flood stage," Nanda replied, "it's not only feasible, it's probable."

The following week, Kern contacted Rod Miller at the National Crime Information Center concerning data pertaining to missing persons. Kern was told that the NCIC does not keep demographic records for missing persons. However, Miller said he would run a line search for all female whites missing as well as one for all female whites missing between the ages of 27 and 40. The computer printout of the NCIC's search was done on Wednesday, March 21, and sent by mail to the Davenport Police Department.

Dead Water

The final anthropology report was received from Dr. Clyde Snow the same day. He had used the bones of the torso to recreate the parameters of the body structure. The woman from which the torso was severed was between five feet and five-six in height and weighed between 120 and 140 pounds. Both measurements were consistent with those of Joyce Klindt.

Lt. Ted Carroll acknowledged the anthropological study had been completed. He told Judy Pochel by phone, "There is nothing inconsistent in the report that would indicate the torso is not that of Joyce Klindt. The report won't hurt us."

Since the disappearance of Joyce Klindt, Lieutenant Carroll and Corporal Kern had followed every lead, from digging up a backyard in Bettendorf on a tip from a clairvoyant to photographing the eight-inch opening of the power-driven meat grinder on Albert Rohse's mink farm. The past three months had been nonstop, and although the two officers had made some startling discoveries while retracing Jim Klindt's steps, the fact was that the trail was twelve months cold.

The chiropractor remained the only suspect, but there was no concrete evidence against him. The chain saw confiscated and later returned to the chiropractor yielded no blood or tissue samples.

With the arrival of spring, the authorities seemed no closer to solving the case. Time had handcuffed the police. Trails not followed were covered with undergrowth and moss. Leads seemed to dissipate in the March winds. The investigation dragged on, past the first anniversary of Joyce Klindt's disappearance. With no new pertinent information the case seemed dead in the water. That made the prosecutor's next move all the more improbable.

13

ARRESTED

On Wednesday morning, March 28, 1984, Scott County Attorney William Davis presented District Court Judge James Havercamp with a summary of how the forty-nine witnesses the prosecution had lined up would testify in an upcoming trial.

At 3:15 that afternoon, Lieutenant Carroll received a phone call from Davis. "It's a go, Ted. Everything's in order. Havercamp just signed the warrant for Klindt's arrest."

After sending Corporal Kern to the courthouse to pick up the warrant, Carroll called Sgt. Daniel Reardon into his office and explained the situation. "I'll be honest, Dan. I really don't know how Klindt will react. I think we've got to treat him as dangerous. Grab a couple of blues and meet me back here as soon as you can."

Reardon returned to Lieutenant Carroll's office a few minutes later with officers Gerald McCabe and Mike Edinger. Kern arrived a moment later, warrant in hand. Carroll's voice was calm. "I think you're all aware we've got reporters camped out back watching our every move. Let's try not to make this a circus. The fewer of them at the arrest, the better. Take three squad cars and head out in different directions. Dennis and I will follow in a couple of minutes. We'll meet in front of Klindt's office at precisely three-fifty."

Dead Water

Klindt Chiropractic Clinic
(Wednesday, March 28, 1984, 3:50 p.m.)

The four cruisers pulled silently to the curb in front of the big white house at 1941 West Third Street. Officers McCabe and Edinger were posted in the rear. Lieutenant Carroll, along with Corporal Kern and Sergeant Reardon, entered the front lobby to arrest James Barry Klindt for the murder of his wife.

Reardon walked to the desk. The receptionist glanced up, her eyes stopping briefly at the badge pinned to the officer's leather jacket. The sergeant smiled and tried not to alarm her. "We've got some paper work for Dr. Klindt," he said in a distinct Chicago/Irish brogue.

The woman drew a worried breath and nodded toward a closed door. "He's in there."

Reardon turned the knob and pulled. The door opened a crack and then slammed shut. Someone was holding the door from the other side. Reardon pulled harder, nearly dragging Jim Klindt into the lobby.

The chiropractor tried to act casual. He greeted the officers with a nonchalant, "Hi there." The relaxed demeanor was in direct contradiction to the dark circles that framed his eyes.

"Doctor Klindt, we have a warrant for your arrest," Kern announced.

Klindt sighed and nodded. "Okay."

"Do you want me to find Bart?" Lieutenant Carroll asked.

Klindt shook his head. "He'll been taken care of."

Corporal Kern then proceeded to read the warrant.

Jim Klindt gasped when he heard the amount of his bond. It seemed obvious he could not post bail. "Can I get my coat?" he asked.

Reardon's voice was stern. "No. I'll get it."

"It's hanging on the vacuum cleaner in my office closet."

Dick Klindt, who had heard the tail end of the conversation, appeared in the doorway. "What's going on?" he asked.

Homicide

"We're arresting your son for the murder of Joyce," Carroll replied.

A pained expression crossed the old man's face. "I'll get his coat," Dick said. He returned a moment later with a corduroy jacket and went back upstairs.

Reardon frisked Klindt, read him his rights, and asked him to place his arms behind his back. The chiropractor was handcuffed.

"Take him away," Lieutenant Carroll said.

Across the hallway, Terry Keuhn had witnessed the arrest. She stood dazed in the doorway of her beauty shop, visibly shaken, tears streaming down her cheeks. When the young woman noticed the lieutenant watching her, she ran out the back door. Carroll turned and followed Klindt, flanked by officers Reardon and McCabe, down the front porch steps. Only a handful of reporters and photographers and a few neighbors were present. The chiropractor, still wearing his light blue smock, smiled but said nothing as he was escorted down the walk and into a waiting squad car. An officer placed a hand on Klindt's head, and the chiropractor ducked into the back seat.

The lieutenant turned back toward the house. The woeful faces of Dick and Geraldine Klindt were pressed against an upstairs window. As the cruiser drove away, it was evident to the detective that the chiropractor had destroyed more than one life.

Klindt had anticipated the arrest. Three weeks prior, he had granted his parents power of attorney in handling his personal affairs. Upon reaching the station for booking, the chiropractor refused to answer questions, phoning his father instead. Dick had found Bart. The boy would spend the night with his paternal grandparents.

The breakthrough in the case had come in January, when tests from Southwest Forensic Laboratory in Dallas concluded

Dead Water

the torso was, indeed, that of Joyce Klindt. A new forensic science using genetic markers was utilized to identify specific cellular traits. Lieutenant Carroll and Corporal Kern had employed the latest scientific methods in forensic testing and anthropologic study to construct a case for the State. But even with the identification probabilities placed above 99 percent, there were no eyewitnesses to the crime itself. The case against the chiropractor was based solely upon circumstantial evidence.

Ted Carroll had dogged Jim Klindt for more than a year. He had conducted dozens of interviews and sorted through hundreds of tips and clues. The detective had done his job well. Jim Klindt was, at last, going to trial.

The arrest, which had taken less than ten minutes, proved anticlimactic. The rush Carroll had expected following the chiropractor's detainment was missing. Carroll would continue on the case, conducting interviews and gathering evidence to strengthen further the State's cause. He would also testify at the upcoming trial. But the chase was over for Ted Carroll, his role diminished. Enforcement had moved to judgment. Gaining a conviction was out of his hands.

Scott County Attorney William E. Davis, forty-three, had remained circumspect in the background ever since he had first learned Joyce Klindt was missing. With the arrest of her husband, the fiery little prosecutor now took center stage.

Bill Davis understood from the onset that without a confession from the chiropractor, proving him guilty would be difficult. The prosecutor also knew that in order to gain a conviction, he would be forced to stretch the bounds of imagination and the law. The revolutionary case against Jim Klindt used forensic methods so complex that just relating the statistical data to a jury would be an imposing task. But before he could do that, Davis would have to educate himself. All of

Homicide

this, along with the rest of his duties, took a great deal of time. His family suffered.

Bill Davis, like Ted Carroll, was longtime married. He and his wife Sharon lived with their three beautiful dark-haired daughters in a large home in central Davenport. Unlike Bill, who was raised in a blue-collar neighborhood in Detroit, Sharon, a blue-eyed full-figured woman of forty-two, had come from Edina, a chic suburb of Minneapolis. Fortunately, Sharon, a spirited woman with a husky voice, had the inner strength to endure the long hours her husband would spend working on the case.

The authorities were all smiles at a joint news conference.

"What makes this case different?" a newswoman asked.

"It's unique," said Realff Ottesen, "because it's the first murder case in Iowa where the identity of the victim could be an issue."

"The case is unusual in other ways, too," added Acting Chief Borgstadt, "because investigators have been unable to determine the exact cause of death. Believe me, we're all relieved the investigation has finally come to an end."

"Why the show of force at Klindt's office?" queried a reporter.

Borgstadt defended the additional manpower. "It's better to have too many officers than not enough, just in case there's trouble."

"What about you, Mr. Davis?" came the follow-up.

"My job has just begun," the prosecutor replied.

The following morning, March 29, Jim Klindt was formally charged with the murder. He made the short walk from the county jail to the courthouse chained to a dozen other prisoners. The rangy chiropractor dwarfed his fellow inmates. Dressed in the same blue lab coat and brown slacks he had been wearing when he was apprehended, Klindt said nothing to the mass of reporters who flocked outside the courtroom's doors. There were so many photographers at the arraignment that they scrambled for position to snap Klindt's picture.

In court, Klindt sat quietly, his hands clasped in his lap. When he was called before Judge Jack Broderick, the chiropractor stared at the floor.

"James B. Klindt. You are formally charged with the first-degree murder of your wife, Joyce A. Klindt. I have set the plea date for April 24.

"I am placing your son, Bartley, in the temporary custody of his maternal grandparents, Eugene and Virginia Monahan."

Reporters spoke with friends and relatives of Joyce after the arraignment.

"I can only hope our love, understanding, and security will be a stabilizing factor in the boy's life," said Mrs. Monahan.

The same day, the Monahans filed a motion with the court that Klindt be denied executorship of their daughter's estate.

The arrest was greeted with mixed feelings. "I knew all along Jim Klindt killed my sister," Bruce Monahan told the press. "I'm relieved he's finally been arrested."

The harsh remark was surprising in light of the fact that Jim Klindt had taken a liking to Joyce's younger brother. Whenever Bruce visited Davenport, he spent much of his time hunting and fishing with the chiropractor.

Dr. Dennis Hagemann appeared less biased. "The court will figure out his guilt or innocence. Jim made it clear about a week ago that an arrest was coming. It's good news and bad news. Joyce was a friend of mine."

Jim Klindt did not fare well in jail. On the morning of April 4, 1984, the chiropractor complained of chest pains and was taken to the jail's infirmary where he was examined by a

Homicide

physician's assistant and a nurse. They learned that Klindt had a history of high blood pressure. (Klindt had once told Elizabeth Reed he could make his blood pressure rise at will.) While arrangements were being made to send him to the Community Health Center, he was returned to his cell. A short time later, Klindt was found semiconscious, slumped over his bed, his chest heaving. He was taken immediately to Mercy Hospital and released after the doctors could find nothing wrong.

Many were surprised to hear that Klindt's attorney, Ned Wehr, who had long been an antagonist of Bill Davis, would not be defending Klindt. It was rumored that Wehr dropped Klindt after learning the chiropractor had failed polygraphs on two separate occasions.

Sources close to the case said that Lawrence Scalise, a prominent Des Moines attorney, had been retained by Klindt to replace Ned Wehr. It was also said that Scalise, a former Iowa State attorney general, could earn in excess of $100,000 for defending Klindt. Davis's 1984 salary as county attorney was $41,800.

Scalise and his talented young assistant, Melody Haines, were at Klindt's side on the morning of April 24, when Klindt entered a plea of not guilty. At that time, Scalise asked that his client's $1 million bail be reduced.

Prosecutor Bill Davis opposed the bond reduction. He presented the pre-trial release papers that Klindt had signed when he was freed on drug charges the previous year. "Is this your signature stating you would not leave the country?" Davis asked.

"Yes," Klindt replied.

"And did you leave the country?"

"Yes."

Dead Water

The prosecutor knew that Klindt had vacationed in the Bahamas during the summer of 1983 with Terry Keuhn and Bart.

Scalise argued Klindt had known for a year that he was a suspect in the murder case and although he left the country, he did return. Therefore, bail should be reduced.

Scott County Jail Administrator David Clearman testified that a package of magazines had been left for Klindt on April 2, with maps of the United States and Canada inserted between the pages.

Judge Havercamp took the request for bond reduction under advisement and at the same time approved Scalise's request to push the June 4 trial date into August to accommodate the defense attorney's heavy workload.

"Are you going to seek a change of venue?" Havercamp asked.

Scalise replied, "At this time, Your Honor, we simply don't know."

After the bail reduction hearing, Davis said, "I had Clearman introduce the maps to point out the mobility of the defendant. I ask you, what was he planning?"

Havercamp later rejected the bond reduction request, citing Klindt had violated his pre-trial release agreement by traveling to the Bahamas and had also pressured a witness in the upcoming trial to change her testimony.

On Friday, May 3, Klindt wrote to Michael Shinkle, the Davenport attorney representing the Joyce Klindt estate, in response to Shinkle's questioning Klindt's right to sell the couple's property to pay legal expenses. The note, badly spelled and nearly incoherent, was written on jail stationery and read as follows:

Homicide

>Scott County Detention Center
>416 West Fourth Street
>Davenport, Iowa 52801
>319-326-8750
>
>Joyce's name is only on the house
>and Scout II — he isn't dead, any way as
>no death certificate has been signed, and
>3 witness' have come forward to attest — we
>are checking to see if false accusations
>you are making about her death may be used
>against you, as increasing & aggrivating my
>povrety level, hoping to hear any more
>inflammatory retoric, with your signature
>for futher possible action.
>
>   Sincerely
>
>   James

Shinkle immediately brought the letter to the attention of Ted Carroll, telling the detective that if these alleged witnesses existed, it would shortcut the necessity of dealing with Joyce Klindt's estate. "All we wanted to know," said Shinkle, "was if the property Klindt had put up for sale was also half Joyce's. If it was sold, we wanted an accurate accounting."

When the information contained in the letter found its way into the press, Acting Chief Borgstadt was forced to respond. "If Klindt will give us the names, we will check it out. We will work just as hard to prove him innocent as we would to prove him guilty."

When Jim Klindt would not reveal his eyewitnesses, Lieutenant Carroll attempted to find them on his own. He phoned Lawrence Scalise's law office in Des Moines to ask for the witnesses' names. The detective was told the lawyer was out of town.

Rumors of eyewitnesses had been circulating for months and the Davenport police had few clues as to their source. Unfortunately, Carroll was forced to leave the investigation. He was scheduled to attend classes at the FBI Academy in Quantico, Virginia, the following week.

Detective Larry Bankson took Carroll's place. Bankson had followed the case since its inception and like all good detectives, was well-briefed and mentally prepared. But the search for eyewitnesses was more like a wild goose chase, and the detective soon found himself dealing with people who lived in some very out-of-the-way places. Bankson conducted the first such interview with Marsha Crofton.

Up until St. Patrick's eve, 1983, the Croftons, Marsha and her husband Jack, had lived together in their rural Dixon home some fifteen miles northwest of Davenport. At one time the couple had been close friends with Joyce and Jim Klindt. In fact, Jim Klindt had kept his airboat parked in the Croftons' garage until the fall of 1982.

It was that fall, about the time Klindt started dating Terry Keuhn, that the two couples had a falling out. Exactly why is unknown. Even the Croftons gave different accounts. Jack, purportedly, broke off the friendship because he disapproved of Jim Klindt's cocaine use and philandering ways. That makes little sense in light of the fact that Jack had put up with Klindt's drug use and womanizing for years. Rumors persisted that Jack became upset when he learned Klindt had once turned his affections toward Jack's wife. Marsha, on the other hand, told police the neighbors had complained about the airboat being an eyesore, that Klindt had taken the gripe personally and severed relations with the Croftons after he moved the boat. In the same interview, Marsha stated that the boat was kept out of sight in the garage.

Homicide

On Thursday afternoon, March 17, 1983, Jack Crofton went on a hunting trip. That evening, Marsha Crofton left her husband for good. She spent the night in Davenport. The next morning, the day Joyce Klindt disappeared, Marsha admitted to being in Princeton. Jim Klindt, who was also in Princeton on the morning of March 18, was spotted at the Crofton house that afternoon, even though he no longer stored his boat there.

Davenport Police Department
(Friday, May 4, 1984, 3:11 p.m.)

Detective Bankson: "Did you know Joyce Klindt?"

"Yes I did. She was my friend," Marsha Crofton replied.

"What were the circumstances of your friendship?"

"We used to go boating with the Klindts, sometimes other people. Bart would usually go too. We had good times together. My ex-husband, Jack, would go on the airboat with Jim almost every Sunday. The Klindts would stop by our house once in a while when we lived in Dixon. That was about the extent of it."

"Your husband and Jim were friends?"

"Yes."

"Did Jim ever come out to your place when your ex-husband wasn't there?"

"Sure. He'd come out to pick up his airboat. He stored it in our garage. When we left, we locked the house, but we didn't always lock the garage."

Crofton went on to say that Joyce Klindt was a loving mother. "Just a real nice person."

"Do you remember the day you left your husband?"

"Sure. He went hunting with a bunch of his buddies on Thursday afternoon. When he left, I left him."

"St. Patrick's Day 1983?"

"Uh-huh. I came to Davenport that evening. I remember making green Jell-O, and I was wearing a green jumpsuit."

"Did you stay in town that night?"

"Yes. I returned home the next day, about noon or so, and picked up some clothes. Then I drove to Wisconsin."

"So, your house was empty that weekend?"

"Why are you stressing that so much, my house being empty?"

Bankson ignored her. "Did Jim have a key to your house?"

"No."

"Okay. You went back to the house on Friday, the eighteenth?"

"Yeah, to get some clothes. Must have been before noon."

"You were definitely at the house on the eighteenth?"

"That morning ... that morning, uh-huh. Are you guys, are you thinking he came out to the house and he took Jack's chain saw or something?"

"I don't know. It's speculation," said Bankson.

"Oh dear."

"Have you heard that Jim says there are witnesses who have seen Joyce alive?"

"Yeah. I wonder who they are."

"You're not one of them?"

"No. I haven't talked to Joyce since she called me crying one night in December of '82."

"Well, Marsha, thanks for stopping in."

"I probably wasn't any help."

About that, she may have been correct. But Marsha Crofton certainly gave Bankson something to think about. Was it possible that Klindt had gone to the Croftons' the morning of March 18, 1983 to "borrow" Jack's chain saw and returned it that afternoon? The police had also heard rumors that a blonde was driving the Jetta on the afternoon of March 18. Marsha Crofton was a platinum blonde.

Homicide

On May 7, Bankson drove to Dixon to interview Croftons' neighbors. His first stop was Pat Learn's. Learn stated that she had seen Dr. Klindt's International Scout drive by her house and park in front of the Croftons' garage around 3:00 p.m. on March 18, 1983. She said the chiropractor only stayed for about five minutes, and she thought it strange he would be out there when no one was home.

Bankson's next stop was at Rosann Mohr's. "I was walking my new baby past the bay window in the front room. It was mid-afternoon when Klindt arrived," Mohr said, adding that Marsha Crofton had once characterized Jim Klindt as "mean."

"Did you ever hear Jim Klindt supplied drugs to ... to a man that would do anything for Klindt?" Bankson asked.

"Yeah. From what I heard, he was kind of a side-saddle guy," Mohr replied. "Like a little leech that would go with Klindt all the time. I only saw him one time when he was out here, and he was small, seemed a lot younger than Jim.

"Jack used to go with Jim a lot when they went on their hunting trips and stuff. They slacked off a year or so ago. I don't think Jack was too taken with Jim anymore. Klindt's not a real likable guy all the time."

On May 10, Bankson finally caught up with Jack Crofton at the J. I. Case plant in Rock Island. The short interview took place in the lunchroom while Jack was on break. Crofton was hesitant to talk. He acted as if he still considered Jim Klindt a friend.

"Look, I don't know what happened on March eighteenth. I was on a hunting trip. I haven't seen Jim in months. I can tell you one thing. The man is squeamish. He doesn't even like to clean his own game."

"But you did hunt with Jim Klindt in the past?"

"Lots of times. But we went our separate ways a year and a half ago."

"About the time he started dating Terry Keuhn?"

"That was part of it," Crofton replied. "After Jim met her, he didn't have time for his friends. Just sort of lost interest in everything and everybody except Terry."

"Do you own an orange and white sixteen-inch Stihl chain saw?"

"Yeah, it's in my basement."

"Can I see it?"

Crofton laughed. "Sure. Come on out. But you better hurry. It's seen its best days. I've cut a lot of wood with it in the past few years."

Arnold's Body Shop
1730 North Division
Davenport, Iowa
(May 30, 1984, 3:30 p.m.)

On the afternoon of May 30, 1984, Corporal Kern and Lieutenant Carroll spoke with DeWayne Arnold, owner of Arnold's Body Shop. Kern asked the questions.

"Mr. Arnold, could we speak with you a moment?" Kern asked, flashing his badge.

"You the officer who called?"

Kern nodded.

"Well, like I told you on the phone, I did an estimate on Klindt's '81 Volkswagen Jetta on January fourth last year for American Family Insurance. I'm sure, because I checked the file after you called. I made copies," he said handing some papers to Kern.

"I'm not too good at remembering dates, but the weather was still cold the next time I saw Klindt. He had a check made jointly to me and him for the car repair.

"Klindt wanted me to sign the check, you know, endorse the back. I told him I couldn't do that. That practice would leave me open to a civil liability and tax problems."

Homicide

"What'd Klindt say?"
"He didn't pursue the issue. Said he'd found it laying in the house and he needed cash. That's all. I didn't even look at the check."
"Could it have been a check for other work you might have done? Another car?"
"No. He had the Cadillac touched up once, but that was a year before and the work had already been paid for. Funny you should ask," Arnold continued, "His dad, Dick, phoned me and wanted to know if I had the check. I told him I didn't."

As the trial date drew closer, it became apparent a fair trial could not be conducted in Scott County. In retrospect, the block headline which had appeared in the March 29 edition of the *Quad-City Times*, was neither more nor less inflammatory than most others the paper had printed during the past year and a half:

CHARGE: KLINDT SLICED UP WIFE
CHIROPRACTOR HELD ON $1 MILLION BOND
IN BIZARRE TORSO CASE

From the onset, the story had been sensationalized by the press. The newspapers stood accused of irresponsible and highly unwarranted journalism. As a result, the Quad Cities was polarized as to the guilt or innocence of the chiropractor. Klindt's legal counsel had no choice but to seek a change of venue in the upcoming trial.

In a written ruling, made public on August 10, 1984, Scott County Judge James Havercamp granted Lawrence Scalise's request for a change of venue. Klindt's defense attorney had earlier petitioned the court to move the trial to an area where publicity and notoriety were not so great, citing a public opinion poll showing that most of the Quad City residents had heard about the case and that nearly half believed Klindt to be guilty. The edict was in large part a bitter denunciation of coverage by the *Quad-City Times*. Judge Havercamp denounced the extensive and sensationalized publicity:

> Newspaper articles in the *Times* have to a great extent, by number, headline, content, and positioning, sensationalized the event, and have been seemingly calculated to require readers to form an opinion and to make judgments considering the merit of the State's case, and the involvement of the defendant. Where the defendant's right to a fair trial clash with the Fourth Estate's right to publish news, in order to serve both, the community involuntarily forfeits its right to judge.

In a most unusual filing, Bill Davis leveled a first-degree murder charge against Klindt, even though no death certificate had been signed.

PART TWO

TRIAL BY JURY

Record-setting temperatures came in August, cloudless skies and blazing sun. Sirius had arisen. The Dog Days of Summer were at hand.

14

VENUE OF DOUBT

The trial was slated to begin Monday, August 13, 1984, in Keokuk, located in the Eighth Judicial District, 120 miles downriver from Davenport. Keokuk, a small city of thirteen thousand, is in the extreme southeastern tip of Iowa, one of two county seats in Lee County. The other is Fort Madison.

Keokuk, pronounced Keel'kuk by the locals, was named after the Indian chief who led the area's Sac and Fox tribes. Known as the "Gate City," Keokuk was a stopover for settlers traveling west, as well as a jumping-off point for Union soldiers heading into battle during the Civil War.

On Sunday afternoon, August 12, Bill Davis packed his bags, kissed Sharon good-bye, and began the long trek to the trial site. Traffic was sparse on U.S. 61. The temperature soared, and the sky was a white-hot blue. Heat radiating from the pavement created the ever-present mirage of water. Radial tires ticked across seams of sticky tar.

Although Highway 61 abandons the Mississippi for long stretches, the road, like the Mississippi, touches all the major

Dead Water

cities on Iowa's southeastern border. Twenty miles west of Davenport the highway angles back to the river, through Muscatine and across a broad sandy flood plain. For the next few miles the rolling hills, with rows of corn and soybeans, give way to flat irrigated fields of melons and tomatoes. Then the road climbs into the hills and turns south.

Davis found his concentration, which had been on the trial, broken as he descended into Fort Madison. The Iowa State Penitentiary loomed a fortress off to his left. The walls, sheer sandstone cliffs thirty-five to fifty-five feet high, were topped by coiled razor-wire. Seven guard towers overlooked the rectangular compound.

In the eyes of the prosecutor, this was the ideal venue for a trial. The citizens of Fort Madison understood law and order. They were confronted by the "walls of justice" every day. If Jim Klindt was found guilty of first-degree murder, he would spend the rest of his life here, without hope of parole, with no chance of escaping punishment.

Two hours and forty minutes after leaving Davenport, the prosecutor's blue Ford station wagon rolled, along with the river, into Keokuk. At the north edge of the city, the highway merged with Main Street, widening into a four-lane thoroughfare. For a few blocks, gleaming white colonials and large brick homes lined the roadway. Farther south, the sprinkled green lawns and trimmed hedges gave way to small bungalows and patchy brown grass. As the zoning turned commercial, storefronts stretched along the west side of the street. The recession was manifest and many of those buildings displayed fluorescent signs taped to interior windows that read "for sale or lease." One such wooden structure, its windows broken and boarded up, had been blackened by the heat of a suspicious fire. The Mississippi flowed, out of sight, along the eastern edge of town, past huge mansions, before curling beneath the industrial belly of the city and through Lock and

Trial by Jury

Dam Number 19. There was little traffic Sunday afternoon, and Davis hardly touched accelerator or brake as he coasted down Main Street toward the river.

At the far end of business district, the prosecutor swung left into the Holiday Inn parking lot. The hotel, a square building five stories tall, was within walking distance of the Lee County District Court rooms. More important, for the sake of the state, the lodging was inexpensive. As soon as Marty, the prosecutor's secretary, found out the trial site, she had booked a block of rooms large enough to accommodate the State witnesses and numerous guests who would travel to Keokuk to observe the trial.

Davis stepped from the air-conditioned station wagon onto the burning blacktop. The air was so hot it hurt to breathe. He hurried inside, checked in at the front desk, and took the elevator to the fourth floor. The slow-moving cab, which seemed ten degrees warmer than the lobby, smelled of Roger's cleaning solution. The ventilation was poor and the prosecutor found himself holding his breath. When the door finally opened, Davis gulped the hallway air. A moment later he inserted the key in the lock and entered a small suite. After tossing his clothes on the bed, he turned down the thermostat and headed for the lounge.

Later, when Davis returned to the room and hung up his clothes, he discovered he had packed only one pair of pants. He phoned Sharon, who was leaving for Des Moines to visit her sister, asked her to buy him three pair of slacks and ship them to Keokuk via Greyhound bus.

Lee County District Court
(Monday, August 13, 1984, 7:55 p.m.)

As in so many river cities, a good number of the buildings in Keokuk have withstood the test of time. The century-old red brick federal post office, which houses the Lee County District

Court, is a prime example. Built in 1889 and renovated at a cost of $250,000, the post office is listed in the National Historic Registry. Its Romanesque exterior carries into the courtroom, where arched windows and ornate woodwork have the feel of a church. Spectators are seated on pews of cherry and the judge's oak bench, flanked by white glass globes on brass standards, rises above the courtroom like an altar. Twin marble fireplaces grace the interior wall.

Klindt smiled at reporters as he was escorted, unmanacled, into the courtroom by two Lee County Sheriff deputies. The lanky chiropractor was dressed in a charcoal gray suit and stiff white shirt. The half-Windsor knot of his necktie was snugged just beneath his protrusive Adam's apple; a scarlet handkerchief adorned his breast pocket, and gold cuff links gleamed at his wrists.

Sixty-eight potential jurors and a pack of eager reporters crowded into the courtroom. The carnival-like atmosphere was dampened when the air conditioner failed to operate during the first day of jury selection. The temperature outside reached ninety-three degrees. The courtroom seemed even hotter. The prosecution and the defense jockeyed to gain an edge.

Defense Attorney Lawrence Scalise appeared relaxed as he peered over the top of his gold-rimmed glasses. From time to time he showed his teeth in a wide grin and dropped trivial facts about his personal life. "I'm the father of seven, you know. My youngest is only three," he said sitting down on the edge of the defense table.

Mr. Scalise's manner was a little too folksy for "King James" (Judge Havercamp), who had set a strict code for behavior the first day of the trial when he scolded reporters for bringing cameras into HIS courtroom during jury selection. His stern voice crackled from the bench. "Counselor, this is

Trial by Jury

not your living room. If you're too tired to stand, perhaps we should take a recess."

Larry Scalise and James Havercamp were old acquaintances. Both men had graduated from the University of Iowa Law School. Caught off guard by the swift rebuke, Scalise jumped to his feet. "Sorry, Your Honor."

Jim Klindt seemed relaxed, but his cool demeanor was belied by his hands. He would pick up his pen, make a note, lay it back down, and push it across the legal pad. He would clasp his hands as if in prayer, then fold them on his lap. On occasion, he would drum his long fingers silently or run the tips of them along the trim of the table's carved edges.

Scalise, graying, and rumpled from the heat, hammered away at the contention of reasonable doubt, asked personal questions about families, and even reproached Richard Nixon, announcing, "No one is above the law."

His antithesis, Bill Davis, dapper in his light gray suit and sporting a neatly trimmed salt-and-pepper beard, questioned candidates about their knowledge of the river, particularly at flood stage. "Have you ever known anyone who just ... disappeared?" he asked.

The slightest hint of humor brought relief to gallery and attorneys alike. A couple of times, a tight-lipped smile crossed Judge Havercamp's normally placid face.

"Do you want to serve as a juror?" Scalise asked one candidate.

"I don't really have a choice, do I?" the man replied.

An outburst of laughter broke the tension.

Each hour was punctuated by the solemn gong of the clock in the courthouse tower. Prospective jurors were asked the same repetitive questions, and their answers became more patterned as the day dragged. Some fanned themselves for relief while others read books.

It was not long before the boredom had become more unbearable than the heat. By evening, the white-haired bailiff had tilted his chair back, rattling his keys as he stared at the ceiling. Even Klindt, who had removed his coat for the afternoon session, was yawning. Selection went slowly, with only sixteen prospective jurors interviewed by late evening.

Tuesday, the air-conditioning was working, and selection went more smoothly. At the mid-morning recess, the assembly got its first glimpse of the "other woman" when Terry Keuhn, who had been sitting in the rear of the courtroom, rushed to embrace Klindt. The courtroom buzzed when he bent to kiss her. The couple walked hand-in-hand up the aisle, where they were met by Terry's mother, Ruth, on leave from her job in the Scott County Courthouse. The trio slipped down a hallway and disappeared into a room set up for the defense.

By evening the jury was set. There were seven men and five women, ranging in age from twenty-four to seventy-one. Even though Davis had hired a psychologist, a so-called expert, to help, jury selection had gone poorly. The cards were already stacked against the prosecution.

That night, conversation over dinner lagged, though Davis made no qualms about being unhappy over jury selection. The only humor was the prosecutor's story of Sharon's sister trying on trousers for Bill at Younkers in Des Moines. Following dinner, Davis retired to his room. Before climbing into bed, he reviewed Wednesday's slate of witnesses and the questions he would ask. A man who required little sleep, Davis lay awake most of the night.

The following morning, Assistant Scott County Attorney Gary Sissel made the opening statement. Wearing Coke-bottle glasses and a conservative navy blue suit, Sissel spoke in a bland monotone, droning on and on as he meticulously laid out the State's case. "Your Honor ... ladies and gentlemen of the jury ... the State will prove, beyond doubt, that James B.

Trial by Jury

Klindt did willfully and with malice aforethought murder his wife, Joyce Klindt.

"The State will prove motive. It will show the defendant's greed and his ongoing affair with another woman ... There are inconsistencies ... The defendant's story is filled with lies and deception."

An hour into the monologue, Bill Davis grew concerned. Sissel was floundering. The prosecutor watched the jury grow restless. Was it possible, Davis wondered, to lose a case before testimony had been heard?

Sissel continued to ramble until Judge Havercamp interrupted. "How much longer is your opening statement, Mr. Sissel?"

"Your Honor, I would think ... a ... probably ten to fifteen minutes."

"These people have been sitting here for two hours," the judge said in an irritated tone. "Let's take a fifteen-minute recess."

Downcast, Bill Davis shuffled out of the courtroom, mumbling to himself and shaking his head from side to side. Judge Havercamp caught up with the prosecutor in the hallway and berated Davis, blaming him for the inordinate length of Sissel's opening statement.

After the break, Sissel continued to ramble, closing with the recorded argument between the couple the night before Joyce Klindt disappeared. "You're going to hear Jim Klindt say over and over how much he hated his wife, and at the end of the tape the defendant tells his wife, 'I have to get rid of you.'"

Despite Sissel's long-winded opening, it seemed the State had built an incontrovertible case. Through it all, Klindt appeared smug and unshaken as he listened to Sissel, making notes and at times shaking his bald head in disagreement.

In a succinct opening statement, Lawrence Scalise questioned the validity of the State's evidence. "The best evidence, the bottom-line evidence," he stated, "is that the torso is not that of Joyce Klindt."

Scalise continued by questioning the way the State had built its case. He turned to the jury. "This is the first case I've ever been involved in whose outcome will be based on statistics. It is crucial that you listen intently to the technical evidence to be presented by Benita Harwood and Kimball Thompson."

In closing, Scalise confronted the damning tape which Joyce had left with the Reeds the night before she disappeared. "Unpleasant things are often said in the heat of argument," he told them, forewarning the jury that the recording was peppered with "four-letter words."

But immediately after mentioning the tape, which he believed to be the most damaging piece of evidence the defense had to overcome, Lawrence Scalise changed the subject. He lowered his voice to just above a whisper as if he what he was saying was a well-kept secret. "There is a substantial amount of money missing, over $30,000 from the Klindt home." The insinuation was clear: Joyce Klindt had taken the money, left town, and was, indeed, still very much alive.

Then it was back to the tape, where Scalise challenged Joyce's motive for setting up the recorder in the first place. "She intentionally caused 'Jimmy' to lose his temper and baited him with leading questions. She pushed and pushed and pushed."

In the end, the defense attorney acknowledged the tape clearly showed the disdain the defendant held for his wife. But in the next sentence, he reminded the jury "that while hate is contemptible, Jim Klindt is not being charged with hate."

The prosecution's first witness was Doren Shifley, a thin little man dressed like a patriot — white jacket, blue shirt, and narrow red leather tie. Shifley testified that Joyce and Jim Klindt had first come to his law office on December 10, 1982. He said Dr. Klindt wanted to petition for a divorce. The

Trial by Jury

lawyer said he explained to the couple that in Iowa all divorces are "no fault," that there's a ninety-day waiting period, and that they would have to come to a mutual agreement on the final decree which would divide the assets and determine the custody of Bartley.

"Did Joyce return to your office?" asked Davis.

"Yes, on December fifteenth," Shifley replied using his index finger to push up the too-large plastic-rimmed glasses which constantly slipped down the bridge of his nose. "Joyce came in to sign the Acceptance of Service papers."

"Did she seem different from the first meeting?"

"Yes. She appeared upset, near tears. I think she had finally come to the stark realization that she'd be forced from her home and lose custody of her son."

Shifley said he was subsequently contacted on March 11, 1983, by Michael Shinkle, an attorney who shared space with Seymore Raben. Shifley was informed that either Sy Raben or Shinkle would be representing Joyce Klindt in the pending divorce action, and Shinkle asked Shifley not to take default against Joyce if the ninety-day waiting period had run its course. After agreeing to Shinkle's request, Shifley said he phoned Jim Klindt, informing his client Joyce had retained Sy Raben and the March 17 court date had been postponed.

Judy Pochel, the reporter for the *Rock Island Argus*, was the next to testify. She said she had interviewed Klindt twice in person and spoken to the chiropractor by phone on several occasions about the disappearance of his wife. Pochel seemed apprehensive as she waited for the prosecutor to begin direct examination.

"When was the first time you interviewed the defendant?" asked Davis.

"The day the police released the information that his wife was missing."

"What was the conversation about?"

"He said that she was gone, she took everything he had, and he was glad she was gone."

"Was he always helpful?" the prosecutor asked.

Pochel grinned. "Well, he was almost always nice," implying that Klindt had been less than cooperative at times.

"And you tried to interview him again?"

"Yes. The day the torso was found, I phoned him. I was told by his associate, Dr. Hagemann, that Jim was at a convention in Chicago. I had a friend living there, and he phoned all of the hotels in the city but couldn't find Dr. Klindt or a chiropractic convention."

"And when was the next time you got hold of him?"

"Not till the following Monday, by phone."

"What did you talk about?"

"I asked him for an interview and he finally consented."

"When did you interview him?"

"On April twenty-second in his office."

"Tell me about the interview," said Davis.

"It was off the record. I asked him about the taped argument. He admitted making the statement that he was going to 'cut her up in little pieces,' but said that he was just being dramatic. He said his wife was upset because he was getting custody of Bart. That when he got home that morning he found her in the bedroom with a gun to her head. He said it was a marriage gone bad."

"Anything else?"

"Yes. He said he gave her $2,000, loaded her clothes in the car, then went to the store to get a part for his airboat. He was gone about fifteen minutes, when he returned the clothes were back on the porch. So, he loaded them again, put the boat part in the garage, and the dog got out. While he chased the dog, she put her clothes back on the porch again. When he caught the dog, he loaded her clothes in the car one more time, then

Trial by Jury

she smiled and told him, 'You better get up to Princeton and move the boat. It's half mine you know,' and left."

"Okay, so he went to Princeton. Then what did he tell you?"

"He said he put the part on the boat and took it out on the water. He tried to fish with a net, found a hoop net that had a turtle in it. He took the turtle, he never said what he did with it, put five dollars in the net, and lost his keys in the water. So he couldn't start the boat. It got tangled in some trees, he took an axe he had on the boat and chopped it free. Then he got the boat started, I don't know how, without keys, and went home."

"Then what happened?"

"Well, when he got there he found that $30,000 was missing, so he went to look for his wife."

Davis stopped her. "Did you say $30,000?"

"Yes."

"Thirty thousand? No more, no less?"

"Yes. He said he drove her car to Moline when he found her clothes missing and moved the seat."

"Back or forward?"

"He pushed it forward. Then he went to the airport and Terry picked him up."

"This was all off the record?"

"Yes."

"Do you have the notes from that interview?"

Pochel smiled sheepishly and fidgeted. She obviously knew the question was coming, and she had dreaded it. "No, the company destroyed them."

"Why?"

"Because you found out about the notes and threatened to subpoena them."

"So you destroyed them. When?"

Pochel lowered her eyes. "In June."

Dead Water

Davis shook his head. "But you did review them before writing your article, didn't you?"

"Yes."

"Did you interview him again?"

"I phoned him, but he didn't want to talk. He hung up on me."

"But you're persistent aren't you?"

Pochel nodded.

"Anybody else ever hang up on you?"

"You did."

Davis grinned. "You called him back?"

"Yes. He agreed to talk."

"Was the substance of this interview the same as the first one?"

"Yes, but he did change some of the story."

"What did he change?"

"I told him we were going to print the first interview. He told me he wanted to make a couple of changes. He asked me not to quote the $30,000 amount because he didn't want people to know that he kept that kind of money in the house. Not to tell the story about the turtle, and he told me the gun was pointed at the floor."

"He changed part of it?"

"Yes. The first time he'd told me it was pointed at her head."

Scalise asked no questions of Judy Pochel and she was excused.

"The prosecution calls Richard Lamer to the stand."

Lamer was in charge of the evidence locker at the Davenport Police Department. The officer verified that no one had tampered with any of the evidence relative to the case. He explained that he held the only key and all requests to get into the evidence locker had to be made through him.

Trial by Jury

"Has anyone ever tried to break into the locker?" Davis asked.

"Yes," Lamer replied.

"And who was that?"

"You, Counselor."

This standing joke between the two men brought laughter to the courtroom.

Clifford Reed was the next to testify.

"Were you a personal friend of the defendant?"

"Yes."

"First name basis? You call him Jim?"

"Yes, for thirteen years."

"Did you hunt and fish with Jim?"

"Yes," Reed replied, unable to bring himself to look at the defendant.

"Without your wives?"

"Yes."

"Have you ever been on the defendant's airboat?"

"Yes, but only once. Right after he bought it."

"Tell us about the airboat."

"Well, the airboat is designed to go over shallow water. It's propelled by a powerful engine with an air propeller instead of a propeller in the water. You sit out in front. Goes very fast."

"How many people can you get on it, do you know?"

"Not more than three."

"I believe you told me once it would go over wet grass, so it doesn't need water at all?"

"That's correct."

"They also have another boat, don't they?"

"Well, Jim's had quite a number of boats. I can't remember all of them. I think the one he's got now is some sort of Hawaiian day cruiser."

"Were you aware that your friends, the Klindts, were having some marital discord?"

"Yes."
"When did you find out?"
"The week of March sixth."
"How did you find out?"
"My mother-in-law told me."
"When was the last time prior to the week of March seventeenth that you saw either of the Klindts?"
"Not since January."
"Okay, let's focus on time. A couple weeks before March 17, 1983, did you have occasion to see Joyce Klindt?"
"Yes. We gave Joyce a key to the house and a spare room to keep her stuff in."
"Why?"
"So she would be free to come and go, whatever she put in that bedroom would be private, we wouldn't—we weren't about to pry into her private life."
"Did she, indeed, put things in there?"
"Yes."
"Okay. This particular item has been marked for identification purposes as State's Exhibit 15. Do you recognize it?"
"It's a tape recorder."
"How is it you recognize this particular General Electric hand-held tape recorder?"
"Joyce handed it to me."
"When?"
"The night of March seventeenth."
"What year?"
"19 ... last year, '83."
"Who else was present?"
"My wife, my mother-in-law, and Joyce."
"Did you request her to give it to you, or did she offer it to you?"
"No, I asked for it."

Trial by Jury

"Anything connected with this particular tape recorder when she did that?"

"There was a tape in it."

"Did you listen to the tape."

"Most of it, yes."

"And did you also take the tape?"

"Yes."

"What did you do with the tape?"

"I kept it until the next night."

"Okay. What did you do with it the next night?"

"I gave it to the police."

"Did you recognize the voices on the tape?"

"Yes."

"And who were those voices?"

"Jim and Joyce Klindt."

"Why did you ask for the tape?"

"Well, I heard enough of it to be concerned."

Clifford Reed then recounted the week of March 13, 1983, as he remembered it. He told of the items Joyce had left at the Reed home and the events that took place on the day she disappeared.

The final witness of the day was Kenneth Gamb. Reverend Gamb testified that Joyce had an appointment for counseling on March 18 and that she neither showed, nor canceled. Under cross-examination, Scalise got Reverend Gamb to admit that Joyce Klindt had missed an appointment the previous week. Under redirect, the minister acknowledged that Joyce had phoned to cancel the first appointment, but she did not cancel the second.

The trial was going badly for the prosecution. Davis had enough experience to tell just by looking at the jurors' faces. What the prosecutor did not know was that things were about to get worse.

Davis left the courtroom in no mood for conversation. He turned down a ride to the hotel, preferring to walk instead. The prosecutor realized he had made a mistake as soon as he stepped from the air-conditioned courthouse. The late afternoon heat struck him in the face. He stripped off his suit coat and walked south on Main Street.

Thirsty and wanting to be alone, Davis turned into a saloon and waited for his eyes to adjust to the darkness before moving to the bar and ordering a Bud Light. When he tossed a ten dollar bill on the counter, a voice boomed from behind him. "Don't take his money, Shelley. It's counterfeit."

The prosecutor wheeled and squinted at the huge man sitting in a corner booth. "I guess they're not too damn picky about who they let in here," Davis said.

"Obviously not," the big man countered, roaring with laughter. "Goddamn it, Counselor, don't you ever return a call? I've been trying to get in touch with you for the past two nights."

Harry Forrester, a businessman living in Keokuk, was originally from Des Moines. He and Davis had become friends playing intramural basketball at Drake University. Davis had gone on to law school, graduating top in his class in 1970.

The prosecutor stuck out his hand. "How are you, Harry?"

"A hell of a lot better than you, Counselor. Who's the wizard that helped you pick the jury?"

The prosecutor's eyes narrowed. "Why?"

"Keokuk's a small town, Bill. I know most of those jurors. The insurance salesman's a publicity hound, and I'd swear a couple of others have parents who are first cousins. The map says it's Iowa, Bill. But it ain't. It's Missouri. You won't get a conviction down here."

Davis chugged his beer and turned to the bartender. "Get us two more."

Trial by Jury

The two men had talked for over an hour when Davis glanced at his watch. "Christ, I was supposed to meet Sissel at the hotel fifteen minutes ago."

Forrester laughed. "I heard about his opening statement. Let him wait."

Davis surprised himself by coming to Sissel's defense. "I'm afraid that's my fault, Harry. We're not all cut out to be trial lawyers. Gary will find his niche. He's a damn fine attorney."

The assistant prosecutor was pacing the lobby when Davis pushed through the hotel's revolving door. "Sorry I'm late, Gary. Ran into an old friend. Where should we eat?"

"I hear the Verity Room's good."

"Let's go. I'm starving."

The two prosecutors walked across Fourth Street and down the steps to the basement restaurant. An eight-foot lithograph of an old paddle steamer hung on the wall in the vestibule. They were seated at a corner table covered with checkered oil cloth. A candle flickered through a red glass centerpiece.

Davis ordered a scotch. Sissel, a teetotaler, sipped on a glass of ice water with a lemon slice. "Something bothering you, Bill?"

"We're in trouble."

"What do you mean?"

"I mean we're in danger of losing this case."

"Oh, I don't know," Sissel said, "seems like we're in pretty good shape to me."

"You must be watching a different trial than I am."

A woman's voice interrupted the conversation. "Mr. Davis?"

The prosecutor looked up at the waitress. "Do I know you?"

She smiled. "No, but I've seen your picture in the paper."

Davis smiled back. "I'm flattered."

Dead Water

"There's a phone call for you. The man says it's urgent. You can take it in the lobby."

The prosecutor glanced over at Sissel. "Did you tell anybody we'd be eating here?"

Sissel shook his head.

Davis was puzzled. "Neither did I."

He left the table to take the call, returned a moment later and drained his scotch.

"Jeepers, Bill. You look like you've seen a ghost."

"No," said the angry prosecutor, "but somebody has. That was Scalise. He wants to meet with us in his motel room right away. You know those witnesses we couldn't find who said they'd seen Joyce alive. One just surfaced ..."

Unlike Davis's secretary, no one on Lawrence Scalise's staff had bothered to make reservations in Keokuk. The defense team had underestimated the allure of the trial. An entourage of reporters had taken every available room in the small city. Scalise was forced to stay in a cut-rate motel on the north edge of town.

"Nice room, Larry," the prosecutor said looking around at the wealthy lawyer's spartan accommodations.

Scalise grinned. "Not much, is it? Still, it beats the hell out of sleeping on the street."

Just barely, Davis thought.

"I'm sorry I have to put you through this, Bill. Honest to God, I just found out an hour ago."

"Cut the bullshit, Larry. Who's your witness?"

15

SIGHTING

Bill Davis was still half asleep. Last night, he and Sissel had grilled Jim Klindt's best friend, Jeffrey Ryan, for nearly two hours in Scalise's hotel room. Ryan claimed he had seen Joyce Klindt alive in the spring of 1984. Davis had not arrived back at the Holiday Inn until well after midnight, spending the next three hours trying to prepare a defense against what he believed to be perjured testimony.

Elizabeth Reed was the first witness to testify on day four of the trial. Reed was impeccably dressed in a maroon suit and white blouse. There was little doubt from the beginning of Bill Davis's direct examination that she was the State's star witness.

The prosecutor tried to get Mrs. Reed to relax by asking her personal questions about family members and about how the relationship with the Klindts began. Reed was nervous, but she spoke in a calm clear voice of the thirteen-year friendship she and her husband, Clifford, and her daughter, Heather, had shared with Joyce and Jim Klindt. Davis allowed her time to reminisce before asking her any emotionally-charged questions.

"Then you sort of lost track of Joyce after she and Jim came to dinner that night in January of 1983. When was it you saw her again?"

"On March ninth. We went to dinner. On the way to the restaurant Joyce indicated she didn't have any money."

"Was that unusual?"

"Yes. We had always gone dutch until that night."

"What did you talk about over dinner?"

Dead Water

"She related some things that were pretty painful to her ... going on between the two of them. And she told me ..."

Scalise had been waiting for an opening, any chance to interrupt the smooth exchange. He attempted to fluster the witness.

"Objection, Your Honor. That's hearsay."

"Sustained."

Mrs. Reed digressed. "Joyce said she had to take Bart somewhere that night ... that she'd be over about eight o'clock. Joyce lived for Bartley."

Reed said that after she had paid for dinner, she gave Joyce a check for $200 to retain a divorce lawyer.

"Did you see her again after that evening?"

"Yes, Joyce called again Friday. Said she had tried to retain Sy Raben as her lawyer, but that she wouldn't know for sure until he got back into town on Monday."

"She called me about ten-thirty Sunday morning and told me she was at Jim's office and she had found a divorce decree down there, and she and Geri were looking at it."

Elizabeth stated that on Sunday evening, Joyce had handed her a stack of personal papers. The witness spent the next few minutes examining and identifying the State's exhibits of Joyce's clothing, personal effects, and papers left at the Reed home during the week of March 13, 1983.

"On either Sunday or Monday," Elizabeth continued, "I gave Joyce a key to our house. Joyce told me her marriage was over, that she was tired of all Jim's paramours."

"Objection," said Scalise.

"Oh dear! Is that hearsay again? Sorry ... On Monday, Joyce came to the house to change clothes and drove to see Sy Raben. She had a two o'clock appointment.

"A half-hour later ... forty-five minutes, while she was gone, Geri ... Jim's mom, called to see if Joyce had gone to see the attorney. Geri told me she had offered Joyce an

Trial by Jury

apartment in their home to live in. Joyce and Geri had a very nice relationship. Geri told me she was glad Joyce had gotten an attorney."

Scalise interrupted again. "That's hearsay."

Judge Havercamp glanced up. "On what grounds?"

Scalise thought for a moment. "Oh well, I guess she is going to testify later," he said sheepishly.

Elizabeth then identified the sealed envelope containing the audio cassette that Joyce had left with Clifford Reed the night before she disappeared. When Reed told of her confrontation with Jim Klindt that evening, she said she called him a liar several times. During that part of her testimony, Reed, both anguished and angry, glared through glistening eyes at Jim Klindt as she recounted the showdown. She then spoke of Geri Klindt, of how upset Mrs. Klindt was that evening, and finally of driving to the police station with her husband, Clifford.

During Scalise's cross-examination, Elizabeth repeated the events of March 18 yet again. The defense attorney focused on Joyce's physical appearance and hair color. Mrs. Reed admitted that Joyce's hair was more blonde than brown. "It was not Swedish blonde, it was more of a strawberry or dishwater blonde."

Scalise accomplished what he had set out to do, confuse the jury as to Joyce Klindt's physical appearance. By the time she stepped down, Elizabeth Reed had spent three hours on the witness stand.

Michael Shinkle, Sy Raben's associate, then testified that he had spoken to Joyce Klindt by phone and that he had told her that if Raben could not represent her, he would. Shinkle added he had telephoned Doren Shifley and asked him not to take a default before hearing from Raben.

Davis then called the defendant's mother, Geraldine Klindt, to the stand. Mrs. Klindt proved Lieutenant Carroll correct. She was, as the detective had predicted, a hostile witness.

Dead Water

After several moments identifying jewelry and other articles that Joyce had left with Elizabeth, Davis began the heart of his direct examination. "Were you aware that your son and daughter-in-law were going through the process of a dissolution of marriage?"

"The day ... or the day after it was filed."

"Okay. How was it that you knew?"

"Joyce came down and told me they'd filed for divorce."

"Did she tell you where they'd gone?"

"To a Mr. ... a ... Shifley."

"Did she tell you if she'd gone with Jim?"

"Yes."

"Did she tell you who her lawyer was?"

"No."

Davis backpedaled. "I hope I didn't jump ahead or lead you. It was Mr. Shifley who was going to represent your son. Was that your understanding?"

"I'm not sure, a ... if it's not contested, isn't that the way it is?"

"You didn't have any understanding as to who was being represented at that time?"

"No."

"Merely that they'd filed?"

"Yes."

"And they'd gone to Mr. Shifley?"

"Yes."

"Okay. And you talked to your daughter-in-law on a fairly frequent basis after they'd filed that action?"

"Well, she came down almost every day."

"Didn't you call her on the phone occasionally too?"

"No," Geri replied.

"Never?" asked Davis.

"Once in a great while."

"Did you ever call the Reed home looking for her?"

Trial by Jury

"No."

"Davis was surprised. "Never?"

"I can't recall that I ever did."

The prosecutor tried to jar her memory. "How 'bout the week of St. Patrick's Day, 1983? I know it's a year ago and it's tough to remember, but ..."

"I can't recall."

Davis was growing frustrated. "Never ... at no time during that month did you ever call?"

Geri paused for a long time before answering. "I can't recall ... making the call."

"How did the dissolution proceed, or how did those kids proceed ... after the divorce was pending? Did they change things about their lifestyle?"

"I really couldn't say."

"Well, did you talk to your daughter-in-law on a daily basis?"

"Yes."

"Did she advise you ever that they were going to be able to reconcile?"

"She thought they might."

"Did you talk to your son on a daily basis?"

"Yes."

"In fact, he practices in the same building that you and your husband own and live in. Is that correct?"

"Yes."

"And did you talk to him about the pending dissolution?"

"No."

"Would he have talked to your husband?"

"Not that I know of."

"Did you have concerns about your grandson."

"None at all."

The prosecutor eyed her suspiciously. "Why not?"

Dead Water

"Because I knew he would be taken care of by one of the three of us."

Davis followed up quickly. "And just who are the three of you?"

"James, myself ... or Joyce ..." she said, obviously stumbling over who the third person would be, "if she decided she wanted him."

The prosecutor's dark eyes flashed. Had the jury heard her falter? "But you thought you entered into the picture of taking care of him?"

"I thought it could be possible."

"Why was that?"

"You don't know how things are going to come out."

"But both your son and your daughter-in-law at that time are mentally healthy and able-bodied, are they not?"

"Yes."

"But you thought it was in the realm of possibility at that time that Bart could become your responsibility?"

"I wasn't sure of anything."

"Were these times of turmoil in your house?"

"No."

"Just that no one was keeping you advised?"

"That's right."

The prosecutor turned his attention to the divorce decree. "Did you ever let Joyce into Jim's office when he wasn't there?"

"No."

A few minutes ago, Elizabeth Reed had testified Geraldine had told her that she and Joyce had discovered the edict in the chiropractor's office on a Sunday morning. Someone was lying and Bill Davis felt he knew who.

"Were you aware that she did go into his office?"

"No."

"She never advised you that indeed she had gotten into his office and photocopied the proposed decrees?"

"I can't recall that at all."

"Did she ever advise you that one time she got in, found the proposed decrees and hand-wrote them out, that she had copied them by hand?"

"No, I can't recall that."

"Do you recall her ever calling you and telling you that she had a photocopy of the proposed decree and indeed he was going ahead with it?"

"I cannot recall that."

Frustration again crept into the prosecutor's voice. "Did you ever recall your son becoming upset upon learning your daughter-in-law had retained an attorney?"

"I cannot recall him becoming upset."

"Do you recall being present and him discussing with you that indeed she had gotten a lawyer?"

"No," Mrs. Klindt said, growing adamant.

Davis persisted. "Do you recall ever telling Dr. Hagemann that indeed that had happened?"

"No," she said emphatically.

"Do you recall a conversation in that particular office, the building where you live and where your son practices?"

"NO."

The woman was getting testy and Davis was seething. More important, the line of questioning was going nowhere. Geraldine Klindt was supposed to be corroborating Elizabeth Reed's testimony. Unfortunately, her memory had gone on vacation.

"Dr. Hagemann also practiced there, did he not?"

"Yes."

For the first time in quite a while Davis had found something that Mrs. Klindt could answer in the affirmative, something she could still recall. "In fact, you've known him since he was ten, eleven years old?"

"Yes."

"And he rented space from your husband, did he not?"

"Yes he did."

"For a long time?"

"Yes."

"How many years?"

"I think three, I'm not sure."

"Since he had become a chiropractor?"

"Yes."

"In fact he'd come to your husband to be treated as a child? Is that right?"

"I think so, but I'm not sure."

"He's a lifelong friend?"

"Yes."

Davis started to relax. "And you don't remember having a conversation with him to that effect?"

"No I don't. I can't recall that."

"And you don't recall your son ever expressing any alarm or concern because indeed ..."

"No," she answered before Davis finished the question.

"... his wife had retained an attorney?"

"Definitely not."

"When did you learn that she had retained a lawyer?"

"The afternoon of the day it was filed."

"What was filed?"

"The divorce decree."

"The day the divorce decree was first filed?"

"Uh-huh."

"So as far as you know, Joyce never did get a lawyer?"

"That's right."

"And as far as you know the only lawyer ever involved in this was Doren Shifley?"

"At that time, yes."

"Okay. How about any time later, prior to March 18, 1983? From the time they filed till March 18, 1983, were you ever informed that indeed your daughter-in-law had retained an attorney?"

"Yes."

"And when was that?"

"Tuesday, March 15, 1983."

"And how did you find out?"

"She came down that evening and told me that Bartley wanted to see me ... and in the process of our conversation in the living room, she said she had paid or retained a lawyer."

"Did she tell you who the lawyer was?"

"Yes."

"And who was that?"

"Sy Raben."

"Did she tell you why she retained a lawyer?"

"No."

"There was no further discussion ..."

"No."

"... about the pending divorce?"

"No, no."

Davis shook his head, realizing the woman had just said "no" before he finished his question. "Did she talk about custody of Bart?"

"No."

"Is this the woman, the same woman, you say you talked to on a daily basis?"

"Yes."

Fuming, Davis paused and changed the subject. During the lengthy exchange it was obvious the prosecutor felt she was lying, that her emphatic responses were in direct contradiction to her deposition.

Geri Klindt, single-minded and defensive, stated that the only person who seemed excited by Joyce's "leaving" was Elizabeth. She also stated that while they were inside Jim's house on the evening of March 18, 1983, Jim called the Monahans and then the police. According to Geri, the Reeds and Celeste Ralfs were in the living room at the time.

She repeatedly denied any knowledge concerning her son's divorce or his reaction to Joyce's retention of counsel. The prosecutor's patience was growing thin. "Any problem with your memory?" he finally asked.

"Not a bit," Geri said smiling.

Davis was still upset when Dr. Dennis Hagemann took the stand. Jim Klindt's former associate had the face of a minister. Hagemann wore a gray suit, wire-rimmed glasses. His short dark brown hair was neatly parted.

"Hello, Doctor," Davis said, trying to calm down.

"Hi."

"Could you tell us a little about your schooling."

"I graduated from the Palmer College of Chiropractic and Iowa State University."

"And before that?"

"Davenport West."

"Did you know Jim Klindt then?"

"Yes. We were classmates."

"For how long?"

"Since fifth grade."

"Could you tell us about your business arrangement with Dr. Klindt?"

"We shared space, patients, and a common waiting room."

Hagemann seemed poised and confident. Davis leaned back in his chair.

"Doctor, were you aware of the Klindts' divorce action?"

"Yes."

"Were the ninety days almost up?"

"Yes."
"How did you learn about that?"
"Joyce told me."
"And did you, in turn, tell Joyce anything about March seventeenth?"
"Yes. The defendant had marked the morning section of his calendar for that day in large letters, "OFF.""
"Was that unusual?"
"Yes. He normally works on Thursdays."
Davis nodded. "I see. And on March eighteenth, did you have a conversation with anyone?"
"Geri Klindt."
"About what?"
"She told me Jim had called her around 9:30 and said that he and Joyce had made up, that she was leaving for a while. Geri thought she might be going to Pennsylvania to see her brother."
"Where did this conversation take place?"
"At the office."
"Did she say anything else?"
"She told me that when Jim found out the divorce was being contested, he had stormed upstairs saying Joyce would get everything. She described him as a beaten pup with his shoulders rounded and his head down."

Before stepping down, Hagemann also testified that Jim had told him the story of losing his keys in the river and about Joyce taking $34,000 from the house.

Davenport police dispatcher Evelyn Martin followed Hagemann. Thin and bespectacled, she looked more like a schoolteacher than a police employee. In a quiet voice, she recounted her phone conversation with Dr. Klindt. The $4,000 the chiropractor said he had given Joyce before she left town made quite an impression on the woman.

"We wanted to buy a van and we needed $4,000. I remember wishing we had that much money."

"Did you make a report of that phone call?" Sissel asked.

"Not right away."

"Why?"

"Sergeant Lynn told me the officer at the scene would handle the report."

"And were you subsequently asked to file the report?"

"Yes. In April, Sergeant Lynn informed me that the Detective Bureau had requested my report."

"How did you make your report?"

"Well, the tape of the conversation had been erased, so I had to recall it from memory."

Policewoman Gayle Girt then testified she had been sent to the Klindt home on the evening of March 18, 1983. Scalise tried to rattle the officer when she told the jury Klindt seemed rehearsed.

During the morning recess, Davis coached Sissel on how he wanted Jeffrey Ryan questioned. "Don't add credibility to his testimony," said the prosecutor. "Use phrases like "this person," when he talks about the sighting, rather than "Joyce."

Sissel nodded in agreement. Still, he was nervous when the muscular little mechanic took the stand. The assistant prosecutor started slowly, almost stalling, as he led Ryan through the background questions of his lifelong friendship with Jim Klindt.

Ryan's memory failed him when he got to the day Joyce disappeared. The man could not recall if the chiropractor had even come by his house, let alone whether he had given him a tranquilizer or not. Davis wondered, could there be some microbe in Keokuk's water that was feeding on brain cells?

The prosecutor turned sideways in his chair to catch a glimpse of Klindt. The doctor wore an arrogant smile.

Trial by Jury

The more Sissel pressured Ryan, the more the little man's eyes twitched. Soon Ryan became restless, and his eye contact wavered. He was unable to look at Sissel and seemed to have developed a sudden interest in the ceiling.

Davis took copious notes and fidgeted in his chair. He knew what was coming, and there wasn't a damn thing he could do about it. Sooner or later Sissel would be forced to confront the sighting. The assistant prosecutor was walking on eggs.

Sissel asked the question hesitantly. "Have you ever had a meeting with a man named John Dolan?"

"About a month ago."

"Who is he?"

"A private investigator working for Jim's lawyer."

"Did he tell you that one of the witnesses who was supposed to have seen Joyce, had 'crapped out'?"

"Yeah," Ryan said agitated.

"And did you tell him anything?"

"Yes."

"What was that?"

"I told him, 'I'd like to keep this off the record, but I've seen Joyce since this has all taken place.' He asked me where, when and how, so I told him."

"Now, when did you think you saw Joyce Klindt?"

Davis shook his head as soon as he heard the question. Sissel had just given the witness credibility by mentioning the missing woman's name.

"Early this spring. I can't tell you the exact date."

"What do you mean by 'early spring'?"

"End of April, first of May. It was still chilly."

"What day did you see this person?"

"Sunday, I believe."

"What time?"

"Three, four o'clock in the afternoon."

"Where did you see this person?"

"Corner of Locust and Brady ... in Davenport."
"Which direction were you going?"
Ryan thought for a moment. "West."
"Did you get to Brady?"
"I was stopped at the light at Brady, in traffic. She was next to me."
"What kind of vehicle were you driving?"
"A 1966 Volkswagen van."
"What kind of car was this person in?"
"A silver Camaro."
"About what year?"
"Between '78 and '81."
"What lane were you in?"
"Inside."
"Where was the Camaro?"
"Outside, near the curb."
"Did you get a long look at this person in the Camaro?"
Ryan shook his head. "No, sir."
"What did you see of this person?"
"I was looking around. I looked down, saw this face look towards me. It just flipped into my mind, that's Joyce. You know? She saw me at the same time and looked away. She pulled her car as far ahead as she could."
"Now, how long did you see the face of this person?"
"Looked at her, looked away."
"Glance?"
"Yeah, glance."
"Did you get the license number?"
"No."
"The color of the plate?"
"Yellow, I think. Yellow background, white letters."
"Could you read the state? Was it Iowa?"
"No."

Trial by Jury

"What action did you take to obtain identification of the vehicle?"

"My first thought was to catch it, but I couldn't. I turned right out of the center lane, but I couldn't catch it."

"Do you have a sight problem?"

"I wear glasses to watch TV and stuff."

"Nearsighted?"

"That's what they call it, nearsighted."

"Did you have your glasses on?"

"That, sir, I could not tell you."

Sissel unloaded. "Did you go to the police with this information?"

"No."

"You didn't go to the police?"

"No."

"Do you know any of the officers involved in the case?"

"Ted Carroll. He's interviewed me."

"Did you call Ted Carroll?"

"No."

"The county attorney?"

"No."

"The highway patrol?"

"No."

"The FBI?"

"No."

"When was the first time you advised someone in law enforcement of this sighting?"

Ryan hesitated. "Uh ... last night."

"Why didn't you call Lieutenant Carroll?"

"The way the case was going, I didn't think Lieutenant Carroll was looking for her anymore."

"Isn't it a fact, that you told Lieutenant Carroll that if Jim had done anything wrong you hoped the police would be unable to prove it?"

Dead Water

"No. What I said was that Jim was my best friend and I hoped he wouldn't have to go to jail."

"Mr. Ryan, at what time last night did you first reveal this information to us?"

"Uh, about eleven."

"Did you talk to anyone else about this before that?"

"John Dolan, Larry Scalise ... Jim."

"Melody Haines?"

"And Melody Haines," Ryan repeated.

"Everyone but us," Sissel said sarcastically.

The questioning had gone better than Davis had hoped. He continued to make notes, while Scalise, as he had done throughout the trial, saved the witness's credibility by asking a series of leading questions during cross-examination.

"Isn't it true," Scalise said rising to his feet, "that the reason you didn't tell the police was because you didn't think the police would believe you since you were Jim's best friend?"

"Yes."

Having made the point the defense attorney abruptly changed the subject. "Did you get wet when you rode the air boat?"

"Yes."

"Because of the design, it sprayed water, didn't it?"

"Yes."

"How did you keep things dry in the airboat?"

"Plastic bags."

Scalise raised his eyebrows. "Garbage bags?"

"Yeah."

"Did Jim keep garbage bags on the boat?"

"Yes."

"So it was not unusual for Jim to put garbage bags on the boat?"

Ryan turned toward the jury. "Used them all the time."

"Thank you, Mr. Ryan. No further questions."

Trial by Jury

It had been another difficult day for the prosecution. Elizabeth Reed had been convincing, but Geraldine Klindt had been a stalwart. Davis had never been able to get the defendant's mother off dead center. And even though Hagemann's testimony had directly contradicted Mrs. Klindt's, it was at best a wash. Gary Sissel had finally shown some moxie, but Lawrence Scalise's cross-examination of Jeffrey Ryan had helped to reinstate Ryan's credibility. All-in-all the defense scored more points.

After questioning Geraldine Klindt and watching Jeffrey Ryan testify, Bill Davis was only sure of one thing. Tomorrow would not get any easier.

16

BEST FRIENDS?

Finley Gunn, an old "river rat," opened the testimony Friday morning. The court waited while the assistant prosecutor struggled to set up a slide projector. Gunn, who lived on the Mississippi in Princeton, walked to the screen and pointed out Kernan's Restaurant and the Princeton Beach Marina. He described the sloughs north of Princeton and said no one was boating the day of March 18, 1983, that the water was high and rough.

Gunn also explained the different kinds of fishing nets. He told the jury that gill nets are illegal and that fishermen must pay a fee before putting commercial nets in the water. It was a subtle way of saying that Jim Klindt not only fished with an illegal gill net, but that he was not licensed to fish with any commercial net.

In the cross-examination, Scalise got Gunn to concede a gill net could be set in the sloughs above Princeton, even if the water was high.

Following Gunn's testimony, Davis searched for his briefcase. It was not to be found. Before Gary Sissel began questioning Katie Ryan, the prosecutor sent Rick Chase back to the hotel to look for it. While Chase was gone, Davis watched in horror as another key State witness fell to the defense. Once again, hostile was the word.

Katie Ryan stated that she was Joyce Klindt's best friend. On the stand, she sounded more like the chiropractor's bosom buddy. Ryan testified she went with Joyce to Jim's office and waited outside while Joyce got the divorce decree. Then the

Trial by Jury

two women went to Thoms-Proestler where Katie made a copy for Joyce.

She said she found nothing unusual about Jim calling her at 9:30 the morning of March 18, 1983, saying Joyce had left town. Ryan added she had known for some time that Jim had filed for a divorce. She said she never told Joyce that Jim ran around on her, that she presumed Joyce knew. She also said that Joyce worked out and that the two women often rode bicycles and took long walks, up to ten miles, together.

During cross-examination Katie Ryan shredded the State's case.

"Have you ever seen Joyce nude?" asked Scalise.

"Yes."

"When was the last time?"

"Probably the summer of 1982 on Jim's cabin cruiser."

"Did you ever notice a small blue birthmark just above her waist?"

"No."

"How tall is Joyce?"

"Five-six, five-seven."

"About 115, 120 pounds?" Scalise asked, leading the witness.

"Yes."

"Who's bigger, Diana Iossi or Joyce?"

"Diana is much bigger."

Scalise stood and walked to a table immediately in front of the bench. Davis knew what was coming. He jumped to his feet and moved to the bench. "I object to these photographs, Your Honor," the prosecutor said. "They lack foundation."

It suddenly dawned on Davis that he was out of order, that it was Sissel's responsibility to lodge the objection. He looked up at Havercamp. "Sorry, Your Honor."

The judge was as frustrated with the assistant prosecutor as Davis. "I understand."

Davis slunk back to his chair.

"I want to show you, for identification purposes, what has been marked as 'Defendant's Exhibit G,'" Scalise said, handing a photograph to Katie Ryan. "You want to tell me what it is?"

"The torso."

"And what is this, labeled 'Defense Exhibit H?'"

"The same picture, only bigger."

"Are these true and accurate representations of what they purport to show?"

Katie Ryan looked at the pictures of the torso and then at the defense attorney. "Yes," she said nodding.

"Is it Joyce Klindt?"

"No."

"How can you be so sure?"

"The hairline, the color, the shape, it's just not the same."

"How can I phrase this delicately? What color is her hair, and by that I mean pubic hair?"

"Blonde, but sometimes she shaved it."

The photograph that Katie viewed was actually a picture of a picture. Scalise had used a Polaroid camera to photograph one of 35mm photographs already entered into evidence. The Polaroid he had taken came out darker than the original and had a reddish hue.

"If there are no objections, I would like to introduce these into evidence."

There was no response. Davis and Sissel huddled, trying to figure out how to keep the bogus pictures out of the jurors' hands. Scalise waited, jiggling the photographs to show his impatience.

"No objections," Sissel finally said.

The wily defense attorney had what he wanted. The photographs were accepted into evidence. He walked over and handed them to a juror.

During redirect, Sissel scolded Katie Ryan.

"You were slated to be a witness for the State?" he asked.

"Yes."

"When you arrived in Keokuk, who did you talk to first, Mr. Scalise or Bill Davis?"

"Mr. Scalise."

"And where did you spend the last two days, with the State's witnesses or in the defense room?"

"With Bart."

"You heard the news on April 16, 1983, that the torso had been found?"

"Yes."

"Did you ever call the Monahans?"

"No."

"You did know the Monahans?"

"Yes."

"You didn't think it was important to call them, to give them hope?"

"I don't know what I thought."

"Mrs. Ryan, have you in fact ever seen the torso itself?"

"No."

"So you really don't know what those pictures represent, do you?"

"No."

Davis looked up wistfully. Sissel knew as well as he that Katie Ryan had never seen the torso. Therefore, she could not possibly have known if the pictures that Scalise had shown her were a true representation or not. If Sissel had objected at the time, it might have meant something. As it stood now, Ryan's negative response came too late to have any impact on the jury.

"Did you ever contact the police or county attorney's office to help identify the torso?"

"I thought they would contact the Monahans."

Dead Water

"So as the best friend of Joyce Klindt, you figured this and you figured that and never came forward to help with identity, did you?"

"As an outsider, I didn't think ..."

Sissel interrupted nastily. "YES or NO?"

"Nope," she replied casually.

Katie Ryan had testified about as the prosecutor had expected. Davis, however, was angry that Scalise's Polaroids were placed into evidence without a battle.

During the morning recess, Rick Chase carried in Davis's valise. "You're not going to believe this, Bill. When I went back to get your briefcase, I felt something was missing from your room. At first I couldn't figure it out, then it dawned on me. Joyce's skeleton was gone."

Davis paled. "Jesus, did you find it?"

"Yeah. It was in the room maid's cart. She said she didn't check to see what was inside the plastic bag, thought it was garbage."

The prosecutor breathed a sigh of relief.

Fortunately, the next witness worked in the Scott County Attorney's office. Davis would finally have a friend on board. Ruth Keuhn, the "blonde-haired" mother of Terry Keuhn, took the stand.

"Hi, Ruth."

"Hi, Bill," she said unsmiling.

"Where do you work, Ruth?"

"In your office."

"But you're not working now, are you?"

"No, I've been on a leave of absence since June."

"And I might add," said the prosecutor, "it's an unpaid leave of absence, isn't it?"

"Yes."

"Do you have any children, Ruth?"

"Yes, three daughters and a son."

Trial by Jury

"And your youngest daughter, what is her name?"
"Terry."
"Is Terry dating Jim Klindt?"
"Yes."
"For how long?"
"About a year."
"This is August of 1984, Ruth. That means Terry started seeing the defendant back in August of 1983?"
"I really don't remember."
"How about March of 1983, the fifteenth, sixteenth, seventeenth, and eighteenth?"
"Yes."
"Ruth, do you remember the night Detective Carroll and I came to your apartment and talked with you and Terry?"
"Yes."
"Was it before or after Joyce Klindt disappeared?"
"After."
"A short time later, did you and Terry quit keeping house together?"
"Yes."
"Was there family discord?"
"I was concerned, that's all."
"Is that why Terry moved out?"
"I don't think so."
"Didn't she give you an explanation?"
"No."
"Wasn't it because the defendant told her to move?"
"I'm not sure."
Davis was bewildered. This was a friendly witness? "Did you know that Jim Klindt was married?"
"Yes."
"Was the relationship between the defendant and your daughter kept secret?"
"Well, they weren't open about it."

Dead Water

"So they didn't go out in public?"

"I don't know where they went."

"Do you remember what you told Ted Carroll that night we came to your apartment?"

"Ted didn't talk to me that night."

"Do you remember telling me, while Lieutenant Carroll was sitting at the table, that once, when Jim Klindt was in your apartment, there was a knock on the door and he hid in the closet?"

"No."

The prosecutor's face grew red.

"Do you remember coming to my office a few months ago and asking for a photocopy of your testimony?"

"I didn't get a copy."

"That's not what I asked. Did you sit across from me at my desk and read it?"

"Yes."

"Did I ask you if it was accurate?"

"I'm not sure."

Davis slammed down his legal pad. "NO FURTHER QUESTIONS."

He paused briefly to give the defense a chance to cross-examine Keuhn. Scalise smiled and politely declined. Ruth Keuhn rose quickly and exited the courtroom, looking at the floor on her way out.

"Call Ted Carroll," the prosecutor snarled through clenched teeth.

Bill Davis continued to fume as Lieutenant Carroll took the stand. He knew Ruth Keuhn had deliberately lied under oath. At that point, he was actually considering charging the her with perjury.

Lieutenant Carroll quickly corroborated the prosecutor's contention. The detective said he had called Bill Davis at home and gotten him out of bed to interview Ruth and Terry Keuhn.

Trial by Jury

He stated they had gone to the Keuhns' Bettendorf apartment that night and that Ruth Keuhn had stated Jim Klindt had once hid in a closet when someone knocked on the apartment door.

Duane Manlove, Joyce Klindt's personal physician, took the stand. He confirmed that Joyce was an asthmatic, but explained that between attacks an asthmatic could function fairly normally.

Shirley Burmeister followed Manlove. The tall waitress with bleached hair was about to tell the jurors why Scalise had asked Jeffrey Ryan about garbage bags.

"Do you remember the morning of March 18, 1983?" Davis asked.

"Yes. I was washing windows at Kernan's Restaurant."

"In Princeton?"

"Yes."

"What kind of day was it?"

"The weather was bad. It was cold and windy, kind of misting, and the river was high."

"Did you see something out of the ordinary that day?"

"Yes. I saw a man loading garbage bags onto an airboat."

"What does an airboat look like?"

"It's a small boat pushed by a fan."

"He was loading garbage bags, you say?"

"Yes. I watched him for about an hour. He was carrying black garbage bags down to the river and placing them in the airboat."

"What happened then?"

"He took off like a bullet and headed south."

"Did you make a comment to someone?"

"Yes. I turned to Roger Becker, a part-time cook at the restaurant, and said, 'Hey, Roger, who's that crazy ass out on the river?'"

"What did Roger say?"

"He said, 'That's Dr. Klindt.'"

"Did Mr. Klindt return?"

"Yes. He made four or five trips out on the river. Each time, he would load a black garbage bag into the airboat."

"Can you stand and show us how he carried them?"

"Well, some of them he carried in just one hand, but one of them was heavy. He held it out in front of him, like this," the waitress said placing one fist on top of the other.

When the defense declined to cross-examine Burmeister, Marilyn Lampo was sworn in and seated. Lampo was a thin woman in her early fifties. She seemed deathly serious and barely moved her lips as she spoke.

"Where do you live, Mrs. Lampo?"

"On a acreage just north of Cordova, Illinois."

"Is that on the east bank of the Mississippi River?"

"Yes, we live right by the river."

"What is directly across the river from you?"

"A bunch of islands and sloughs."

"I mean on the Iowa side?"

"Princeton is to the southeast."

"Do you remember the morning of March 18, 1983, for any particular reason?" Davis asked.

"Yes."

"Anything unusual happen?"

"Yes, I was getting ready for work and I heard a noise. When you live on the river it's easy to distinguish one sound from another. I can tell the Delta Queen from a towboat in the middle of the night. I knew it was an airboat, because the propeller in back pushes the sound out ahead of the boat. I went to the window and looked out."

"What did you think when you first saw the boat?"

"I was surprised. There were no other boats on the water. The river was very high and rough. It was very swift and there was a lot of debris."

"But you don't worry about floods where you live, do you?"

"No, we live about forty, forty-five feet above the river."

"Was there anyone else at home at the time?"

"Yes. My daughter Lori was home from college on spring break."

"And what did you say to Lori?"

"I said, 'Why would anyone in their right mind be out on the river on a day like this?'"

The last witness of the day was Lori Lampo. She verified her mother's story.

"And then you came to the window?" Davis asked.

"Yes. When I first heard the boat, I thought it was a Hovercraft," Lori said. "You know, a boat with an inflated skirt that floats on a cushion of air. But when I saw it, I was surprised. It was unlike anything I had ever seen before. The seats were set low and the oversized propeller was enclosed in a large cage and extended well out over the water."

Throughout the day, Scalise tried to get those witnesses living in the Princeton-Cordova area to admit that fog limited visibility on the March 18, 1983. While all said it was misting and overcast, not one would concede that the view of the opposing river bank, some three-quarters of a mile away, was obscured.

But even with three eyewitnesses divulging that Jim Klindt was out on the flooded river the morning his wife disappeared, it was still not a good day for the prosecution. Katie Ryan had sounded positive when she said the torso was not Joyce Klindt.

The day was not a total loss, however. At last, one of the prosecutor's prayers had been answered. The weekend was at hand.

17

THE SCARLET WOMAN

At 8:30 on Monday morning, Benita Harwood was called into chambers for a private interview to determine her credentials. The serologist had a youthful face, flashing dark eyes, and pouty red lips. She was poised and knowledgeable, answering a series of difficult questions put to her by Bill Davis, Lawrence Scalise, and Judge Havercamp. She spoke precisely, rarely using contractions. When the session was over, there was little doubt as to her qualifications. At 10:15, Harwood, having been duly sworn in, was examined and testified for the jury.

"Ms. Harwood, what do you do for a living?" Davis asked.

"I am a forensic serologist."

"Who are you employed by?"

"I'm employed by the Southwestern Institute of Forensic Sciences in Dallas, Texas."

"Just what is that?" asked Davis.

"It is what most people would refer to as a crime laboratory. There are nine criminalists that work in various areas in the field such as ballistics examination, fingerprint identification, document examination, trace evidence analysis such as paint comparison, arson analysis, and gunshot residue analysis, as well as blood and body fluid analysis."

"And what part of the lab do you work in?"

"I work in the identification of blood and other fluids."

"Now, who is your boss, the main guy who runs the whole show?"

"Dr. Charles Petty."

Trial by Jury

"Is that the same Charles Petty that Jack Klugman refers to on his Quincy TV show?"

"Yes, it is."

"Who owns the lab or institute?"

"It is a county-run agency. Dallas County is the funding body. Dr. Petty is the chief medical examiner."

"A serologist; has to do with blood, doesn't it?"

"Blood or other body fluids."

"And blood is a tissue?"

"Yes, it is a living tissue that is transported throughout the body, that carries oxygen to other tissues."

"You did get some things from Davenport in the mail?"

"Yes, I did. On November the eighth of 1983, I received by Federal Express two different samples, one of tissue and one of bone from Dennis Kern of the Davenport Police Department. They were packaged and shipped in dry ice."

"Then what did you do?"

"First, I analyzed pieces of the vertebrae using the absorption-elution technique. That is, I added a commercially-prepared antisera and let it sit overnight. The next morning, I washed the samples in a cold saline solution, heated them to fifty-six degrees Celsius to break the chemical bond and added the appropriate A, B, and O cells and looked for clumping."

"What did you find?"

"That the blood type present was type A."

"And then you analyzed the deep-muscle tissue sample?"

"Yes, by electrophoresis."

Davis shook his head. "You just used a word I don't understand. Can you explain it?"

"Electrophoresis is an analysis in which the sample is placed in a medium such as starch and an electric current is run through it."

Davis smiled. "Gave it a shock?"

"About four hundred volts in one case."

"Okay. In the muscle tissue that we sent you, did you find any, what do you call them, genetic markers?"

"Yes, I found six different enzymes, genetic markers. On the bottom line of the chart I prepared, you will see the combined phenotype incidence, .0027."

"What is a phenotype?"

"Phenotype is an express type of individual, the type that we see when we obtain the results in each of these systems."

"How did you arrive at the number, .0027?"

"I multiplied the frequency that each of these individual markers were found together."

"Can you translate that number into something I might understand?"

"This would indicate that this phenotype would occur in only about 27 out of 10,000 individuals."

"Then what happened?"

"I was asked if this tissue could be associated as being an offspring of a couple."

"And then you received the whole blood samples we had taken from Joyce Klindt's parents, the Monahans?"

"Yes."

"What did you find?"

"In this instance, the Monahans are 107.8 times more likely than a couple chosen at random to produce offspring with a phenotype the tissue possesses."

Bill Davis wondered if the testimony that Benita Harwood had given was too difficult for the jurors to understand. There was no doubt in the prosecutor's mind that Lawrence Scalise would try to muddle her words even further.

"I've noticed, ma'am, that something is missing in the tissue sample taken from the torso that was found in the blood samples of the Monahans," Scalise said.

"I believe you are making reference to the fact that I was unable to detect the AK phenotype."

"You did not find it at all. You got zero for the tissue. Is that significant to you or not?"

"Not really, when we know it is going to occur in 95 percent of the population."

"Let's take the reverse of that. It is significant that only 5 percent of the Caucasian population does not have the AK genetic marker, is that true?"

"Yes."

"So the Monahans both have it, the torso does not."

"That does not mean AK was not there at one time. It may be ..."

Scalise cut her off. "I don't want you to speculate. The truth is you didn't find it."

"I did not get a typing in the AK system."

"Well, ma'am, let's go back a little bit. You got a B.S. degree, right? A bachelor of science?"

Here we go, thought Davis. He is going to try to discredit her.

"A bachelor of science," Harwood replied.

"Okay. So do you take an internship someplace like doctors do?"

"No."

"You went right to work in a blood bank?"

"Yes, cross-matching blood for transfusions."

"For two years?"

"Yes."

"And then you went to work for Doctor Petty?"

"That's correct."

"And your supervisor, I believe you told me earlier, is a geologist?"

"He is my administrative supervisor, yes."

"And what's his name, Stone?"

"Dr. Irving Stone."

"Yeah," Scalise joked, "that would fit with a geologist, wouldn't it? He doesn't do work on blood, does he?"

"No."

"A guy who works on rocks doesn't do any blood work."

"No, he does not."

"And does he follow your report with respect to your work?"

"He is my administrative supervisor, not my technical supervisor."

"And your technical supervisor is?"

"Ultimately, Dr. Petty."

"Well, Dr. Petty doesn't review your work as you do it, does he?"

"No, he does not."

"And just to keep this going here ... you have kind of applied genetic principles to reach your final conclusions, haven't you?"

"Yes, I have."

"Will you tell the jury what training you've had in genetics, formal training?"

"My formal training was my medical technology training in the genetics of the ABO system."

"The blood system?"

"Yes."

"The fact is, ma'am, your med-tech training didn't qualify you for the electrophoresis work you're doing today, or the genetics work you're doing today, or the statistical work you're doing today?"

Harwood remained composed. "It gave me a background on which to build additional information in the field."

"Sort of on-the-job training?"

"Yes."

"Isn't it true, even if a sample is frozen, that bacteria continues to operate?"

Trial by Jury

"That's correct."

"Have you ever done testing on a tissue sample that had been in a river prior to testing?"

"Not that I can remember. This is the first time I've had a sample that was ..."

"Contaminated?" Scalise interjected.

"In this condition prior to my analysis," Harwood corrected.

"Can bacterial contamination and oxidation interfere with your readings?"

"I don't think from the strength of the readings I got that there was any interference, but that is always a possibility."

Lawrence Scalise gained few concessions from Benita Harwood. He did challenge the accuracy of the statistical data she had relied on in calculating her conclusions. He also pointed out that the Dallas institute she represented was little more than a "gun for hire," that she was paid both to run the tests and to testify.

Despite that, Bill Davis was satisfied with Ms. Harwood's performance. She had not allowed Scalise to unnerve her. Her testimony was concise and to the point. Any credits the defense attorney scored were earned by twisting numbers.

Still, Bill Davis needed to catch a break. The trial was in the second day of the second week. During that time, the prosecutor had suffered from an ineffective staff, had fought with hostile witnesses, and had been stung by perjured testimony. He was beginning to feel like the owner of a puppy in a house with white wall-to-wall carpeting. Every day held a new surprise. Today was no exception. Except, on this particular morning, the puppy moved in with the defense.

"The prosecution calls Theresa Keuhn."

Bill Davis was actually looking forward to questioning Terry Keuhn. The jury would hear the truth this morning. The petite brunette with the dimpled chin was too ingenuous to lie.

Davis thought back to a week ago and the stir that had rippled through the courtroom when the "other woman" received a simple kiss from the defendant. The prosecutor was wondering what kind of impression that had left on the jurors. The thought was interrupted when the bailiff swung open the oak door and Terry Keuhn waltzed into the chamber.

There were gasps, followed by titters. The young woman was wearing a bright red suit. The prosecutor did everything in his power to keep a straight face. And he would have, had he not looked at Lawrence Scalise. The defense attorney was having a coronary.

"Would you state your name please?" Davis said grinning.

Keuhn smiled back. "Theresa Ann Keuhn, K-E-U-H-N," she said in a squeaky voice.

"How old are you, Terry?"

"Twenty-six."

"Where do you live?"

"1941 West Third Street in Davenport."

"Tell the jury about your living arrangement."

"I rent and have my beauty shop there."

"Who else lives there?"

"Jim's parents, Dick and Geri Klindt."

"Did you replace someone when you set up shop there?"

"Yes."

"Dr. Klindt's chiropractic associate, Dennis Hagemann?"

"Yes."

"Are you married?"

Keuhn giggled. "No."

"You know the defendant, right?"

"Yes."

"Are you romantically involved with him?"

"Yes."

"Do you remember the day of March 18, 1983?"

"Yes."

Trial by Jury

"Tell us about it."
"Jim called me about 1:30 from Kernan's."
"From Princeton?"
"Yes."
"Where were you at the time?"
"At my job at Family Affair Fashions in Davenport."
"Did you have an appointment at that time?"
"Yes, a haircut."
"What do you charge for a haircut?"
"Eleven dollars."
Davis did a double take. "Eleven dollars. Gee, that's pretty steep," he said, running a hand through his thinning hair.
Keuhn laughed. "Yeah, especially if they don't have much hair."
"What did the defendant say?"
"He asked me to pick up some hamburgers and Coke and meet him at his house."
"Did you?"
"Yes."
"What happened?"
"When I got there he got in the Winnebago, and I followed him to the Village Shopping center across from North Park. We parked in front of Alexander's and had lunch in the Winnebago."
"What did he say?"
"He told me Joyce had left for a trial separation. That he had given her $2,000 and loaded her clothes and she left."
"What was your reaction?"
"I was happy. I hugged him."
"Then what happened?"
"I went back to work."
"Did you hear from the defendant again around 4:30?"
"Yes."
"What did he ask you to do?"

"To pick him up at the airport."
"And did you pick him up?"
"Yes."
"How many vehicles does Jim have?"
Terry looked confused. "How many?" she said rolling her eyes and guessing. "Three?"
Davis realized this was a math problem for Keuhn. He counted on his fingers. "Well, there's the Scout, the Winnebago, the Jetta and ..." The prosecutor waited.
"Oh, the Cadillac," Terry squealed as if she had just figured out the theory of relativity. "Four ... he has four," she said proudly, holding up her fingers and hiding her thumb behind her palm like a preschooler.
"Did he tell you why he was there?"
"I didn't ask."
"Did he tell you how he got to the airport?"
"I didn't ask."
"Didn't you wonder why a man with four vehicles would ask you to pick him up at the airport?"
"No. I never question Jim."
"Did he tell you where to go?"
"No, I told him I had to go."
Davis was puzzled.
"At Jumer's," Terry explained. "I had to use the rest room." More titters.
"Did he tell you where to drive the car?"
"To Randall's in North Park."
"Did you have any further conversation?"
"He called Bart."
"Did he ask Bart if his mother was there?"
"No."
"What happened then?"
"We went into the motor home."
"Did you talk?"

Trial by Jury

"A little. I think he was confused as to what to do."
"What do you mean?"
"I think he wanted to call the police."
"Did he tell you why he was looking for Joyce?"
"He said she took a lot more than he thought."
"Do you mean money?"
"Well, what else would she take?"
"I don't know, Terry," Davis sneered. "You were the one having the conversation. Did he say how much money she took?"
"No."
"Why did you go into the motor home?"
"For privacy."
"Did you remain clothed?"
"No. We made love."
More gasps, followed by whispers. Havercamp gaveled the courtroom silent.
"And you were only in the motor home ten minutes?"
"It wasn't very long."

The next witness, Diana Iossi, Joyce Klindt's cousin, identified the GE hand-held tape recorder and told how she and Joyce tested the recorder to make sure it was working on the afternoon of March 17, 1983.
"How big was Joyce?" asked Davis.
"About my size. Five foot four and maybe 130 pounds."
"Did you ever exchange clothes with her?"
"Yes, I still have a black bra I borrowed from her."
"What size is it?"
"34B."
The prosecutor hoped the jurors were listening, because Katie Ryan had testified that Diana Iossi was much bigger than Joyce.
"What color was her hair?"

"It's hard to say. She was always doing something to it. I think it was naturally a light brown. But she had this streak of gray in front that she made look silver."

Mrs. Iossi was followed by Dennis and Thomas Mosher and the three Bettendorf police officers who arrived at the scene after the two fishermen had discovered the torso.

Sharon Campbell, a 7-Eleven employee, told of informing Jim Klindt about co-worker Connie Caven sighting someone who looked like Joyce. Caven testified that the chiropractor had offered to pay her to go to the Davenport police and give a deposition which in the chiropractor's words would "save his ass."

Ted Carroll was the last witness on Tuesday. He spoke of the extensive interviews he had held with the defendant and of the many lies Jim Klindt had told him. It was interesting to note that Carroll and the prosecution always referred to the defendant as Mr. Klindt rather than Dr. Klindt, a subtle attempt to deny the chiropractor any status.

At last, a day had gone well for the prosecution. After watching the spectators file out of the courtroom, Bill Davis collapsed on one of the cherry benches, laid his bifocals on the seat beside him, leaned back and closed his eyes. Television newswoman Kathleen Seith sat down next to Davis. There was an embarrassing crunch. The prosecutor was about to learn that he had a bigger problem than broken glasses.

18

IN ABSENTIA

Bill Davis arrived at the optometrist's office five minutes before closing. The receptionist recognized him immediately. "You've become quite a celebrity down here."

Davis smiled. "It's quite the case, isn't it?"

"It sure is. Have a seat. Dr. Hunter will be with you in a minute. He's just finishing up with a patient."

"Come on back, Counselor. Let's have a look at those glasses," Hunter yelled. "Hell, this ain't so bad. At least you didn't break a lens. Let's see if we can find some frames. How's the trial going?"

"Okay, I guess," Davis replied. "I really can't discuss it until it's over."

"I understand," Hunter said winking. "Would you be interested in hearing what I know?"

"Sure. I can't talk, but I can listen."

"Well, I have this friend, Frank Donaldson, who runs a little company here in town. He has a woman who works for him that's sitting on the jury. Blew his mind when she got picked. Said she hasn't made an on-the-job decision in the past five years. He can't imagine her finding this Klindt fellow guilty."

Davis sagged. The optometrist had just rekindled Harry Forrester's ominous prediction. Starting with the change of venue, the prosecutor had not caught one break that would help him convict Jim Klindt. It now appeared that gaining a guilty verdict in Keokuk would be impossible.

For the past year, the Klindt case had dominated Bill Davis's life. It had enveloped him, driven him. Now, with the wag of his tongue a total stranger had stripped the prosecutor of his motivation. The letdown was immense.

That night, Davis shunned the crowd of reporters in the hotel lounge, walked down the hill to the Cellar, and ordered a scotch. The alcohol did little to numb his dejection.

It was late by the time the prosecutor returned to the Holiday Inn. Discouraged and restless, Davis paced the confines of his small, dimly lit room. His thoughts drifted back to his youth, growing up in a tough neighborhood in Detroit, working his way through college, and arguing with the dean just to get into law school. It seemed to Davis that he had fought for everything he had gotten in his life, culminating with his surprising upset of the incumbent, former State Senator Elizabeth Shaw, in the 1978 race for Scott County Attorney. The prosecutor sat on the edge of his bed, gulped a stiff drink and decided if he was going to lose this case, he would go down fighting.

Still, Davis slept poorly. He awoke before dawn, his mood as dark as the night, and studied the slate of witnesses. A phone call interrupted his breakfast of black coffee and Tylenol at 6:30. It was Judy Pochel.

"You hurried off so fast last night, I didn't get a story. Do you know you haven't issued a statement to the press since last weekend?"

Davis exploded. "You want a story, Judy, I'll give you a goddamned story. Write about a man who's being held on a $1 million bond and is on trial for first-degree murder. Tell them the son-of-a-bitch rides from jail to the trial in the front seat and his handcuffs are removed before he gets out of the car. Tell them he has the run of the courthouse and he's driven unrestrained to McDonald's for lunch everyday." The prosecutor slammed down the receiver.

Wednesday, August 22, brought more testimony about the river, this time from the Army Corps of Engineers. After

Trial by Jury

lunch, Davis tried to find heart, to rally himself, to fight and convict a man he knew to be guilty. But the day was little more than a blur of witnesses.

On Thursday morning, Officer Rick Chase testified as to his involvement as the initial evidence technician in the investigation. After Chase stepped down, Davis inadvertently set up the last comic relief the jury would have for quite some time.

"Your Honor, I request that Officer Chase be allowed to stay and operate the movie projector during the testimony of the next witness."

"After seeing Mr. Sissel's problems with the slide projector, I welcome the idea," Havercamp quipped.

Even Sissel chuckled.

Dr. Kimball Thompson took the stand and explained the autopsy. The film was more graphic than the slides taken when the torso was pulled from the river. Even with the lights dimmed, Davis noticed several of the jurors had difficulty watching.

Joyce Klindt's mother, Virginia Monahan, was spared the trauma. As a witness, she was not allowed to view the trial until she had given her testimony.

Mrs. Monahan was sworn in following lunch. Wearing a bright-colored dress and large hoop earrings, she seemed detached and failed to shed a tear. During cross-examination, she strengthened the defense's contention the torso was not her daughter.

"Do you recall ever seeing any small moles or bluish birthmarks on Joyce's back?" asked Scalise.

"No."

"What color was Joyce's hair?"

"Dishwater blonde."

Because of a travel conflict, Dr. Clyde Snow, the next scheduled witness, could not reach Keokuk until the following Monday. Judge Havercamp took the opportunity to grant the jury a long weekend.

On Monday, August 27, the trial entered its third week. Clyde Collins Snow, a world-famous anthropologist, testified first. Despite Snow's expertise, the severed bones he had reassembled consisted of little more than a woman's pelvis. Exact measurements were impossible.

Snow conceded under cross-examination that there were hundreds of thousands, even millions of women in the general population with bone structures similar to those of the torso.

The second expert for the prosecution, Michael Liesch, was the chief medical technologist with the blood center at the University of Iowa Hospital in Iowa City. It was understood that if the State did not call the med-tech, the defense would. Liesch said the samples he received from the torso were too contaminated with bacteria for accurate testing.

During cross-examination, Scalise got Liesch to admit that he actually got a positive reaction for blood type B the first time he tested. Liesch acknowledged that was true but said that because of the contamination the tests were inconclusive.

Michael J. Peterson of the Iowa Criminalistics Laboratory in Des Moines said he examined samples from the torso in May 1983 and found type A blood. Scalise cast doubt on Peterson's testimony because the samples were shipped to him in a formaldehyde solution.

"Could the formaldehyde affect your test results?"

"I don't know," said Peterson.

"What else did you find in the samples you received?"

"Crushed shells, rotting vegetation, mold, and silt."

"You're the same guy who tested the blade from the chain saw taken from Dr. Klindt's garage, aren't you?"

Trial by Jury

"Yes."

"Find any human blood or tissue or bone on it?"

"No."

"No further questions, Your Honor."

The prosecutor had failed to accomplish the one goal he had set at the beginning of the trial to prove without a doubt — the torso and Joyce Klindt were one and the same.

The week dragged on. Witnesses came and went. Bill Davis was tired. Scalise was tired. The jury was tired.

The final day of testimony found the courtroom packed. Joyce Klindt was about to testify against her husband in absentia. The recording of the argument between Joyce and Jim Klindt the night before she disappeared was the final piece of evidence introduced by the State. The defense had tried on numerous occasions to stop it from being played to the jury. Lawrence Scalise lodged another objection. Judge Havercamp overruled for the umpteenth time.

Scalise then made one last-ditch attempt to have the audio cassette ruled inadmissible. "The tape is hearsay, I can't cross examine a tape."

The motion was, at best, ludicrous. Havercamp gave Scalise a deadpan look, somewhere between disdain and disbelief, and quietly overruled.

Lieutenant Carroll was called back to the stand. He relinquished the tape to Davis.

Scalise had taken great pains during jury selection to make sure the panel was aware of the tape's explicit contents. Despite his efforts, neither the jury nor the gallery was prepared for the graphic language and verbal abuse they heard. Unfortunately, the tape brought a different reaction than Davis expected. At times the jurors smiled, as if embarrassed at eavesdropping on a domestic dispute. The prosecutor felt sure, however, the animosity exhibited by the defendant would eventually play on the jurors' minds. After the forty-five minute tape ended, the prosecution rested its case.

Bart Klindt, a six-foot one-inch eighth-grader, was the only witness for the defense. Scalise's direct examination was brief. He asked Bart to recall the events leading up to and what took place on the day of March 18, 1983. He was also interested in the relationship between the boy and his dad.

Bill Davis also asked very few questions. "You haven't seen your mother since March 18, 1983?"

"No, sir."

"Not a card?"

"No."

"Not a telephone call?"

"No."

"Nothing further, Your Honor."

In final analysis, Bart Klindt was little more than a character witness for his father. The defendant, James B. Klindt, did not testify on his own behalf.

The trial was winding down. Only the closing arguments remained. Bill Davis watched Jim Klindt embrace Bart, kissing the boy on the lips. It seemed a forced display of affection to the prosecutor. He wondered if Klindt was playing to the jury. It was hard for Davis to believe that a man who could murder and dismember his wife held affection for anyone but himself.

Klindt seemed to have gathered a following during the hearing. The rangy chiropractor had the charisma of a cult leader. Friends and family had backed him with a fierce determination throughout the trial. Davis mused. Was it out of loyalty or fear?

On the other hand, the defendant's physical appearance had deteriorated. The chiropractor had seemed relaxed during the first few days of the trial, but first-degree murder is a heavy charge. By the beginning of the third week, Klindt's

Trial by Jury

complexion had gone sallow. The energy he had shown at the beginning was no longer evident. He rarely smiled, and not even the steady diet of McDonald's hamburgers for lunch had kept him from losing weight.

That night the prosecutor lay in bed and worried. The possibility of conviction seemed remote. Still, it seemed inconceivable that a man could commit a crime of this magnitude and walk — or was it?

19

DEADLOCKED

The closing arguments were made Wednesday, August 29, 1984. There were no surprises. Sissel, to whom words were more important than time, spoke for forty-five minutes, reviewing every statistic, every circumstance ad infinitum. He talked slowly and paused often, ending his summation as he had begun, without emotion. "Ladies and gentlemen of the jury ... there ... is ... no ... reasonable ... doubt."

In comparison Lawrence Scalise seemed poised and relaxed. He could smell an acquittal. He exchanged smiles with Klindt and continued to beam as he swaggered onto the stage. As he spoke, he removed his bifocals and crossed the gold bows as if he were going to put them in his pocket. He never did, continuing to hold them in a subtle show of control. "I promised Bill I wouldn't talk for more than forty-five minutes," Scalise said, poking fun at Sissel and grinning at Davis as if they were old friends. Then the smile was gone along with his folksy manner, replaced by a brash self-assuredness. He went on the attack. "The prosecution has taken much of the tape out of context. I challenge you, the jury, to evaluate the recording as a whole."

Scalise proceeded to cast doubt on the compilation of statistical evidence. "Dr. Lenth's numbers are skewed. There is a missing Illinois woman who has been totally left out of the equation," he argued. "And remember, Benita Harwood could not find any 'AKs' present in the torso's tissue sample. I ask you, why?

"This case is historic," Scalise continued, "because it is the first time in my twenty-six years as a lawyer, it is the first

Trial by Jury

time ever, in my memory, I've ever seen anybody attempt to prove that someone committed murder, beyond a reasonable doubt, by statistic. Not by direct evidence, mind you, eyewitness evidence, not by circumstance, but by statistics. I'll tell you something ... We don't do that in this country."

It was a solid close. The defense attorney seemed convinced that if he could discredit the identity of the torso, he could get an acquittal.

As Bill Davis stood for his rebuttal, he already knew he would never convict Jim Klindt in Keokuk. He had seen it coming at the start of the trial when he lost control of the jury. He had felt it in the hallway when Havercamp reproached him. He had heard it from a friend in the smoky little bar on Main Street and from the optometrist who repaired his glasses. He had sensed it at night when sleep would not come. The prosecutor understood he had mismanaged the case. He had relied too heavily on others. It was no longer his to win. The best the State could hope for was a tie. With his back against the wall, Bill Davis argued for a mistrial.

In contrast to Scalise, Davis was energetic. He could not allow the jurors to know his mind. His rebuttal was scintillating. Since Iowa law allowed him to address only those points Scalise had made in his summation, Davis focused first on the tape, speaking directly to the jurors. "I've never had the victim testify in a murder case, but you did, you heard her own words."

In confronting the attack on Dr. Lenth, Davis warned the jury not to be fooled, saying, "The defense is using false logic. They're telling you that an elephant has four legs, therefore all four-legged animals are elephants. You and I know that isn't true.

"And Benita Harwood didn't say there were no 'AKs' present. She just said she couldn't find any. Counsel," he said pointing at Scalise, "is the only one to say there weren't any

'AKs' present. Not finding something doesn't mean it isn't present."

Davis closed with a flurry. "We didn't intend to prove Joyce Klindt dead by the statistician or by the pathologist or by the anthropologist," he bellowed, pounding his fist on the table, "OR BY THE TAPE," he roared, pointing at the recorder. "ALL the evidence, as a whole, not part, not one piece, but ALL the evidence, proves Joyce Klindt was murdered by the defendant."

The stirring rebuttal was the high point of the trial.

The jurors, seven men and five women, emotionally drained and pale, were given a long list of instructions by Judge Havercamp and sent to the jury room to decide the fate of a man charged with one of the most grisly and heinous crimes ever committed in the state of Iowa.

On Friday afternoon, August 31, after twenty-three hours of deliberation, the jury foreman, H. Wayne Nelson, sent Havercamp a note informing the judge of the difficulty the panel was having reaching a verdict. Havercamp called the jurors back into the courtroom and quizzed Nelson.

"Are the members of the jury presently discussing the differences between themselves?"

"Yes, sir."

"Are you in a frame of mind conducive to agreement?"

"Yes, sir."

"Since you began deliberations, have you made progress toward reaching an agreement?"

"No we haven't. No, sir."

"Well, let me remind you of instruction nineteen, the Allen Rule, which stipulates in effect that the prosecution has put a lot of time and money into this case and does not anticipate a hung jury."

The jurors were then sent back to the jury room, where they remained until 7:30 that evening. They were asked at that time if they wanted dinner brought in. Instead, Nelson requested that the jury be excused for the Labor Day weekend. Judge Havercamp obliged.

"Are you surprised by the length of the deliberations?" a reporter asked Bill Davis.

"We did our job, we're confident they'll do theirs. If the verdict is not in our favor, we'll live with it. We'll be displeased, but they have to do what they think is right. They should take their time."

The prosecutor scratched his beard. "The three-day weekend should help the jurors clear their minds," Davis added. "Spending time with their families may help them relax and be ready to decide the matter Tuesday."

On September 4, the jurors returned to the courthouse to continue their deliberation. During the morning session, Nelson asked for a rereading of testimony of several of the State's witnesses. Havercamp thought the request was too time-consuming and tried to narrow its scope. "I assume there's some disagreement about Mrs. Reed's testimony. Would reading it again aid in deliberations?"

"It would probably help. Yes, sir," Nelson replied.

Havercamp relented. The rereading of Elizabeth Reed's testimony took three hours. The jurors filed back into the jury room and continued to debate until 5:30 that evening. At that point, Nelson sent Havercamp a final note stating the jury appeared hopelessly deadlocked.

The judge called the jurors back into the courtroom and asked the foreman, "Do you believe there is any useful purpose to be served by continuing to deliberate at this time?"

"No, sir," Nelson replied.

"I think it is safe to say it is inconclusive," Havercamp said. "With the jury not being able to agree, I declare a mistrial."

Klindt bowed his head as the judge rendered his decision. Geraldine Klindt and Terry Keuhn, sitting in the front row, showed no emotion. Davis, however, ripped off his glasses and slammed them on the table, outwardly disgusted — inwardly thankful.

Judge Havercamp excused the jury saying, "Thank you for your time. I know you did the best you could. I ask that you not discuss the matter with reporters, so as not to prejudice the next jury that will hear the case."

The jury had heard the testimony of sixty-three witnesses, reviewed more than one hundred and sixty exhibits, and had failed to reach a verdict after thirty-two hours of deliberation. They filed out of the courtroom looking tired and relieved.

The mistrial gave the State an opportunity to retry. According to Iowa law, the prosecution had ninety days to exercise this option, unless Klindt waived the time period.

Klindt was returned to the custody of Lee County Sheriff Donald "Bud" Arnold before being sent back to the Scott County Jail.

"Someone must have believed that indeed, Jim Klindt did kill his wife," Bill Davis told the press. "I am disappointed, but I intend to try this case again. Obviously some people think he is guilty, otherwise they wouldn't have been deadlocked.

"We will start from square one, and I will retry the case," he continued. "One thing we'll do differently is to take a little more time educating the jury. Maybe they were not ready for all the expert testimony. A plea bargain is the furthermost thing from my mind."

The press interviewed the jury foreman, H. Wayne Nelson, immediately following the trial. He ignored the judge's plea for self-censorship. "We tried," Nelson told her. "We decided not to decide. It's like kissing your sister."

"What about the tape?"

"It didn't seem to make much difference to most of the jurors. A lot of things are said in the heat of a family dispute. Early on, we discussed the possibility that Joyce Klindt might have used it to set up her husband. The torso made us change our mind."

"Were you ever close to a conviction?"

"I prefer not to discuss that," Nelson replied. "Obviously some of the jurors believed Klindt was guilty or we wouldn't have had a mistrial. I personally don't believe the State presented enough evidence to be sure beyond a reasonable doubt.

"The State had plenty of witnesses," Nelson continued. "It might have been better off without some of them. But the prosecution and the defense both did a fine job. I feel let down today."

After the interview, Nelson sought out Bill Davis. "You did a fine job, Mr. Davis," he drawled offering his hand.

"I'm only sorry I couldn't convince you that the torso was Joyce Klindt," the prosecutor replied.

"Oh, I don't think there's much doubt that the torso was Joyce," Nelson replied.

The prosecutor glanced up, stunned. "You're kidding?"

"No, we all thought it was Joyce. I think your problem is you put too many eggs in one basket. The tape isn't the answer to getting a conviction. You wanna get a conviction, you'd better put the whole thing in order. We were so confused, we didn't know whether we were coming or going.

"It's not that we liked Jim Klindt. We thought he was arrogant. We didn't care much for Mr. Scalise's attitude either. But neither one of them could hold a candle to your assistant.

"You had another problem, Counselor. There were a couple of real asses on that jury."

Davis smiled. "I'm sure there were."

"Yeah, we had some real knock-down drag-outs in the jury room. It was hostile as hell in there. One man, I won't mention his name, threatened to kill me.

Dead Water

"Well, I gotta get going," Nelson said. "Can you believe it? The trial's only been over an hour and I've already been offered two paid speaking engagements."

The last remark irked Davis. Harry Forrester had been right. The jury foreman was a publicity hound. Davis was well aware of most of the prosecution's shortcomings. But Nelson had given the prosecutor some valuable insight: the jurors had understood the complicated expert testimony. They believed the torso to be Joyce Klindt.

In retrospect, the prosecution had overlooked a most important element of the trial. Bill Davis had spent so much time hammering home the identity of the victim, he had neglected to get a conviction. The prosecutor had assumed it was a foregone conclusion that if he proved the torso was Joyce Klindt, the jury would logically presume Jim Klindt had killed her. What was a stone connection for Davis was a quantum leap for the jury.

Davis was not the only one who misread the jurors. Lawrence Scalise too had failed to recognize the conclusiveness of the statistical evidence presented. The fact was, the jury believed the torso was Joyce Klindt. Scalise had spent most of the trial arguing against the identity of the torso. Too little time had been spent on convincing the jury of his client's innocence.

There seemed to be several reasons for the failure to convict Jim Klindt. There is little doubt that the change of venue hurt the prosecution's cause, not because the trial was moved, but rather where it was moved. Keokuk is the only city in Iowa that lies east of Missouri. The locals speak a distinct dialect, a mixture of river jargon and Ozark twang. The folks from Keokuk readily admit that they identify more closely with Missouri, which remains very much the "show me state."

The logistics of the trial were also a nightmare. Just getting to Keokuk presented a problem. The city is a winding three-

Trial by Jury

hour drive from the Quad Cities, and no major airline serves the community. This lack of efficient transportation created scheduling problems. The prosecution, therefore, allowed the State's witnesses to appear at their convenience. Because of the random testimony, the trial did not unfold in a smooth chronological order, confusing the jurors as to the sequence of events. The fact there were no witnesses scheduled to testify on Friday during the second week of the trial supports that contention.

The out-of-the-way venue also made the trial the most expensive in Scott County's history. Understanding this, Bill Davis tried to cut costs by eliminating such things as overnight stays by witnesses.

It was now obvious to Davis that the jury did not care for the way the State had presented its case. The testimony had been muddled and at times contradictory. Too much emphasis had been placed on Klindt's moral character, too little on the murder itself. In the end the prosecutor was fortunate to get the mistrial.

Following the trial one of the jurors, Judy Redinbo, leaked a story acknowledging that of the numerous ballots taken, the majority had always leaned towards acquittal. On one such ballot, Jim Klindt had come within two votes of being a free man.

PART THREE

VERDICT

The long hot summer gave way to a crisp blue autumn. Colors faded and fell from grace.

20

TRY AGAIN

On October 22, 1984, Judge Havercamp named the venue for the second trial. He selected Sioux City, the district seat of Woodbury County, some 370 miles from Davenport and God only knows how far from Keokuk. Bordered on the west and southwest by Nebraska and on the northwest by South Dakota, the community of 88,000 sits beside the Missouri River in northwestern Iowa.

Bill Davis was determined not to squander a second chance to convict Jim Klindt. Upon learning that Dennis Kern had a brother on the Sioux City police force, he sent Kern and Rick Chase to the trial site a week before the hearing was to begin. The Sioux City police were more than happy to accommodate two fellow officers.

Chase took along his personal computer and set up an elaborate information bank dividing Sioux City into sectors. This was critical in jury selection because it allowed Davis to

Verdict

pinpoint neighborhoods, thus giving him a feel for the affluence and probable education levels of prospective jurors.

While in Sioux City the two policemen also checked out the Woodbury County Courthouse, designated site of the second Klindt trial. Erected in 1918, the eight-story structure is listed in the National Historic Registry and was recently nominated for National Landmark status. Designed by William E. Steele, a member of the Frank Lloyd Wright Group, the building is one of the finest examples of Prairie School architecture. Narrow, elongated, blonde bricks make up both the exterior and inner walls, and enormous lead glass windows disperse light throughout the earth-toned interior.

Deciding the courtroom looked too cheery, the lawmen ordered black crepe curtains to cover the huge rectangular windows. Next, they moved the defense table so it was difficult for the jury to view the defendant. In order to see Klindt, the jurors would be forced to turn their heads acutely to the right.

The prosecution did this with the express purpose of controlling Jim Klindt. In Keokuk, Davis had learned too late that Klindt was an excellent non-verbal communicator. Using nothing more than his eyes, quaint smiles, and nods, the defendant had influenced several members of that panel. Following the first trial, the prosecutor had told Sissel he would not have been surprised if Klindt could have gotten a date with a couple of the women jurors.

Since the defendant would probably not be testifying, the prosecutor wanted to depict him in an aggressive light. One way to achieve this was by alluding to guilt by association. The officers mounted the projector screen above and behind the defense table. Whenever the jury viewed anything gruesome, such as slides of the torso or the edited video of the autopsy, they would be shown on the large screen just over the defendant's right shoulder.

Dead Water

Bill Davis arrived in Sioux City on Sunday afternoon, November 4, and immediately summed up his job as prosecutor. "My burden isn't to prove how he killed her, or where he killed her, but that he did kill her."

On Monday, November 5, jury selection began. All went smoothly. Whether the data stored in Rick Chase's personal computer gained the prosecution a physical edge in the selection process was moot, because the psychological advantage was enormous. Time after time jury selection was interrupted in order to bring Davis a new printout. The brain trust for the defense had no idea these were just reprints of the same register. Fearing Davis would gain the upper hand, they ended up scratching prospects that Davis also wanted to eliminate, while accepting many the prosecutor wanted to keep. The result was a jury whose makeup seemed favorable to the prosecution.

In a day and a half—twelve jurors—ten men and two women, and two alternates were chosen. The jury, ranging in age from twenty-five to sixty-four, included a high school teacher, a nurse's assistant and a retired nurse, two semi-retired men, a bank bookkeeper, an advertising copywriter, a welder, a draftsman, a grain elevator operator, a livestock buyer, and the owner of a feed company.

Two familiar figures were missing at the second trial. Melody Haines was absent from the defense, replaced by one of Lawrence Scalise's peers, the eminent John Sandre of Drake University. Deputy prosecutor Gary Sissel had decided to remain in Davenport; his wife was in her final month of pregnancy. He was supplanted by Douglas Wells.

James Klindt was confined at the Woodbury County Jail, a short walk from the courthouse. Bill Davis's complaint of lackadaisical treatment of the prisoner in Keokuk found tighter

Verdict

restrictions placed on the chiropractor during the Sioux City trial.

At 2:25 the afternoon of November 6, Judge Havercamp introduced the court reporter to the jurors and gave them a short admonition before asking Bill Davis to proceed. The prosecutor set the tone for the trial with a snappy twenty-minute opening statement. It was in stark contrast to Gary Sissel's methodical and detailed commencement at the first trial.

Reorganized and rejuvenated after his close call in Keokuk, Davis attempted to simplify the case. "The evidence of this trial will be broken into two distinct parts: First, I will prove by expert testimony that the tattered, cut, and dismembered human remains found in the Mississippi River are Joyce Klindt, and second, that the actions of Jim Klindt during the day his wife vanished were not consistent with his statements following her disappearance."

Davis had planted the seed in the jurors' minds. Certifying the torso was Joyce Klindt was important to the case, only if it linked Jim Klindt to the crime.

"I will prove," the prosecutor continued, "that Jim Klindt killed his wife, butchered her with a chain saw, and dumped her into the river. You are going to find out he had a reason. You are going to find out he had a motive."

In conclusion, Davis told the jury the case was a bit like a crossword puzzle that needs to be put together a piece at a time in order to form the true picture. It surprised some that the prosecutor glossed over the audio cassette emphasized as the major piece of circumstantial evidence throughout the first trial.

Lawrence Scalise followed the same format he had during the first trial, casting doubt that the torso was Joyce Klindt. He spoke of experts being only about 55 percent sure that it was Joyce Klindt—that it took a statistician to tie it all together.

Scalise also gave advice to any juror who might begin to think that Jim Klindt had committed the crime.

"I want you to look for the answers to these questions: where, how, when, and lastly, why," he said, ticking them off on his fingers. Like Davis, Scalise barely mentioned the infamous tape.

Dennis Mosher was called as the State's first witness. Mosher spoke of the river, of the life of commercial fisherman, licenses needed, illegal nets and finally of finding the torso. The next witness, Mosher's father, Thomas, gave a similar account.

The Bettendorf patrolman, Gary Richardson, who was the first police officer at the scene, related his initial viewing of the corpse. Det. Christopher Kauffman acknowledged he also saw the torso and that the police action at the scene had been video taped by a local TV station. The video cassette was then played for the jurors.

On Wednesday, November 7, day three of the trial, Rick Chase testified first, showing an edited videotape of the autopsy, which was also narrated, highlighting the main points of the procedure.

Pathologist Dr. Kimball Thompson was the first of the expert witnesses. His choice of schooling may have bolstered his credibility. Thompson had graduated from Creighton Medical School, located downriver from Sioux City in Omaha, Nebraska.

Dr. Thompson spoke of his direct examination of the torso and his use of swab smears to determine that the victim had not been sexually abused. He said tests of the torso for drugs also proved negative.

As for physical appearance, Dr. Thompson stated there was no appendectomy scar, evidence of medical sterilization, or intrauterine devices present. There were, however, both stretch

Verdict

marks and an episiotomy scar, indicating the woman had given birth.

During the slide presentation showing photographs of the torso prior to the autopsy, Bill Davis asked a macabre question.

"Doctor, are you able as a pathologist ... to look at those cuts and determine what may have made them or what did make them?"

"In this particular case, at least, this cut and the patterns on the ends of the leg bones suggested to me that it was made by a mechanical saw, probably a chain saw."

In his cross-examination, John Sandre ignored the brutal aspects of how the torso came to be. He was interested only in disproving the torso was Joyce Klindt. Sandre, clever and well-versed, eventually forced Dr. Thompson to recant some of the presumptions he had laid out in earlier testimony.

The defense lawyer got Thompson to admit that the first tissue sample he had removed from the torso was classified by the University of Iowa Hospitals as having Type B blood. (Joyce Klindt had Type A blood.) By alluding to the fact that bacteria was present in that initial specimen, Sandre concluded it was therefore possible the whole torso could have been contaminated.

Once Thompson had agreed to the possibility of that hypothesis, Sandre continued to hammer. "Doctor, from your examination, what I would like to do is discuss with you several things that appear to me that you can't say with certainty, but you tell me if I'm wrong, all right? You cannot say with any certainty whether the torso had been subjected to any freezing before the postmortem that you did, isn't that true?"

"That's true."

"You can't say with any certainty how long the torso had been dead and, therefore, in the river, isn't that true?"

"That's correct."

"And as you know, and I wish you would tell the jury, the fact is, cold water retards decomposition, does it not?"

"Well, yes, it will retard decomposition."

"And as I understand it, the best estimate that you can come up with in terms of the amount of time that this specimen had been in the river is somewhere between two weeks and four months, is that correct?"

"That's correct."

"And, as a matter of fact, you can't even say that it might not have been as long as six months, can you?"

"Why, I would be surprised if it was six months, but it is not an impossibility."

"Could have been six months?"

"Could have been."

"As I understand it, Doctor, you cannot say with any kind of certainty whatsoever how old this woman, related to the torso, is. Isn't that correct?"

"No ... Well, it's related. The age estimate is based on what I have said."

"And the certainty that you expressed with respect to age estimate is between the ages of eighteen and forty, correct?"

"That's correct."

"I understand that age estimate, that's basically formed on the basis of when a woman's reproductive years are, correct?"

"Yes. And then, you know, the appearance, the — you know, mature appearance of the specimen that we have."

"So this torso could have belonged to a woman who is anywhere between eighteen and forty years of age?"

"That's correct."

"That's a very wide range, isn't it, Doctor?"

"Yes."

"Now, Doctor, with respect to some of the things that, from your examination as well as your training and expertise, you

Verdict

can tell us for certain that the torso had pubic hairs the color of red-brown, isn't that true?"

"Yes."

"Not blonde, but red-brown?"

"It was red-brown."

"You also find scarring that is consistent with an episiotomy, correct?"

"That's correct."

"If it was an episiotomy, that would tell you, presumably, that this person had at least one child, correct?"

"That's correct."

"It wouldn't tell you whether this person had two, three, or four children, would it?"

"That's correct."

"Another thing you told us, Doctor, I think you told us before, is that this individual had hips of thirty-nine inches. That's what you have talked to us about so far, is it not?"

"In my report I said that the maximum measurement was thirty-nine inches, but as I reviewed for the deposition, I discovered that number was based on the width of the lateral wound {the deep cut made by the chain saw just above the buttocks crease} which was nineteen inches. At that point it's 50 percent of the circumference, making that at that point of the wound circumference approximately thirty-eight or thirty-nine inches ..."

That led to a lengthy discussion as to exactly where hips are actually located. The doctor was inclined to talk in medical terms, finally saying the hips are located "above the buttocks and below the waist." Sandre pointed out that the area that a layman commonly thinks of as the hips is the buttocks and that measurement of the torso at the buttocks could have been "forty-one inches or more." Dr. Thompson conceded that possibility.

There followed a long exchange about the birthmarks found on the torso. Again, the doctor acknowledged there was considerable confusion about the subject, that most physicians referred to any bluish skin discoloration with a vascular component as a birthmark.

An argument then ensued on when birthmarks are formed. Dr. Thompson stressed that most of what are commonly called birthmarks do not occur at birth but from twelve years of age to early adulthood.

Throughout the cross-examination, Sandre, as any good defense attorney would, continued to cast doubt on the accuracy of the other two blood tests (both of which came back blood type A) because bacterial contamination might have been present, as well as the discrepancies between lay and medical terminology in such areas as hip measurement and birthmarks. At one point, the defense lawyer even challenged the doctor's credentials by making sure the jury recognized that Kimball Thompson was not a forensic pathologist.

Bill Davis's redirect was short and to the point. He made certain the jury understood that the first blood tissue was so contaminated that, according to the written report of Mike Liesch of the University Hospital Blood Bank, "A positive ABO determination of this admitted tissue sample is not ascertainable."

The prosecutor also made it clear that there were only a few forensic pathologists in the entire state of Iowa, noting Thomas Bennett, who would testify later in the day, was one of them. Still, Davis was not able to totally undo the damage Sandre had inflicted upon the prosecution's first expert witness.

Thompson was excused and Davenport radiologist Robert Picchiotti took the stand. Picchiotti said he had X-rayed the torso, which consisted largely of the dead woman's pelvis. He explained that the streaks of black in the soft tissue indicated the presence of air. He said he had made notes on two slight

Verdict

medical abnormalities he found present: spina bifida occulta (an anatomical defect in the bony arch of the back bone) and pars interarticularis (a discernible difference between the bone density of the right and left pedicles).

Dr. Picchiotti said these subtle defects were cited only for identification purposes. In other words, if a previous X-ray were found in the dead woman's medical file, this would aid in the comparison. The doctor also said that for all practical purposes, the woman's pelvis was normal.

When Sandre, in the cross-examination, asked if the streaks of black indicating air in the soft tissue meant there was bacterial contamination present, Picchiotti replied, "Without a doubt."

Picchiotti was followed by Dr. Robert F. Godwin, a dermatologist in private practice in Davenport, Iowa. Since Godwin had not been present at the autopsy, he had to draw his conclusions from photographs.

A major argument flared on the definition of birthmarks — what they were, and when they formed. Godwin said that the two small bluish markings on the torso could be any of three possibilities: a contusion or a bruise; a vessel malformation referred to as hemangioma; or a traumatic tattoo, arising from an injury in which foreign material becomes embedded beneath the skin.

Under cross-examination, when Dr. Godwin was pressured by Sandre to admit the two "birthmarks" most likely appeared early in life and were probably hemangioma, Godwin sidestepped. When Sandre reminded Godwin that Dr. Thompson, in examining the torso at the autopsy, had called them "birthmarks," Godwin informed Sandre that Dr. Thompson was not a dermatologist.

Dr. Duane Manlove, Joyce Klindt's personal physician, then testified on Joyce's asthmatic condition. He said that asthmatics understand their particular condition better than the average patient, and that when an asthmatic, like Joyce, feels an attack coming on, he or she knows what medication to take.

The final witness of the day, Dr. Thomas Bennett, a pathologist, was also the Iowa State Medical Examiner. Dr. Bennett's qualifications were unquestionable. He was a board-certified anatomic, clinical, and forensic pathologist.

Dr. Bennett explained that forensic pathology is "where you look at sudden, violent, unnatural or unexpected injuries and deaths and the instruments that cause them." He said that he received a set of thirty-four tissue slides from Dr. Thompson, identified as "Jane Doe." Bennett examined the slides through a microscope to determine if the tissue had ever been frozen. He stated he found no traces of crystallization that would normally be found in artifacts that had been frozen.

During cross-examination, Sandre trapped himself. He presumed that slow freezing would be less likely to leave evidence of ice crystal formations in tissue. "Slow freezing can be a little more hidden than quick freezing, can't it?" he asked.

"Actually," said Dr. Bennett, "the reverse is true. The slower tissue is frozen, the more the tendency for larger crystals to form. It's like the crystals have time to build upon themselves. That's why when you quick-freeze something, they get very, very small crystals. They may not even show up."

The testimony concluded at 2:30 in the afternoon. In reality it had been little more than parrying between the defense and the expert witnesses. A major part of the day was spent trying to determine the dermatological aspects of the torso.

Up until Dr. Thomas Bennett's testimony, neither the prosecution nor the defense had scored many points. But Bennett's testimony laid waste to Sandre's earlier assumption that the torso might have been frozen and in the river for up to six months. Bennett's testimony was a classic example of one expert backing up another. The prosecution had closed on a winning note. Bill Davis had the defense on the run.

21

CONFLICTS OF INTEREST

When Bill Davis picked up a copy of the *Sioux City Journal* Thursday morning, he was furious. The "Wickersham brothers" were at it again. Two "ambulance-chasing" lawyers had come to Sioux City for a media blitz, arguing the true identity of the torso was that of a Cedar Rapids woman murdered by her husband. Davis had first met the attorneys in Keokuk and consented to allow a family member of the Lynn County victim to view pictures of the torso. Although the woman had said the torso was definitely not her sister, the lawyers refused to believe her. One had called Davis on Sunday, the day the prosecutor left for Sioux City, asking the prosecutor to run further tests on the torso. They argued. Davis hung up on him.

Testimony resumed at 8:43 a.m., November 8. Corporal Kern was first to take the stand. The chief evidence technician gave the jury a slight break from the complicated expert testimony.

Kern explained that he had not become involved in the Klindt case until October 1983, that he had been attending FBI school in Quantico. He spoke of the search for a qualified laboratory that could not only do traditional ABO blood typing but also had the serological expertise to perform analysis of blood subgroupings on partially decomposed tissue that had been immersed in water and subsequently frozen. He said that the Southwest Institute of Forensic Science in Dallas came highly recommended.

Dead Water

Kern told of Federal Expressing to Benita Harwood samples of muscle tissue and vertebrae that Dr. Stephens had removed from the torso, as well as whole blood samples taken from the Monahans and from Bart and Jim Klindt.

He spoke of the credentials of Clyde Snow, the forensic anthropologist, of driving overnight with Lieutenant Carroll to deliver the torso to Dr. Snow at the Oklahoma State Medical Examiner's office, and of the results of Snow's report.

Kern then told of telephoning the motor vehicle departments in all fifty states looking for Joyce A. Klindt or Joyce A. Monahan, of making contact with the National Crime Information Center in Washington, D.C., and of obtaining Joyce Klindt's dental records.

Sandre interrupted Kern's testimony on numerous occasions, always with the same complaint.

"I object, Your Honor. That's hearsay."

Havercamp overruled, explaining after the final objection, "I disagree, Mr. Sandre. I think it is not being offered to prove the truth of the matter asserted, but rather to provide a foundation or basis for the statistical or probability expert to follow."

Still, in his cross-examination, Sandre tried to discredit Kern and the information he was providing, especially the numbers of missing women reported by the NCIC. Sandre said the list was incomplete.

Dr. James W. Hanson, head of the Division of Medical Genetics at the University of Iowa, was sworn in following the morning recess. After the doctor had given his educational background, Bill Davis made it clear that Hanson was neither a witness for the State nor the defense, but rather for the court. Dr. Hanson's testimony was in large part a monologue.

"Doctor ... you are here both at my invitation and Mr. Scalise's," said Davis. "Would you explain to the jury, genetics?"

Verdict

"Before you all die," Hanson jested. "It could take a long time. I'm going to try to make this reasonably brief and clear."

Dr. Hanson tried to bring his complicated testimony down to the level of the audience. "Chromosomes are packages of genetic information that are found within every cell in our body ... A chemical called DNA controls genetic destiny, the DNA molecule is a blueprint of life ... Amino acids are the building blocks for proteins which tell the cell how to carry out various chemical processes, like turning sugar into energy.

"Genes come from a person's parents," Hanson said. "They are transmitted from generation to generation ... It is important to recognize that when so-called genetic tests are done, one is not actually examining the gene itself, but rather the 'products' of the gene."

Hanson then talked about one method of genetic testing. "Electrophoresis is one of the most reliable methods that we know of now. It's the type of test in which you expose the material to an electric field and try to separate the different kinds of proteins according to differences in their electric fields ... It is certainly among the state-of-the-art techniques.

"There is a problem with interpreting genetic tests, because there are very few genes that are unique to a single individual. In considering whether a group of genes identifies a particular person, one needs to know how frequent those genes are in other people that are similar to that individual you are testing."

Hanson stated that the scientist must rely on "statistics," finding that frequency as a percentage and multiplying it times the frequency other enzymes are found. Each multiplication makes the fraction smaller and eventually the scientist will reach a high degree of probability as to identification.

Hanson went on to say that if a direct root cannot be found, then it is not uncommon for the scientist to compare the genes of the parents with the offspring to achieve identification.

"What is AK, is that an enzyme?" Davis asked.

"Yes, that's the initials for a specific enzyme, adenylate kinase, which has a particular kind of chemical function in allowing energy production and utilization in the body."

"Does everyone have AK?"

"Well, presumably so, as far as we know," said the doctor. "Not having any of that enzyme activity, we think, could not be compatible with life."

"Am I right in saying; you would be dead without it?"

"Or wouldn't have been alive to begin with," replied Hanson.

"Now problems can occur in the interpretation of genetic testing," the doctor continued. "If the test gives you a misleading result that says something is present and it's not, that's called a false positive. If it gives you a misleading result that says something was missing and it's really present, then that is called a false negative."

In his cross-examinations, Scalise concentrated on a single argument, that not finding an enzyme present in a tissue sample of an unidentified woman that is present in a child would be strong evidence that unidentified person is not the parent of the child. Dr. Hanson agreed under certain parameters.

The enzyme Scalise spoke of, the enzyme tested for and not found, was AK — adenylate kinase.

In redirect, Davis asked, "It is just everyone has AK or they wouldn't be alive?"

"In terms of the actual chemical effect ... as far as we know, AK is a necessary enzyme."

Bill Davis had made his point.

Benita Harwood followed Hanson. The forensic serologist from Dallas, who testified at the first trial, explained her involvement in the case. She said she had typed the torso's blood as A, the same ABO typing as Joyce Klindt. She spoke of the enzymes and antigens called phenotypes found in body

Verdict

tissue. She talked of finding six genetic markers in the tissue sample of the torso's tissue which were used as a means of identifying its genetic makeup. She then compared the incidence the phenotypes found in the tissue sample with the Caucasian population.

Despite the defense's disagreement with Harwood's numbers at the first trial, the serologist refused to back off from her conclusions. She said that only 27 in 10,000 would have the same genetic markers as those found in the torso.

She then stated that she requested and received from the Davenport Police Department whole blood samples taken from the Monahans. She concluded after analysis that, yes, these two individuals could indeed produce an offspring that had the genetic makeup found in the torso, that this couple was 107.8 times more likely than a random couple to produce an offspring with the genetic makeup found in the torso's tissue sample.

Harwood said she also requested and received whole blood samples drawn from Bartley and James Klindt. By looking at the genetic makeup of the father, assumptions can be made as to what genes came from the mother. She concluded the torso could have been the boy's mother.

Expecting a lengthy cross-examination, Judge Havercamp recessed the proceedings for an early lunch. This allowed Davis to get Harwood and Mark Stolorow together. Stolorow, a forensic serologist from Illinois, was invited to Sioux City for one reason: to corroborate the testimony of Benita Harwood.

The county attorney had observed the effectiveness of one expert backing another the previous day, when Bennett sanctioned Thompson. If Mark Stolorow had similar success in validating Benita Harwood's findings, the prosecutor felt sure the jury would be in the right frame of mind to accept the upcoming statistical evidence.

When Davis left Stolorow and Harwood in the sixth-floor law library, he had no idea a major point of contention would develop between the two serologists. An argument flared. Fortunately, Rick Chase was there to referee.

Davis was on his way back into the courtroom when the elevator doors opened. Rick Chase, Harwood, and Stolorow stepped out. The two serologists were in a huff. "Bill, we've got a problem," Chase said.

The prosecutor listened to Stolorow's argument contesting Harwood's calculations.

"Is there any way to get around your objections?" Davis asked.

Stolorow shrugged. "I don't think so."

"Then you think Benita is wrong?"

"I'm not arguing procedure. I just don't think her numbers are valid."

"Don't worry about your differences, Mark. Just answer my questions honestly."

Suddenly Chase interrupted. "Can we help you, Larry?"

Davis glanced up to see Lawrence Scalise duck into a nearby doorway. The stealthy defense counselor, who had viewed the exchange from a distance, had been trying to get within earshot of the conversation. Chase had spotted him sneaking down the hallway.

"Did he hear any of this?" Davis whispered.

"I don't think so," Chase replied.

It was the first time since he had arrived in Sioux City that Bill Davis was concerned. He knew all too well that Scalise would try to pick Harwood's testimony apart during cross-examination. As a peer, Stolorow's backing would advance Harwood's credibility. On the other hand, if the defense attorney knew that two expert witnesses were at odds it could be devastating. If Stolorow showed even a whiff of reservation during direct examination Scalise would sniff it out.

22

THE NUMBERS GAME

As Davis expected, Scalise attacked both Harwood's methodology and her results. First, he argued that Harwood had used too low a frequency ratio, that blood type A occurs in 37 percent of the Caucasian population rather than 27 percent and that change alone would lower the probability that the Monahans were the parents of the torso from 107 times more time likely to seventy times more likely than a couple selected at random.

"That's literally millions and millions of people, isn't it?"

"Yes, it would be a large number," Harwood replied.

The defense attorney spoke of contamination and claimed that bacteria itself gives off enzymatic activity.

"Bacteria does affect blood typing, does it not?" Scalise asked.

"Bacteria in its putrification of a substance causes a very high acidity level to be produced in its breakdown. This is turn causes hemolysis, or the bursting of the red blood cells. I found no evidence of that."

Scalise then spoke of the frequency that each separate enzyme found in the torso's tissue sample occurred in the Caucasian population in a percentage basis. Miss Harwood had to agree that if each enzyme reading was taken by itself, it would hold little significance in proving the torso was Joyce Klindt. Only when taken as a statistical whole and compared with the Caucasian population in general did the enzymes become significant.

"So the best you can say, Miss Harwood, is that you cannot exclude the torso as being the mother of Bart Klindt and the offspring of the Monahans, true?"

"That is correct."

"Let's face it, Miss Harwood. What you're doing is not an exact science, is it?"

Harwood's answer was curious. "I don't think genetic identification will ever be an exact science ... such as a fingerprint."

At times, Scalise loomed over Harwood, causing numerous objections by Davis and rulings by Havercamp. In reality, the defense attorney's statistical logic was severely flawed.

Davis was satisfied with the flow of the trial. Benita Harwood's performance was solid. She had been more convincing than in Keokuk. Scalise had treated the woman with such lack of respect that he must certainly have looked a villain in the eyes of the jury.

Mark Stolorow, the serology coordinator for the Illinois Department of Law Enforcement, Bureau of Scientific Services, Training and Applications Laboratory, took the stand. A scholar and an author, Stolorow had the curriculum vitae and list of published works to make him a shoo-in for membership in the "Who's Who" of forensic serology.

The serologist had published papers on electrophoresis, the same process used by Benita Harwood. He also said he had worked on several dozen cases during the past fourteen years in which the body delivered from the morgue to his laboratory had been submerged in water.

Stolorow assured the jurors that if tissue contamination was present it would be obvious to the serologist "through the course of the procedure and appearance and behavior of the sample during testing."

"Would you employ the same methods as Benita Harwood?" Davis asked.

Verdict

"I'm familiar with the general procedures that she used. I don't know if I can fairly answer from my own knowledge of her hands-on work in this case, whether it is step-by-step, plate-by-plate, that I would use exactly the same procedures that she does, but I don't mean to split hairs here. In general, the procedures she uses are the ones we use and are generally accepted by the forensic science community."

Despite his differences with Benita Harwood, Mark Stolorow's succinct testimony was extremely damaging to the defense. His answers were precise and more important, easy for the jurors to understand. He never paused, never stuttered. In less than ten minutes, Stolorow had countered every point Scalise had gained against Harwood. By the time he finished, the only question the defense wanted to ask Mark Stolorow was how soon he could be on a plane out of Sioux City.

Scalise glanced over the top of his gold-rims. "Nice to see you again, Doctor."

"It's Mister," Stolorow replied, correcting the defense attorney.

Havercamp, realizing that Scalise wanted no part of Mark Stolorow, dismissed the witness.

Clyde Collins Snow, the globe-trotting forensic anthropologist from Oklahoma, followed Stolorow. Like Harwood, Snow had learned from his testimony in Keokuk. He proceeded to show slides of the defleshed and reassembled skeletonized remains of the human torso.

Bill Davis asked, "What kind of finding were you able to make?"

Snow said that he was able to draw several conclusions. He estimated the age of the torso to be twenty-seven to forty, with a mid-point of thirty-three and one-half years, the height five feet to five feet six inches, and the victim's weight from 125 to 145 pounds.

Dead Water

While Scalise was folksy and very clever, Sandre was just plain shrewd. In his cross-examination, Sandre flattered Snow and then attacked. "Doctor, your credentials are obviously superior. You don't need me to say that for you, but let me ask you this: Your correct specialty is forensic anthropology, is that right?"

"Yes, sir."

"You are not an anatomist, are you?"

Dr. Snow replied that while he did not have a degree in anatomy, physical anthropology overlaps with anatomy and the two are closely related fields.

"So you would say you are also an anatomist?"

"No, I would not say ..."

Sandre cut him off. "Are you a physiologist?"

"No, sir."

"Would you say you are a biochemist?"

"No, sir."

"And you are not a pathologist either, are you?"

"No, I'm not a pathologist."

"You are not a medical doctor, is that true?"

"No, sir."

"Now I take it, Doctor, that part of your work in forensic anthropology involves really examining remains and using the training and scientific works that have been published and the tests that are available in your field to make estimates with respect to those remains, correct?"

"Estimates of age and sex, race, stature, yes, sir."

"All the estimates you made for us here today?"

"Not only from training and using the knowledge of the scientific field, but also based on experience," said the doctor.

"Of course ... Thank you. And that's why you told the jury about certain scientific principles, and some of them have names like symphysium — pronounce that to me."

"Pubic symphysis."

Verdict

"There's another method called Dr. Steele's method, is that right?"

"Gentry Steele. That is the one I referred to in using the fragmentary statural estimates."

"There is the Gilbert and McKern study that you employed, correct?"

"Yes—based on my age estimate from pubic symphysis."

"There is also one called the Snow regression method?"

"Yes, sir."

"Maybe named it after yourself, I don't know," Sandre said caustically.

Snow was unruffled. "No, I didn't name it after myself. Generally those things get in when you publish a paper."

"And after you do all of that arithmetic, you are nevertheless left, are you not, Doctor, with an estimate as opposed to a precise figure?"

"That's largely the nature of any kind of scientific endeavor," Snow said flatly.

Sandre continued, noting that by using a combination of two formulas to achieve a particular measurement, the scientist doubles his chance for error, not that it mattered, because in the end, "You sort of eye-balled it."

The doctor took offense. "Well, I don't like the term 'eye-balling.' I think it's based on a lot of experience ... seeing a great many bodies, more or less in this shape, and being able from my own scientific observations to narrow that down."

"But not on the basis of any scientific ..."

"I didn't use any formulas."

Having made his point, Sandre backed off. "Whether you take the ranges that you first came up with and reduced them, you are still talking about millions and millions and millions of adult women human beings, correct?"

Dr. Snow acknowledged the fact and after a few more exchanges, was excused.

During recess, a meeting was held in the judge's chambers. Sandre strongly objected to the testimony of the next witness, statistician Russell Lenth.

"I believe I've already made that ruling in writing and given a copy to counsel," Havercamp replied.

"That's correct," said Scalise.

Havercamp shook his head. "All right, if you must, Mr. Sandre. Go ahead."

"I just wanted the record to reflect that I'm incorporating the entire thing once again, if that's all right?" Sandre asked.

Havercamp's reply was laced with sarcasm. "Three times is always better than twice."

Sandre then proceeded to lay out his complicated objection, reiterating the evidence collected by Kern was skewed and the statistics to be presented by Lenth were, therefore, misleading.

"Let me remind you, Mr. Sandre," Havercamp replied, "that these same objections were heard and reargued at the proceedings in Lee County, Iowa. I don't think I have anything to add to the ruling I previously made."

Sandre was not finished. "In addition to the foundation objections, Your Honor, the defendant also asserts to this witness's testimony a relevancy objection. I believe it is what other courts have called the 'mystique of the mathematical demonstration.' It creates undue prejudice in the jurors' minds."

Sandre's argument fell on deaf ears. At 3:55 p.m., Russell V. Lenth, the statistician from the University of Iowa, was called to testify. Sandre interrupted immediately, objecting before Lenth had a chance to give his curriculum vitae. The judge acknowledged Sandre, overruled his objection, and the proceedings continued.

"Why don't you tell us what a statistician does. What is a statistician?" asked Wells.

Verdict

"A statistician takes data or the facts that are known, evidence, and tries to demonstrate what is likely to be true and what is not likely to be true."

"And how do you go about doing that?"

"You apply laws of probability."

"Laws and rules that you as an expert know about?"

"Yes."

"As I understand you, people, corporations, and associations rely upon your work?"

"Certainly."

"Could you give these people an example of who would rely on your work?" asked Wells.

"Your Honor," Sandre intruded, "that's objected to as self-serving."

Havercamp frowned. "Objection is overruled."

Lenth named the types of businesses and sciences that employ statisticians.

"Doctor, were you contacted by us to do some statistical analysis ... with regard to this case?"

"Yes."

"And did we provide you with data, information which you termed facts, in order to do that analysis."

"Yes."

"Did you do the analysis for us?"

"Yes, I did."

"Did you come up with some conclusions?"

"Yes ... I prepared a report from which this chart was made."

"Doctor, what information did you have, what data, facts did we provide you with?"

"You provided me with ..."

"Excuse me, Doctor," said Sandre, interrupting for the third time. "Your Honor, I will assert the same objection previously

Dead Water

urged in chambers and I ask that it remain standing as to this portion of the testimony, particularly that as to hearsay."

"Your standing objection was to all his testimony," said Havercamp, annoyed. "You either have a standing objection or you don't. If you want to continue to reurge it, you can reurge it every sentence. Do you want it to stand?"

"I want it to stand, Your Honor."

"It will stand."

Lenth then described the data he was provided with, explaining not all information was usable. The chart, State's Exhibit No. 153, was received into evidence.

Name	Age	Summary of Likelihood Computations Mother x Not Strl x Type A x OSP =				Lkhd	%
Klindt	33	1.00	1.000	1.000	.500	.500	98.15
Fransi	27	1.00	.839	.362	.00764	.00232	.46
Tharp	29	1.00	.772	.362	.00764	.00214	.42
Khatib	37	1.00	.542	.362	.00764	.00150	.29

The first column listed names, representing the four missing women from a four-state area who could not be eliminated by Dennis Kern as possible identities for the torso: Joyce Klindt, Peggy Fransi, Nancy Tharp, and Nahida Khatib. The second column indicated the age of those women as of April 18, 1983; the third, motherhood; the fourth, those not surgically sterilized, the fifth, blood type; the sixth and seventh, the calculations of Benita Harwood.

Lenth explained he arrived at his end calculations, column eight, the likelihood of the torso being Joyce Klindt, by using the product rule.

"How do you demonstrate to a first-year statistics class, freshmen in college, the products rule?" Wells asked.

"Well, the easiest thing to do is probably to flip coins."

Verdict

"Okay. Fair enough. If I have a penny right here, one coin, and if we presume it is a fair coin, if I flip that coin in the air ... what's the probability in statistical terms it is going to come up heads?"

"It would be one-half, or one out of two."

"If I gave you a dime ... and we each flip our coins ... what's the possibility of both of them coming up heads?"

"To figure that out what you must know that there are four possible outcomes of the experiment. It they are fair coins, the probability they would both come up heads is one in four."

"Using multiplication, is there a shortcut in the way you can figure that?"

"The shortcut method is to observe the probability of heads for the penny is one-half, the probability of heads for the dime is one-half ... Because the penny and the dime are what's called independent, you can multiply those two numbers together ... that's one-fourth ..."

"If I gave Mr. Sandre a nickel ... and all three of us flipped our coins at the same time, how do you figure the probability they're all going to come up heads?"

"The probability would be one-half times one-half times one-half; that would be one-eighth."

"Is that what you used to calculate the figures there?" asked Wells, pointing to the column "Other Six Phenotypes."

"Yes, it is."

"And what do those figures mean?"

"These are the probabilities. Again, we do not know the tissue phenotypes of these individuals. These are the probabilities that these individuals would match the torso in all six phenotypes.

"I notice the next column is entitled 'Likelihood,' and there is an equal sign before it. How did you come to calculate that particular column?"

"Well, very much in the same manner. Each of these numbers in the phenotypes was obtained as a product of six numbers in Benita Harwood's calculations."

"Those were the six phenotypes that Benita Harwood identified?"

"Yes. And again, it is reasonable to assume that the incidence of motherhood, the incidence of sterility and blood type, and these other tissue phenotypes are independent. Consequently, I simply multiplied these numbers together."

"What is the definition, in statistical language, of likelihood?"

"It is the possibility of observing these factors."

"It doesn't have anything to do with percentages?"

"No ..."

"And your total is correct as far as you know, the math is right?"

"Yes."

"Okay, so what does your last column, percent of total show you?"

"My last column says there's a 98 percent chance that the torso is Joyce Klindt."

"And that's the bottom line?"

"Yes."

"Is it statistically valid?"

"Yes. Of course, there is always subjective information that could not be quantified, such as where the body was found and the date since last seen."

"Could you clarify that?"

"Okay. The body was found in the Quad Cities and that's where Joyce was last seen ..."

"Objection, Your Honor. That's outside the scope of the witness."

Havercamp agreed. "It is improper foundation ... Sustained."

Verdict

John Sandre, who opened the cross-examination by admitting, "I don't understand a lot about figures," proceeded to give his statement validity. The defense counselor seemed destined to prove the "mystique of mathematical demonstration" he had spoken of in the judge's chambers.

He tried to argue from the standpoint of logic, using the standard words of a lawyer. It truly bothered Sandre that absolutely nothing was known about the other three women involved in the study, that they were only statistics. He finally forced common ground by getting Lenth to admit that a statistical study is no better than the accuracy of the numbers provided.

"Let's start from the beginning, Doctor. You base your entire calculations on several assumptions. One assumption is that there are only four people on this planet who could possibly be that torso, isn't that correct?"

"That's right."

"And that's information given to you by Corporal Kern?"

"That's right."

"That's assumption number one. You also operate from a basic assumption, and that is as to the truth and accuracy of the work done by Benita Harwood, correct?"

"That's right."

"That's assumption number two. Assumption number three is the reliance of certain figures provided to you, either by Corporal Kern or by the National Public Health Service, or somebody of that sort, correct?"

"Yes."

Sandre then pointed out that a letter had been sent to Lenth cautioning him on using the figures concerning mothers who were surgically sterile.

Lenth acknowledged, "There were some standard errors reported with the figures."

"And you were provided with a national average incidence of type A blood in white persons of .362, correct?"

"Yes."

"Okay. Now if any of these matters are in error, Doctor ... your ultimate conclusion is in error, too; you would agree with that, wouldn't you?"

"Of course."

"Doctor, there is a concept known as pair independence, is there not?"

"Yes."

"And as I understand it, you tell me if I'm wrong, the significance of that concept is that in statistics it means you can't validly multiply more than two events together. You cannot multiply six events together."

Dr. Lenth told Sandre he was wrong. "You're referring to the distinction between pairwise independence and mutual independence, and if you have pairwise independence but you do not have mutual independence, that means you cannot multiply more than two of them together."

Lawyers do not deal in probability; they deal in percentages. Sandre quickly went back to assumptions. "Okay. So you have knowns of the torso, we have gone through those, correct?"

"Uh-huh."

"And you have knowns of Joyce Klindt, and we have gone through those, correct?"

"That's right."

"And you add to that equation three people that you know nothing about, except for the fact of their age and whether or not they're a mother, isn't that correct?"

"I'll say again ..."

Sandre interrupted. "Is that correct?"

"That's correct."

"The only two things you know about those other three people, and on the basis of all that, you are asked to make a

Verdict

calculation upon who the most likely candidate that torso is, correct?"

"That's right."

"And you come up with Joyce Klindt, correct?"

"Yes."

"How could it be anybody else, Doctor?"

Lenth looked at Sandre as if he were an idiot. "I don't know how to answer that."

"Do you want to answer the question?" Havercamp asked.

"I didn't think he was going to answer it, Judge," Sandre sneered. "Answer it if you can."

"Well, obviously, it could be someone else, but the point of these calculations is that although it is a 50 percent coin flip here, it is a flip of an extremely biased coin ... that if we were to find out more information about these three people, that they would almost certainly be eliminated from the list."

"Doctor, you don't know anything about the genetic marking of Peggy Fransi, Nancy Tharp, or the other young lady, do you?"

"No, I don't."

"You don't know whether their phenotype incidence is .00764, which is the general average for the whole population, or whether it is something higher or lower, do you?"

"That's a misstatement of probability."

"You don't ..."

Lenth interrupted. "Their phenotype incidence is either one or zero, but the probability that one of these — Peggy Fransi would come up with a one on the phenotype incidence is .00764."

"Well, that's because you already determined the torso can't be Peggy Fransi, correct?"

"NO."

"She can't be Peggy Fransi, then she obviously can't have a very high likelihood of having six phenotypes, isn't that what you are saying?"

"NO, that's not what I'm saying."

"Doctor ..."

Lenth cut Sandre off again. "She either has phenotypes or she doesn't."

"And you don't know?"

"And she almost surely doesn't."

"You don't know that, that's not your field. Have you ever tested her?"

"That's irrelevant."

Sandre was contemptuous. "Is it?"

"Yes."

"Is that your objection to the question, that it's irrelevant?"

"Your Honor," Wells cut in, "I think he's starting to badger the witness."

"I think the witness can take care of himself. Go ahead," said Judge Havercamp, obviously enjoying the exchange.

"Doctor, if you have knowns of the torso and you have knowns of an individual and you have three individuals who you have virtually no knowns of and you try to predict which one of those four people is going to identify most closely with the torso, isn't it a self-fulfilling prophecy that it will be the individual you have knowns about?"

"No, it is not."

"In this case it is not?"

"It is not."

"The same knowns that you identify with the torso are the very SAME knowns that you have for Joyce Klindt."

"Objection, Judge. The question has been answered."

"Objection overruled."

"Twice," said Wells.

"Objection is OVERRULED."

Verdict

"I'll strike the question anyway," said Sandre. "Doctor, knowns and unknowns are sort of like apples and oranges, aren't they?"

"Would you clarify the question, please."

"Well, let me ask you another question.

"Doctor, did you ever hear the story about the statistician who drowned in the river that had an average depth of two feet, did you ever hear that story?"

"I have heard similar stories," Lenth replied coolly.

Bill Davis was pleased with Lenth's performance. The exchanges between the statistician and Sandre sounded more like an argument than a cross-examination, a fact the prosecutor felt sure was not lost to the jury. The defense attorney's clever knack for twisting numbers did little to dissuade Lenth, who remained positive about his findings to the final affront.

In reality, circumstantial evidence is nothing more than a mental compilation of statistics. The "improper foundation" that Judge Havercamp had so judiciously avoided, "subjective information that could not be quantified," could not be taken out of play. For when a jury deals with circumstances it does make a difference WHERE the torso was found, WHEN Joyce Klindt disappeared, and more importantly, WHO had last seen her alive.

23

SUBTLE CHANGES

Friday, November 9, was cold and dreary. The prosecution had spent more than two days establishing the identity of the torso. With that accomplished, Bill Davis set out to prove Jim Klindt guilty of murder.

Between the trials, the prosecutor had used his time wisely. He had recruited psychologist Daniel Petersen to discuss the loss of Joyce with her parents. Davis sensed the Keokuk jury had perceived Virginia Monahan as unemotional. He also felt the State had made a critical mistake by not putting the victim's father, Eugene, on the stand.

Petersen had conferred with the Monahans Thursday night. The psychologist told Joyce's parents not to be afraid to show sorrow when they testified. "It is important to let your emotions flow," he said. "You have nothing to be ashamed of. After all, you've had your only daughter taken from you. It has to be a devastating loss."

The prosecutor felt confident as the grief-stricken father took the stand. Davis kept the questions simple. Monahan testified of his relationship and love for his daughter. He said she never missed sending him a card on his birthday or Father's Day. By the time Scalise rose to cross-examine him, Eugene Monahan wept openly.

The defense attorney quizzed the schoolteacher about his daughter's measurements and hair color. Mr. Monahan said that Joyce was not the petite woman everyone made her out to be and that "Joyce's hair was reddish-brown." It was not the answer Scalise wanted or expected to hear.

Verdict

Because Bill Davis had not asked Eugene Monahan to testify at the first trial, there was little the defense could do but accept the physical characteristics Monahan ascribed to his daughter. The prosecutor's oversight in Keokuk now looked to be a stroke of genius.

Bill Davis had urged Elizabeth Reed to speak with Virginia Monahan about wearing more conservative clothing to the second trial. Elizabeth had recruited one of the Monahan's sons, Jerry, who in turn advised his mother on more appropriate attire. In Sioux City, Mrs. Monahan's apparel was in marked contrast to what she had worn in Keokuk. Gone were the large hoop earrings and the bright-colored dress. Virginia Monahan now conveyed the image of an anguished mother, stepping into the witness box wearing a simple black dress and squeezing a white handkerchief.

Much of her testimony corresponded with that in Keokuk, though she did describe Joyce's hips as being larger than she had indicated at the first trial.

"Well, tell us a little about Joyce's hair," said Davis. "Was she like most women, did she play with it a bit?"

"Most people have brown or red or black or blonde hair. My sons both have red hair. But you really couldn't pinpoint the color of Joyce's hair."

"Do you know for sure what Joyce's hair color was?"

"No, not for sure."

During the cross-examination, Scalise jumped all over Virginia Monahan.

"Mrs. Monahan, your daughter was not red-headed, was she?"

"Joyce could have had a reddish cast to her hair. As I stated, it was ... you really couldn't pinpoint the color."

"You remember taking your deposition with Mr. Shinkle present, do you remember that?"

"Yes, I do."

Dead Water

"Would you read this, ma'am?" Scalise said handing Mrs. Monahan the transcript.

"It says, I said she wasn't red-headed."

"What's your response now?"

"The same, she wasn't red-headed."

Scalise scanned the page. "Would you read this ma'am?"

"I said she didn't like the color of her hair."

"What color did you say it was?"

"You have here, I said it was dish-water blonde."

"That was your answer, wasn't it?"

"Well, as I stated ..."

"Wait a minute, ma'am. That was your answer, wasn't it?"

"That answer wasn't complete."

"Well, ma'am on the very next page, I asked you, 'She wasn't red-headed?' Your answer was 'No. She wanted red hair, but no.' That was complete, wasn't it?"

"Well, that would be a more definite answer than the other."

"Well, ma'am, she wasn't brown-haired, was she?"

"She had some brown in her hair."

"And she wasn't red-headed, was she?"

"Her hair had a reddish cast."

"You've never told me that before today, have you?"

"As I said, you didn't give me time to complete my answer."

"Well, it seems you've changed your answer since Keokuk."

Mrs. Monahan explained, "Joyce's hair got darker as she got older and she was always doing something with the color anyway."

While she testified Virginia Monahan showed both anger and hurt. Now she was crying. Scalise tried to back off, but the damage had been done. Bullying a grieving mother is one tactic that does not set well with a jury.

Although the defense argued with Mrs. Monahan over the subtle changes she had made in her testimony concerning

Verdict

Joyce's hair color and hip size, she was merely reiterating what her husband had previously stated. Together, their testimony helped shore up one of the major problems which had cropped up in Keokuk. They both seemed convinced the torso was their daughter.

After lunch the sledding got even rougher for the defense. Clifford Reed, once a close friend of Jim Klindt, could not hold back his loathing for the defendant. Throughout Reed's testimony, he glared at the man who had betrayed his trust.

Conversely, Elizabeth Reed, the day's last witness, was cool and convincing as she wrapped the jurors around her little finger. Unlike in Keokuk, she was in control of her emotions, accepting the fact that her best friend Joyce was "no longer."

John Sandre failed to gain a point during cross-examination of Mrs. Reed. He could crack neither the woman's story nor her resolve.

The trial was going so well that Bill Davis decided to remain in Sioux City during the Veterans Day weekend. His assistant, Doug Wells, drove back to Davenport to be with his new bride. Rick Chase, a twenty-nine-year-old bachelor, remained with Davis, and the two men continued to work on the case.

Wells arrived back in Sioux City late Monday evening. He found Chase and Davis in the motel bar.

"Don't most people gain weight over a holiday weekend," Chase said, nudging Davis. "Looks like Wells here has lost a little. What do you think, Bill?"

The sexual innuendo found the prosecutor's mind elsewhere. "I'm sorry, Rick. What did you say?"

"It wasn't important," said Chase. "Why so serious?"

"Oh, I was just thinking about Marty getting married last Saturday and me not being there. She's almost like a daughter. You know, when someone's been your secretary for six years it doesn't seem right to miss the biggest day in her life."

Wells ordered a draft beer. "Anything exciting happen while I was gone?" he asked.

The line snapped Davis out of the doldrums. "Well, it's not every day you get thrown out of a laundromat," he said pointing an accusing finger at Chase.

"Rick didn't take a spin in one of the dryers again, did he?"

The young officer seemed embarrassed. "Hell, no," he said defensively. "All I did was sit on a table. The manager of the joint got pissed off and kicked us out."

The look on Chase's face struck Wells silly. The tension built up from his eight-and-a-half-hour drive was released in convulsions. "You mean to tell me that some son-of-a-bitch threw a Davenport cop and the Scott County Attorney out of his goddamned laundromat for sitting on a table?" he roared, tears streaming down his face.

The laughter was contagious. The three men nearly got thrown out of the lounge.

Tuesday morning, November 13, found Davis peppering the defense with an array of State witnesses; Ted Carroll, Evelyn Martin, Gayle Girt, Rick Chase, Dom Giametta and Lea Edwards from Fred's Phillip's 66, and Joyce's cousin, Diana Iossi.

During the afternoon, the prosecutor fought ten more rounds with the defendant's mother. Geraldine Klindt was even more obstinate than she had been in Keokuk. She fought hard to protect her "Jimmy," adding that she thought she had recently spotted Joyce in Davenport.

Davis glared at Scalise. The defense counselor shrugged as if to say, this is the first he'd heard of it.

"I guess I should be getting used to these little surprises," Davis muttered, losing his temper. "But I'm not."

The prosecutor's barrage left Mrs. Klindt's story in shambles. He upbraided her for not bringing the sighting to the

Verdict

authorities and insinuated she was lying. The big woman glanced around, searching for help or, perhaps, someplace to hide.

During the short time Bill Davis had known Geraldine Klindt, he gained great insight into her personality. After watching her in Ted Carroll's lengthy video-taped interview and doing battle with her for two trials, the prosecutor felt he knew Mrs. Klindt pretty well. But while it is easy to lay blame on parents for their children's wrongdoings, Davis held Jim Klindt responsible for his actions. He also understood a mother's desperation in trying to save her only child. Still, Davis found it impossible to feel sorry for the woman. He was more inclined to pity the man who had devoted his life to wife and son. Dick Klindt took the stand.

The defendant's father appeared nervous and frequently glanced at his wife and son while he was questioned by Davis. The prosecutor queried the retired chiropractor about renting space to Dr. Dennis Hagemann and subsequently to Terry Keuhn. The old man's demeanor calmed, and he smiled as he described the hairdresser. "She's a really nice girl. Like her a lot."

"Did she live with your son?" Davis asked.

"I don't know that. Bart did say one time, 'We got a new housekeeper.' I presumed it was Terry."

"Did you advertise to rent space in your house after Dr. Hagemann moved out?"

"No. Jim just sort of moved her in."

"It must have been a lot of work to transform a chiropractic office into a beauty shop."

"Uh-huh."

"Who did the work?"

The old man looked perplexed. "Huh?"

"Did you hire a contractor?"

"Uh, no. Jim did most of the work."

Dick Klindt's testimony ended with his parroting his wife's version of what had happened on March 18, 1983. The defense had no questions.

Jim Klindt's former associate, Dr. Dennis Hagemann, was the last witness of the day. He again refuted Mrs. Klindt's testimony, stating that she had told him the defendant had acted like a "beaten pup" upon hearing Joyce had retained Sy Raben as her attorney.

On Wednesday morning, Bill Davis glossed over Jeffrey Ryan. Jim Klindt's best friend had been a thorn in the prosecutor's side in Keokuk, and Davis was determined not to allow a repeat performance.

In his cross-examination, Scalise continued to argue that Joyce Klindt was still alive. After all, both Jeffrey Ryan and Geraldine Klindt had testified they had seen her since the date she disappeared. But Davis felt sure from watching the jurors' faces that they did not believe either story.

The rest of the day was a repeat of testimony heard in Keokuk; the Lampos, Chuck Seitz, Marie Smith, Finley Gunn, and Shirley Burmeister.

Thursday began with more minor witnesses. Mike Kernan confirmed that Shirley Burmeister had worked the morning of March 18, 1983, when he presented the prosecutor with the waitress's time card. William Marturello's testimony concerned the insurance check for repairing the Jetta that was found among Joyce's possessions at the Reed house. Since it was never cashed, the defendant had persuaded the company to reissue the check in May of 1984.

Tammy Dickinson then testified about Klindt's large purchase of gold chains from Peterson's Department Store and about how the defendant tried to pay for the jewelry with Joyce Klindt's canceled credit card.

Verdict

Between the trials, Bill Davis had tried to figure a way to lay the question concerning Joyce's hair color to rest. He felt that Virginia Monahan had added to the confusion in Keokuk when she had called Joyce a dishwater blonde. The prosecutor had broached the subject with his wife, Sharon, while sitting at home one evening in September of 1984.

"Why don't you find her hairdresser?" Sharon said.

Davis had been dumbfounded by the simplicity of her response. He picked up the phone and called Ted Carroll.

"The State calls Patti Hummel."

Hummel, a five-foot-two, hundred-and-ten-pound beautician took the stand.

"Did you know a woman named Joyce Klindt?" Wells asked.

"Yes," she whispered.

"Could you speak up?" asked Judge Havercamp.

Hummel swallowed hard and nodded. "Yes," she repeated.

"Were you friends?"

"Yes."

"Did you ever go shopping together?"

"Yes."

"Where did you go?"

"We'd go to North Park and shop for clothes."

"Do you know what size Joyce wore?"

"Yes, size nine. She always bought size nine."

"Was she bigger than you?"

"How do you mean?" Hummel asked.

Wells smiled. "Taller?"

"Yes."

"What did she weigh, 110?"

"No, more than that. Maybe 125, 130."

"And was she bigger around the hips than you?"

The hairdresser blushed.

"We're not trying to embarrass you," Wells assured her. "We just want to give the jury a model to go by."

"Yes, she was bigger around the hips than me."

Wells nodded and turned his attention to the color of Joyce's hair. "Are you, in fact, a licensed hairdresser?"

"Yes."

"And did you cut Joyce Klindt's hair?"

"Yes."

"About how often?"

Patti thought for a moment. "I cut it every month and frosted it every three."

"What do you do when you frost someone's hair?"

"You highlight it by bleaching the hair so you have an overall blonde look."

"Is that the same thing as bleaching someone's hair totally?"

"No. You leave a few strands of hair unbleached so the natural color of the hair shows through."

"Was Joyce's hair frosted quite a bit?"

"Quite heavily, yes."

"Did she like her hair frosted?"

"Yes. She felt it complemented the gray in front."

"She had a gray streak in front?"

"She had a lot of gray in front."

"Did you attempt to cover that gray when you were doing her hair?"

"Yes, that was part of it."

"During the time you were cutting, frosting, and working with Joyce's hair, were you able to determine the natural color?"

"Yes, I saw it all the time, yes."

"What was the color?"

"Kind of a light brown, slight reddish highlight, but a good light brown color."

Verdict

Davis had turned so he could watch Scalise's reaction. The defense attorney shook his head, almost imperceptibly, never raising his eyes.

"Was it blonde, dishwater blonde?" Wells asked.

"No."

"No further questions, Your Honor."

The only approach John Sandre could take in his cross-examination was to try to discredit the witness. "Mrs. Hummel, if friends and relatives described Joyce's hair as dishwater blonde, would you disagree with that?"

"I can see how they would say that."

"Yes, but you disagree with them?"

"Yes, it was not dishwater blonde."

"I'm talking about friends and relatives who have known her longer than you."

Wells jumped to his feet. "Objection, Your Honor, the question has already been answered."

"Overruled," said Havercamp.

"Let me finish my question, Mrs. Hummel," Sandre continued. "How about the parents of Joyce Klindt; would you suspect that they ought to know the natural hair color of their daughter at least as well as you?"

"I know Joyce always colored her hair. I don't know when she started to do things to it, so I don't know."

"You don't know?"

"If they would have or not."

"You don't know whether they would know her natural hair color at least as well as you?"

"Probably they would, yes."

That was the only concession that Sandre got from Patti Hummel. As far as Davis was concerned, it wasn't much. Furthermore, the prosecutor did not understand the defense attorney's line of questioning. Joyce's parents had already told the jurors that the color of their daughter's hair was reddish-brown.

The following morning, Davis called Terry Keuhn to testify. Scalise must have said something to Terry about her choice of colors in Keokuk. Today she wore brown. Bill Davis was more blunt in his questioning of Jim Klindt's mistress, treating Terry like a trollop. He refrained from using soft terms like making love, asking instead, "Did you have SEX?"

Finally, the time had come to introduce the tape recording. Davis realized it was not the powerful piece of evidence he once thought. Nevertheless, the recording gave critical insight into the nasty character of James Klindt.

"Doug, give me the tape."

Wells's mouth fell open. "Hell, I don't have it."

The color drained from the Davis's face. He felt sure he was having a stroke. The prosecutor's throat was dry, and he struggled for air. He took a drink of water and wiped the corners of his mouth. "I must have left it back at the motel," he whispered. "Send Carroll and Chase to search my room. I'll stall."

"Is something wrong, Mr. Davis?" Havercamp asked.

"No," Davis replied. "Just a little confusion, that's all."

When Davis stood to introduce the tape, he felt faint.

"Your Honor, Mr. Scalise, Mr. Sandre, ladies and gentlemen of the jury. What you are about to hear is very unusual. It is the testimony of the victim, Joyce Klindt. You are going to hear an argument between her and the defendant ..."

After ten minutes, Scalise interrupted. "Your Honor, we have no objections to the tape's introduction. The State has already established its foundation."

Havercamp agreed.

Verdict

"Your Honor, we have come this far. I see no reason to skimp on establishing a firm foundation, a grounding in reality, so to speak, for the jury."

"That's your prerogative, Mr. Davis," Havercamp replied.

Davis continued to ramble. He spoke at length of the GE tape recorder, that it was in working order, and how the tape came to be. He recalled the testimony of Diana Iossi and the Reeds, of Ted Carroll and Rick Chase. He told of how the tape was stored and that no one had tampered with it.

The filibuster had reached forty minutes by the time Ted Carroll and Rick Chase returned. The prosecutor was exhausted. He requested a five-minute recess.

Davis sprinted toward Chase. "Did you find the tape?"

"No," the officer replied. "It's not in your room."

The prosecutor's chin dropped to his chest.

"Ted suggested, as only he could do, that the little guy with the beard look in his briefcase," Chase added.

The prosecutor spun around, rushed back down the aisle, unlatched the valise and dumped its contents. The plastic rattled as the tape hit the floor.

Following the short recess, the jury listened to the forty-five minute argument between the accused and the victim.

As in Keokuk, Bartley Klindt was the only witness for the defense. He sounded coached.

The trial had gone so poorly for the defense, it seemed logical that James Klindt would be forced to testify on his own behalf. When he failed to take the stand, Bill Davis could draw only one conclusion. The defense attorneys must have thought their client guilty. The honorable Lawrence Scalise was not about to allow the defendant to perjure himself.

The weekend before the final arguments was one that Bill Davis vowed to enjoy. For the first time in a year, he was at peace. The prosecutor had James Barry Klindt dead to rights and he knew it.

24

THE HAMMER FALLS

During his closing argument Bill Davis portrayed Klindt as a spoiled brat. "No one had ever told him 'no' before. He got everything he ever wanted ... All hell broke loose when Joyce Klindt learned of the divorce decree's contents and hired a lawyer to fight him over its terms ... Jim Klindt then used his strong hands meant for healing to murder his wife."

The prosecutor concluded by slapping a placard on a bulletin board initially set up to show the numerous discrepancies in the defendant's story. It read: "JOYCE KLINDT IS DEAD—JAMES KLINDT DID IT."

John Sandre argued the State had not proven its case and asked the jury to find the defendant innocent, "I want to send a message that we do not live in a society where people can be convicted of heinous crimes as a result of maybes, possibilities, and suspicions."

Sandre contended the defense was trying to convict Jim Klindt with a smoke screen. "To introduce indulgent parents and his having an affair, that's absolutely despicable. We're talking about a man's life ... and they want to talk to you about maybe, and maybe doesn't do it."

Lawrence Scalise closed. "The State has not provided a shred of evidence as to how, when, and why this alleged slaying occurred, nor has their investigation turned up one drop of blood. Anyone who had cut up his wife with a chain saw would have been bathed in it. Joyce Klindt dropped out of sight because she suffered the most fundamental rejection, that of her husband and her son. The State's case is a theory and that's all it is ... Jim Klindt is not guilty beyond a reasonable

Verdict

doubt of the chain saw murder of his wife. The torso is not and cannot be a portion of the body of Joyce Klindt, because she is still alive."

On Monday morning at 11:35, following the chief prosecutor's short rebuttal, the jury received instructions from Judge Havercamp and adjourned to the jury room. They deliberated for nine hours Monday, before being sent home at 10:30 that evening.

At 3:25 on Tuesday afternoon, November 20, 1984, the bell, signaling the jury had concluded its deliberations, rang. The courtroom was soon packed with police officers, attorneys, reporters, and relatives. A half-hour later, Jim Klindt, dressed in the same dark gray suit he had worn throughout the two trials, strode quickly down the aisle, taking a seat next to Lawrence Scalise. He appeared nervous and leaned over to talk to the attorney on several occasions.

A short time later, the jurors filed in showing the strain of the two and a half week trial. They had deliberated for fifteen hours over the past two days before reaching the decision. The two women appeared near tears, and not one of the panel looked at the defendant.

Judge Havercamp read the verdict. "The State finds James B. Klindt guilty of murder in the second-degree."

Klindt slumped and hung his head for an instant upon hearing the pronouncement of "guilty," then he snapped upright, as if the words "second-degree" had given him a glimmer of hope. After Havercamp thanked and dismissed the jury, Klindt remained perfectly erect, looking too large for the chair he was sitting in, his eyes lost beneath his furrowed brow, his face devoid of color.

As the verdict was read, Davis watched the Monahans collapse in each other's arms, crying softly. Joyce's aunt and her two cousins wept and hugged each other in the emotion-charged courtroom. "I'm just extremely happy," Mrs. Monahan told reporters in a soft drawl in the crowded hallway outside the courtroom. "We're just happy with what we got."

Earlier, she had told a reporter, "Testifying is something that we have to go through with. There is no verdict that will end the ordeal that me and my husband Eugene have had to endure. It will never be over for us."

"We're finally coming out of a bad dream," said Diana Iossi. "There comes a time when you have to wake up. I think this is what we needed."

During the second trial the prosecution was better organized. Bill Davis served his own cause with tough, at times combative, direct examinations of the witnesses. His mild-mannered style changed. He was not the nice guy who had "tied" in Keokuk. He was an interrogator—grilling and badgering anyone he deemed hostile to the State's cause.

Despite the fact that expert testimony had persuaded the jurors the torso was Joyce Klindt, the prosecution had failed to win a judgment in Keokuk. By breaking the case into two distinct parts in Sioux City, Bill Davis had not only proved the identity of the torso, but he had linked the defendant to the crime.

Since there was no "smoking gun," no blood or death instrument, the prosecution never discussed the when or where or how of the monstrous act. Those were things unknown. What the prosecutor did, after the torso was identified, was to sell the jury on motive and circumstance.

The battle in Keokuk had been fought over banalities—hair color, hip size, and blood type. Obtaining a conviction had been lost to a glut of statistics and the confusing order of the

Verdict

parade of witnesses. The prosecutor had not only been unorganized, he had gotten caught up in the hype. Bill Davis refused to let that happen in Sioux City.

After the trial, jury foreman Jim Goodwin, fifty-two, a self-employed feed salesman, and juror Roger Spencer talked with the press. "The jurors deliberated hard, and we think we came to a fair decision," said Goodwin. "We've done the best job we know how. When it was over, I was totally physically and emotionally drained. I'm very proud of the job our jury did. Not that I'm proud that we're sending a man to prison. That's his doing, not ours."

Spencer, forty-nine, a livestock buyer, contradicted Lawrence Scalise's statement that this was a compromise verdict between acquittal and first-degree murder. "When we finished," Spencer said, "there was no question in anyone's mind who committed this crime. None whatsoever."

"Initially," Goodwin added "I was one of three jurors who favored acquittal, but when we mulled over the testimony and exhibits presented by the prosecution I changed my mind. The legal concept of guilt beyond a reasonable doubt weighed very heavily on me during the deliberations. I had some reasonable doubt. I had to get it cleared up, and I did."

"We talked about the testimony of every witness," said Spencer. "As we did, we built a pyramid that eventually showed overwhelming circumstances that convinced all twelve of us that Klindt was guilty."

Goodwin stated, "Most the jury's time was spent deciding Klindt's guilt or innocence. Only the final three hours were spent deliberating his degree of guilt. Three or so wanted a verdict of guilty of first-degree murder, but the majority felt the evidence was not conclusive enough to warrant such a conclusion. "Deliberate, willful, and premeditated were the words which guided our final decision. The line between the

Dead Water

degrees of murder is so thin that we had a hard time distinguishing."

Both Goodwin and Spencer said that while the debate was lengthy, it was never heated. "Of course we had disagreements," Goodwin said, "or we would have been done in fifteen minutes." Neither man thought it possible to explain the jury's choice of second-degree.

Still, despite obvious perjured testimony during the trial and only circumstantial evidence from which to draw a conclusion, the jurors at Sioux City were able to reach a decision. The American justice system had worked.

The "without a body" conviction was the first ever in Iowa. James Klindt's son, parents, and girlfriend were not in Sioux City when the decision was read. Perhaps, they intuited the verdict. Scalise telephoned Klindt's mother with the bad news. "She took it well," the defense attorney said. "She said, 'Take care of my boy.'"

"This case is the most difficult I've ever tried," said Bill Davis, "perhaps the most difficult ever tried in Iowa." He was pleased with the second-degree conviction, but he could not help but think about what might have been. "Evidently, they thought I didn't prove premeditation. Many times jurors think premeditation means buying the poison or drawing the map. In reality," Davis continued, "premeditation can be almost instantaneous — there just has to be enough time for a prudent person to stop, not to go through with the act." Others, including some of Davis's assistants, disagreed.

One thing was certain. The monkey, "can't win the big one," was lifted — to his great relief — from the county prosecutor's shoulders. Davis, who took a calculated gamble in trying Klindt, never believed the tag to be true. "There are prosecutors who are never labeled as losing the big ones," he said, "because they won't try the big ones." Davis continued

Verdict

by saying that a conviction in a murder case is not something a prosecutor should be elated about. "It's a serious matter. I don't want to treat it like a basketball game."

A moment later, he was accepting the congratulations of a police officer, pumping his hand and saying in an excited voice, "We did it. We did it."

The vanguard case was unusual for three reasons: First, the identity of the victim was in question. Genetic forensics was in its infancy. DNA testing, as we know it today, did not exist. Second, a man was tried for first-degree murder without a death certificate ever being issued. Lastly, and perhaps most staggering, the victim testified against her alleged killer at his trial via the tape cassette.

H. Wayne Nelson of Keokuk, the jury foreman at the first trial, was surprised but elated with the verdict. "I thought the prosecution would be lucky to get a manslaughter verdict. I'm glad they were all able to agree."

All evidence of the prosecution must be given to the defense ten days before the beginning of the trial. New evidence for the defense, however, may be presented at any time during the trial. It was for this reason that Bill Davis could not enter two newly discovered pieces into the record.

One night, in the hotel room, Rick Chase sat up and watched eight-millimeter home movies of the Klindts that Diana Iossi had found. They were taken circa 1975. The prosecution had discovered the films too late and although Davis declined to view the movies, he was forced by law to inform the defense he had them.

Scalise asked Rick Chase, whom he trusted, if there was anything in the films that would help the defense. Chase said no, there was no way to judge hip size or hair color, or see moles and birthmarks from what he had viewed. Scalise, who believed Chase to be impeccably honest, never bothered to watch the films himself, assigning that task to one of his law clerks.

One of the fascinating aspects of the trial was that no one witness had accurately described Joyce Klindt. In reality, Clyde Collins Snow, using little more than the dead woman's pelvis came just as close to calculating Joyce Klindt's height and weight as those who had known Joyce for years.

It seems surprising that the main contention that the torso was not that of Joyce Klindt was that her hip size was nowhere near the 39 inches measured in the autopsy. Many witnesses even considered Joyce Klindt petite.

It was learned in the judge's chambers on Friday afternoon, November 16, after the conclusion of testimony, that Det. Ron Van Fossen had finally obtained the body measurements of Joyce A. Klindt. (Ron Van Fossen is the brother of Lt. James Van Fossen mentioned earlier in the book.) The records were secured the previous Friday from the Ada Gaffney Modeling Agency, where Joyce had once worked as a receptionist, evidence discovered too late to be introduced at the trial.

The records were dated December 23, 1975. Joyce Klindt's measurements at that time are as follows: Height five-foot-five, weight one hundred twenty-eight pounds, bust thirty-five inches, waist twenty-five and three-quarters inches, hips thirty-eight inches, thighs twenty and a half inches, calf thirteen inches, arm ten and a half inches.

One critical piece of evidence never came out at the trial. Sometime in February 1984, Jim Klindt had filed an insurance policy claim with Aid Association for Lutherans for $103,301. The chiropractor left the spaces for date, place, and cause of death blank. The claimant's statement listed Joyce A. Klindt as decedent. James B. Klindt was the sole beneficiary of the

Verdict

insurance policy. Klindt had learned the information on the form could never be used against him because it could not be made public. The insurance claim contradicted what Klindt had maintained all along — that his wife was missing, not dead.

Through it all, Dick Klindt never lost faith in his son. The press caught him sweeping leaves from around his garage on a bleak afternoon in late November 1984, two days after the verdict had come down.

A few feet away his fourteen-year-old grandson was repairing a motor scooter that had been vandalized by neighbor kids. Bart Klindt had tried to go to school that morning but was teased and left early.

The old man's voice was still shaky from the news that his son had been found guilty of murder, on what must have been the blackest day in a father's life. In Dick Klindt's mind, there were still a lot of unanswered questions. "Where is Joyce Klindt?" being the main one. "Maybe she'll show up once she sees Jim being punished," he said, looking at the ground and wiping his nose with a gloved hand.

More than a decade has passed. If Joyce is alive she has not been seen. Evidently, Jim Klindt hasn't been punished enough yet.

* * AFTERMATH * *

There is little doubt the trial was the biggest of Bill Davis's career — and the toughest. "The case has consumed me," he said following the verdict. "Now I can get back to being a lawyer, instead of just being a lawyer on the Klindt case."

But the letdown Davis suffered after the judgment was even more traumatic than the one Ted Carroll had endured following the chiropractor's arrest. The bottle of champagne the prosecutor had ordered to celebrate the imminent guilty

Dead Water

verdict was never opened. It was six months before the depression left him.

With the murder conviction, Joyce Klindt had gained back what her husband had tried to destroy — her identity. In reality, there was not much left of the lower trunk of the "female-white" that Thomas Mosher had spotted floating in the Mississippi River on that cold spring morning in April 1983. Feverish attempts to identify the corpse through forensics and anthropological study had reduced the torso to a few bones and tissue samples.

Following the trial Davis authorized a death certificate and turned the cooler containing Mrs. Klindt's fragmented remains over to her parents for a memorial service. After nineteen months all that Eugene and Virginia Monahan were left with was the somber reality, that this was, officially, legally, and with abysmal finality, their only daughter, Joyce.

EPILOGUE

CONFESSION

On December 14, 1984, James B. Klindt was sentenced to fifty years in the Iowa Men's Reformatory at Anamosa. (Shortly thereafter, the State Board of Chiropractors revoked his license.) It was not until after his transfer to the minimum security facility at Rockwell City on February 20, 1992, that Klindt finally confessed to the murder.

Some say the confession was obligatory, that after all, one of the conditions for parole is to show contrition for the crime. A few, mostly loyal friends and relatives, still believe he is not guilty. The question then becomes, if Jim Klindt didn't kill Joyce, who did?

The out-of-the-blue confession was taken down by Larry Johnson, editor of *The Fort Dodge Messenger*, on July 11, 1992. Jim Klindt had just turned forty-four. The following is a summation of what Klindt said.

"I did it. It's taken me eight years to be able to say that. I did it. And I'm sorry. I didn't intentionally do it. I feel terrible about it. God, am I sorry.

"I blocked it out of my mind for three or four years. Every once in a while it would sneak back into my mind like a little crack of light when you open a door to a dark room. But then I'd shut the door. I guess it's a defense mechanism."

Klindt went on to say he was sorry for the "crazy" sequence of events that took his wife's life and his own freedom, that he was sorry he did not move out of the house after the divorce was filed, that he was sorry he returned home that morning of March 18, 1983, sorry his estranged wife was hiding with a pistol in their bedroom, sorry that he killed her and disposed of her body in such gruesome fashion, and sorry that he had repeatedly lied to authorities about what had happened that day.

"If I'd only called the police ... Hindsight! Do I feel remorse? That's what the parole board asked me. Well, each of my fingers was insured for $100,000. If I could go back and cut my arms off and that would undo this, I'd do it. And my hands are my life.

"I came from a middle class background, and most of my friends were middle class or lower middle class. I wasn't always wealthy, but the first five years or so, my practice was doing well.

"I think Joyce had a dependency on me, and she couldn't see that there was a life for her beyond me."

Immediately after Klindt stated his wife had a "dependency," he speculated she had planned to kill him that morning of March 18, 1983. He says she "wasn't religious" and had refused to baptize Bart, and yet she had an appointment with a minister later that day. He said he thought she had planned to confess murdering her husband to the clergyman. He also stated he believed "the tape" may have been further evidence of his wife's plan to kill him.

"I turned the corner into the bedroom and said hi to Joyce, and as I did, she brought the gun up and pointed it at my head. I ran out of the bedroom, and the pool room was right outside. I picked up the pool ball and threw it back toward her. I was an athlete, and I could throw fairly hard. I wasn't trying to hit her, just to buy a little time. I kept waiting for the concussion when she shot, but it never came. I thought I heard her coming after me and it seemed like a nightmare. I got downstairs and I grabbed a shotgun in the gun room. I yelled at her that I had it — I was trying to get her either to come after me or throw the gun down."

Klindt said he then crept back up the stairs.

Verdict

"I thought I heard sort of a moan, and I thought she was coming, and I'm pretty athletic — or I was — and I did a barrel roll on the floor. But I didn't hear anything more.

"She was a smart woman, so I thought she was down, ready to fire. But then I see her gun. It's just laying there on the floor, three feet away from her. So I'm in the bedroom, and I roll her over, and I see what's happened. She's bleeding from her eyes, nose and mouth. And there's no 911 to call back then, so I'm trying to call the police. I'm dialing. Then she makes a horrible sound and stops breathing. I do CPR. I pump her heart, the whole thing. And the phone's making this horrible squealing sound. I think about calling the police, or my dad, but he's had a heart attack. I don't want to bother him. That's irrational, but I don't want to bother him. I think about suicide, the whole thing. I'm thinking the pool ball's hit her in the head, and how could it have?"

Instead of calling the police, Klindt says he rolled his wife's body in sheets and blankets and drove randomly looking for a place to bury the body, "but the Mississippi was flooded." (That doesn't make any sense, but that's what he said.)

"I didn't know what to do. I didn't want to go back to the house. I didn't want any part of that bedroom ... I mean, I kept thinking that I'm not the kind of person who does this sort of thing. I can't even stand the sight of blood — I cannot STAND it. That's why I became a chiropractor."

Klindt said he was confused, so he invited the woman he had been "seeing" to lunch. "I told her that Joyce left me, and now I'm opening my mouth and everything is snowballing. I was lying and it was getting crazier. I left lunch, I was driving a motorhome and I was looking for something to run into, but I couldn't run into a car, because I couldn't kill another person — I know this sounds crazy, given the circumstances, but I couldn't. And there weren't any bridge abutments."

Dead Water

Klindt went on to say he hid the body in the garage. "She only weighed 118 pounds, but I could hardly carry her. It felt like ten tons — the heaviest burden I've ever had to carry."

Klindt said he then put her body in a wheelbarrow and hid it in the thirty-foot boat in his backyard. Later that evening the Reeds came to the house. "They thought I'd done something to her and demanded that I call the police, so I did."

He then spoke of Officer Girt and the Reeds. "They came out and they searched the house and shined a flashlight into the motor home and on the boat, and asked if it was my boat. I said, 'Yes,' and I was kind of hoping they'd just go to the boat and find her, but they didn't. They (the Reeds and the policewoman) all left, and I left Bart alone — I really hated to do that — and I unhooked the phones.

"I drove out to a gravel road, near the river, and the gravel road was still out of water. I walked into waist-deep water, and I strapped Joyce to a tree with bungee cords and I weighted her down with three ninety-pound cement bags. I drove home and went to bed. I couldn't sleep all night."

The following day, Klindt said he had a fastfood breakfast with his son and saw a few patients before returning to the river.

"She's under the tree and I know the water's going down, so I drive out there with a chain saw and two pieces of paneling and twelve bungee straps ... I think about it, and I just can't see me doing this, but I'm doing it.

"I get in my boat and I look up and there's this nightclub and all these people dancing and having a good time. And here I am. And I'm drifting a while. I'm in this swamp boat with a 472 Cadillac engine. It's a fast boat and I start it up and floor it. I just want speed and noise and cold air to numb me. I get there to the tree. I stop the boat and put on my chest waders, and I'm talking to Joyce, I'm saying: 'Oh God, Joyce.'"

Verdict

Klindt said he then put the body between the paneling, secured it with the bungee cords, and used the chain saw to cut the paneling and the body into pieces.

"I don't know how to start the chain saw. I'd bought it at Farm and Fleet the year before and never used it. And I'm there, reading the instructions about the choke and the switch ... You keep hoping helicopters will fly over and light up the sky and something will stop you. Nothing did."

Klindt then spoke of the day he was arrested. "They did it on a break at my office, very tactfully. The police were very conscientious. Through all of this, I've been treated with dignity everywhere but in the press. I can't say people have been understanding, but they've tried to understand. I can't even understand it myself — things just got out of control so quickly. In an instant, the ridiculous — the insane — happens. I am not the type of person who'd do this, which is really something to say, when you did it. If I'd just called the police ..."

Klindt explained why he did not testify at his trial. He told Mr. Johnson had he done so, he would have lied under oath.

Since entering the Iowa prison system he said he had thought about suicide, but that his newfound Christianity and the other inmates helped him deal with imprisonment.

"Prison — this is hell. And the closest thing we have to heaven on earth is free society America. They [the members of the prison staff] are nice, don't get me wrong. But it's hell.

"The purpose of prison is to make you not want to be there. When you done what I did though, you feel so much pain that prison itself is not comparatively so bad. I've had a clean record in prison — I've followed the rules. Sports indoctrinates you to follow the rules, and except for that one time, I've always followed the rules in life.

"A lot of the men here just feel the system is unfair, and they felt that I was unfairly treated. I obviously don't feel railroaded. I feel my situation was predestined by God, and I feel that by the grace of God, I got second-degree murder.

"He put that in those jurors' hearts, I think. When I was born again at Anamosa, I felt that all my sins were cleansed. Christ absolves you and cleanses you. You feel cleanness and purity.

"I see the parole board in October, and the earliest I could get out would probably be around Christmas. I don't know what they'll do, but that would be something, getting out for Christ's time. I can tell you this: when I finally walk out that door, I'll be pure — pure as you ever want."

* * REBUTTAL * *

One cannot help but note that the confession makes the murder seem like self-defense. This is the third time the former chiropractor has changed his account of coming home the morning of March 18, 1983. Was the gun pointed at the floor, at Joyce's head, or at Jim Klindt? Probably none of the above. Elizabeth Reed testified that Joyce was in the kitchen talking with her on the phone when the chiropractor came through the front door.

All in all, Klindt's admission of guilt seemed nearly as bizarre as the crime itself. Bill Davis's private reaction to the confession was predictable. He laughed. "I think the confession was made for the parole board's benefit," the prosecutor said. "Klindt obviously hopes that a show of remorse will influence their decision. There was no evidence, such as splinters, to substantiate his cutting her up between two pieces of plywood. There is also no doubt that James Klindt killed and dismembered his wife."

Our findings also contradict Klindt's statement about "following all the rules." The former chiropractor lived much of his life outside the law. He fished without a commercial

Verdict

license, employed an illegal net, owned an automatic weapon, used illegal drugs, and admitted skimming thousands of tax dollars. There are further imputations that Klindt attended and bet on illicit cockfights in 1982 and 1983, certainly not a place for a man who recoils at the sight of blood.

Perhaps Ted Carroll was right when he once told Geraldine Klindt that he thought Jim watched too much TV. There is no doubt, Klindt was a "Rambo" of sorts, often wearing camouflage fatigues and holstering a loaded pistol with a bayonet strapped to his leg. And how many men, besides television police officers, use terms like "did a barrel roll"?

Many believe Klindt to be a pathological liar. From the depositions we have read, it seems to have been much easier for him to find God than the truth. One thing is certain. Klindt's arrogance and narcissism have not diminished in prison.

Despite his fabricated confession, we still tried, without success, to interview Jim Klindt. As far as we know, he is the only person who really knows what happened that fatal day. We only had two questions. How did you really kill Joyce? And whatever happened to that one-carat heart-shaped diamond ring she was wearing the day she died?

All of our interviews, and there were many, indicate Jim Klindt has, or at least had, a quick temper. He was employed at Case the summer after graduating from high school. A fellow employee talked of Klindt's frustration while working assembly. "Sometimes, Jim would hurl a ballpeen hammer, smashing anything in sight." Those who played Y.M.C.A. basketball against Klindt spoke of his explosive retaliatory nature. Personal experience (the tennis incident) showed that Klindt had a mean streak.

Those who had hunted with the chiropractor tell stories of him and his friends shooting game from moving vehicles, of gutting deer and hanging them, dripping blood, in back of their vehicles. There is also a documented account of Klindt bedding a young woman in a small community in southeastern Iowa during a hunting trip. Evidently her father learned of the incident. It was not forgotten. When Klindt returned the following year, he was promptly run out of town.

Rick Chase was one of the few police officers involved with the case from start to finish. Now a sergeant on the Davenport police force, Chase is still moved by the crime. "I understand how a man could kill his wife in a fit of anger. But butchering her with a chain saw, the woman who shared your bed and gave birth to your only child, that is something I will never fathom."

Bill Davis went to Klindt's parole hearing in October 1992. The Monahans were there too. Davis was not paid to go. He made the trip out of conscience. It is a long drive from Davenport to Rockwell City. While it is not the county attorney's place to argue for or against Jim Klindt's early release, there is little doubt where Mr. Davis's heart lies.

The prosecutor's desire to attend those hearings is even more astonishing in light of our recent interview with Davis, in which he stated, "I don't think that Jim Klindt is dangerous." (Most of the people we interviewed think Klindt a very dangerous man.) The prosecutor was quick to add that the former chiropractor had not yet paid his debt to society. After saying that, Davis lowered his eyes and stared at the table. When he spoke again, his voice had softened and the rapid-fire speech was gone. "His life was merely interrupted, her life is over," he rued. "He's been temporarily inconvenienced — she's dead."

ARRESTED — Left to right are Jim Klindt and officers Dennis Kern, Gerald McCabe, and Daniel Reardon. Ted Carroll is blocked from view. (Photo courtesy of Lt. Daniel Reardon)